Miniature Orchids
and How to Grow Them

Rebecca Tyson Northen

DOVER PUBLICATIONS, INC.
New York

Bibliographical Note

This Dover edition, first published in 1996, is a corrected, slightly revised and enlarged republication of the corrected printing (1988) published by the Prentice Hall Trade Division (New York) for the American Orchid Society, of the work originally published by Van Nostrand Reinhold Company, New York, 1980, under the title *Miniature Orchids*. For this Dover edition, in addition to correcting a number of typographical errors and updating some botanical names, the author has provided an Appendix, "Orchid Pest Control."

All photographs by the author unless otherwise noted.

Library of Congress Cataloging-in-Publication Data

Northen, Rebecca Tyson, 1910–
    [Miniature orchids]
    Miniature orchids and how to grow them / Rebecca Tyson Northen.
        p.   cm.
    "This Dover edition . . . is a corrected, slightly revised and enlarged republication of the corrected printing (1988) published by Prentice Hall Trade Division (New York) for the American Orchid Society, of the work originally published by Van Nostrand Reinhold Company, New York, 1980, under the title Miniature orchids" T. p. verso. With new appendix.
    Includes bibliographical references (p.   ) and index.
    ISBN 0-486-28920-6 (pbk.)
    1. Miniature orchids. 2. Orchid culture. I. Title.
SB409.75.N67 1996
635.9'3415—dc20
                                              95-36243
                                              CIP

Manufactured in the United States of America
Dover Publications, Inc., 31 East 2nd Street, Mineola, N.Y. 11501

Contents

*Acknowledgments*_____

I wish it were possible to mention all those who have contributed to my 50 years of orchid growing. Wherever I've gone, people have shared their knowledge and experiences. I have benefited from the hours of work and great love orchidologists have put into their publications. The kindnesses and favors of fellow orchid growers have been unending. I sincerely thank each and all. Now, however, I should like to express appreciation to those who have helped in big and little ways with the background and development of this book—those who have taken my husband and me collecting, identified species, answered innumerable questions, allowed me to take pictures in their greenhouses, shared interesting plants with me, and lent me slides. Some are no longer with us but all are included in my expression of appreciation.

My thanks to: The Angraecum House, Mr. and Mrs. David Bennett, Dr. and Mrs. Benjamin Berliner, Lance A. Birk, Black River Orchids, Dr. and Mrs. Ray M. Bloom, Margaret Brown, Heather Campbell, Stephen C. Clemesha, Carmen Coll, Dr. Calaway H. Dodson, Dr. Robert L. Dressler, Frieda Duckitt, Harry A. Dunn, G. C. K. Dunsterville, Geoff Elworthy, Charles Marden Fitch, Dr. Leslie A. Garay, Noel Gauntlett, Ancile L. Gloudon, Great Lakes Orchids, Eric Hagsater, Federico Halbinger, Robert M. Hamilton, Ronald M. Hawley, A. H. Heller, Michael G. A. Hill, Clarence K. Horich, Margaret Ilgenfritz, J and L Orchids, John Jannese, Mr. and Mrs. H. Phillips Jesup, Dr. George C. Kennedy, Mae Lauer, Robert Lester Orchids, Los Angeles Arboretum, Dr. Carlyle A. Luer, Raymond McCullough, Mr. and Mrs. Fordyce Marsh, W. W. Goodale Moir, Dr. Michael J. O'Connor, Orchids Bountiful, G. F. J. Pabst, Dr. Frank Piers, Glenn E. Pollard, Harold B. Ripley, Walter J. Rybaczyk, Charles Schweinfurth, Severin Orchid Farm, Dr. Gunnar Seidenfaden, Eric Simes, Philip Spence, Dr. and Mrs. John M. Stewart, Dr. Joyce Stewart, Dr. Warren P. Stoutamire, José Strobel, Dr. Herman R. Sweet, Dr. Kiat Tan, Dr. Peter Taylor, Walter Teague, Mr. and Mrs. William R. Thurston, C. A. Vogelaar, Leon A. Wiard, Dr. Jeffrey Wood, Dr. Paddy Woods, Ze Lo Wride, and Jacolyn A. Young.

1. Miniature Orchids: An Introduction

Plant lovers looking for new and exciting kinds to grow, and orchid growers seeking more variety, will find unending fascination and beauty in miniature orchids. It has long been proven that orchids can be grown on windowsills and under lights, as well as in greenhouses. Miniature orchids—those ranging in height from $\frac{1}{2}$ inch to 6 inches (1 to 15 cm)—offer everything the larger kinds do. Some reward the grower with jewel-like flowers as translucent as glass, others with blossoms like brightly colored carved wax; some with sprays of many small blossoms, others with flowers as large as the plants themselves.

In the area required for half a dozen big plants, several times that many miniatures may be grown [Plate 1]. Thus they offer the chance to enjoy a wide range of delightful kinds in a limited space, even in an already crowded greenhouse. They are ideal for apartment dwellers and home owners who do not have a greenhouse. Half of the orchid growers in the Greater New York Area, for example, have their plants in windows or under lights.

The cultivation of orchids is no more difficult than that of other plants—the grower has to learn how to handle them, just as he learns how to grow philodendron or coleus. For those who have not grown orchids before, this book describes their basic needs and ways of caring for them and discusses common problems and their solutions.

From among the hundreds of miniatures described in this book, many of great charm are available from commercial growers. Some are rare and one may have to search for them; others are not yet available in this country. American dealers who specialize in species are continually obtaining new kinds through their worldwide contacts. They and licensed dealers in other countries advertise in orchid publications and gardening magazines. Delightful hybrids are also available, although there are relatively few as yet.

Even though you may grow orchids for a lifetime, you can never exhaust the possibilities, for the Orchidaceae offer greater variety than any other plant family. The hundreds described in this book represent only a part of the thousands that exist.

Small orchids far outnumber the larger kinds, and are just as beautiful as their more conspicuous relatives. They are not always easy to find in the wilds, particularly when not in flower. Often they are hidden at the base of larger plants or among the foliage of twigs and branches. Some that would be difficult to see by themselves become conspicuous when they form dense colonies; sometimes they almost take over whole trees. Oddly, neighboring trees may not bear a single plant of those particular species. The tiniest ones may not be as tall as the moss and lichen among which they grow [Plate 2]. Perhaps the best camouflaged are the leafless ones, consisting of only a mass of grayish roots clinging to gray bark, with but a minuscule bract-covered stem from which both roots and flowers arise.

The term "showy," often used to describe large orchids, is just as well deserved by many small ones; indeed, it does not always apply to the large ones, for they can have disappointingly small, even inconspicuous flowers. Nothing could be more eye-catching than a fat-leaved little *Meiracylium*, with its clusters of diminutive rosy blossoms, or a *Sophronitis*, with fewer but larger orange ones [Color Plate C-1], or a *Pleurothallis* that is a bouquet of tiny white or yellow blooms. The astonishing shapes of some are to be marveled at—flowers with tails five times as long as their other parts [Plate 3], or with wild fringes, whiskers, or knobs. It takes a magnifying glass to see the decorations on the little flowers, and for that matter, the fine details of larger ones. And the colors! The orchid world is known for a fantastic array of colors, and the miniatures have every possible range and combination. Many are fragrant: some strongly so; others delicately or deliciously; and a few unpleasantly. They give forth their perfume at various times of the day or evening according to habits developed through evolution and coordinated with those of their pollinators. Sometimes the fragrance is emitted steadily, sometimes in intermittent bursts perhaps more likely to provoke the interest of passing insects.

There is no official designation of what constitutes a "miniature" orchid. In one set of show-judging rules, the miniature category is limited

2. Pleurothallis calyptrostele *is hardly taller than moss.*

3. Dendrobium tetragonum *has tails that give it a length of 3 or 4 inches (8 to 10 cm).*

to plants no taller than 5 inches (12 cm), including the flowers; in another, it is put at 6 inches (15 cm), *excluding* the inflorescence. The latter allows a greater scope and is more realistic, because many small orchid plants have flower stems far taller than the foliage, even up to 2 feet (60 cm) or more. No limit is easy to adhere to; sometimes it becomes a matter of feeling or impression. An obviously large, chunky, heavy plant can have broad horizontally spreading leaves and thus not measure over 15 cm. Yet another plant that is a bit over 15 cm may be so dainty in proportions that it is easily accepted as a miniature. Under optimal conditions, some plants double their height; wild orchids often do this when brought into cultivation where they receive larger quantities of fertilizer, a steadier water supply, or a bit heavier shade. A tiny plant that doubles its size is still tiny, but one that comes close to the size limit for a miniature may exceed the specifications we're setting. The grower will surely not discard a species because of that.

There is also a natural variation in size among individuals within a species; one grower may have a specimen that is 10 cm tall, while his neighbor's plant may be 15 cm. In addition, plants may make larger growth in some seasons, when conditions are just right, than in others. Descriptions of species in this book include the height range as nearly as possible, so that the reader may choose sizes he prefers.

Part of the charm in nature, or in a garden, lies in variety of shapes and habits: Vines and trailing plants contrast with those that grow bushy or tall. So in an orchid collection, plants such as *Dichaea* and a certain type of *Maxillaria* contribute graceful cascades of delicate, ever-lengthening stems clothed with little alternate leaves. Those that climb or ramble, such as *Bulbophyllum* and the insect-imitating *Trichoceros*, present pseudobulbs—each a distinct plant—at intervals along a rhizome. Many kinds spread horizontally to become veritable mats or cushions covered with hundreds of flowers. Tiny monopodials, which grow upward on a single stem, may remain small all their lives, while others that grow rapidly may become too tall. Just as shrubs and vines in a garden require pruning to keep them within limits, so some orchids may have to be trimmed, or separated and restarted.

Flowering habits vary from species to species: There are those that bloom once a year on a certain date, others that flower several times a year. Orchid flowers usually last well, but there are some short-lived ones. Fortunately, many that fade quickly keep forming flowers successively over a long period. A few have flowers that stay fresh on the plant for months, some for nearly a year. In gathering information on species described here, I have taken the flowering times from my own experience and that of fellow growers where possible, but some have had to be gleaned from the literature only, and it has not always been clear whether the dates given were for the country of origin or the United States. Plants from the southern hemisphere usually reverse their flowering season when brought up north. When newly received, they may bloom for the first time according to their habit in nature and change the following year; however, some never do reverse their season. I've done my best to interpret

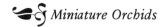

information on flowering times, giving what I believe to be the times that growers in this country can expect blossoms.

Tropical forests, whether of low, warm or of high, cool elevations, abound in many kinds of epiphytic plants—plants that perch on other plants, obtaining no nutrients from them. Orchids share the trunks and branches of trees with mosses and lichens, ferns, aroids, gesneriads, philodendrons, peperomias, anthuriums, and bromeliads [Color Plate C-2]. Their roots receive water from rain, dew, mist, and fog, and obtain nutrients from decaying vegetable and animal matter that is present as humus or is washed down to them along the bark. They also grow on the face of rocks, often on canyon walls and alongside waterfalls. The rock dwellers grow exactly as do those that live on trees; they are given the name lithophyte or are said to be rupicolous. Ancient ruins in tropical countries are likely to have orchids growing on their stones. While there are true terrestrial orchids with roots or tubers below soil level, some apparent ground dwellers merely send their roots rambling among the grasses and weeds and litter of decaying vegetation. There are some that prefer shade, others half-sun, and a few full sun, but fewer grow in the hot lowlands than at higher elevations: the maximum number occur between 3000 and 9000 feet (about 900 and 2700 m), tapering off toward 12,000 feet (3600 m). Many of the smaller kinds prefer a cool climate and are therefore found in abundance at higher locations; and although some of them are able to withstand extended dry seasons, most must have constant moisture.

There are some 30,000 species of orchids, well over 650 genera. If two thirds were miniatures, these alone could number 20,000; some are, of course, extremely rare. Surprisingly, many that were discovered and named in the nineteenth century, the great age of orchid discovery, were not seen again for 50 to 100 years; some have not yet been rediscovered. For the first half of the present century, growers were busy making hybrids, mostly of the large-flowered types. Now they are once more seeking out and growing the species. Some of the "lost" orchids have been rediscovered; many new ones have been found, and still more await discovery.

Sadly, tropical forests are being devastated in the name of expanding civilization, some through utter vandalism. In some countries there is little virgin forest left. Conservationists and governments are working on the tremendous problem of how to save the forests, while at the same time exploring them and learning about the species they hold (not just of orchids but of all living things). Some countries are setting aside national forests and other nature preserves in an effort to save something before it is too late. With habitats being destroyed, it is urgent to grow rare orchids from seed if possible (it isn't always possible to get species to set seed in cultivation, and some do not accept their own pollen, requiring it, instead, from another plant) or to propagate them vegetatively. Accidents can happen, and if a grower loses the only plant in cultivation, there is slim chance of his obtaining the species again. If he has shared divisions, its safety is more secure.

Taxonomists are working to classify species being brought to light, to name new ones, even to create new genera to accommodate some species. They are also revising the present categories, clarifying generic concepts, placing species where they properly belong, and searching out the oldest valid name for each. Often a species was found by different people at different times and in different countries and each time given a name without knowledge of the others; the first name deserves to be retained. Genera that have grown quite huge—some include a thousand species or more—are being divided so that groups sharing distinctive characteristics become separate genera.

Thus today we must give up some of the familiar names and adopt more accurate ones that future generations will learn as a matter of course. Many of the species in this book have recently undergone name changes. I cannot guarantee to have kept track of them all: Some are being changed as this is being written; others will be altered in the future. Most names used herein can, however, be found in past and present books and will undoubtedly be used in catalogs for a long time.

With so many species in the world, it is natural that no two fanciers will own exactly the same orchids. While many catalogs offer the more familiar ones, no two duplicate each others' lists. A grower may search this book in vain for a particular favorite but find many that he has never heard of; actually, that is the fun of growing species. There is always something different to be located. In almost any importation of collected plants, there will be some unnamed or misnamed ones. Not all orchids are in flower when collectors come upon them, and since different kinds can look alike vegetatively, a few may turn out to be something unexpected, even new species or long-lost ones. Not all of those described here will be found in commercial catalogs. The species fan will have to "find" them himself—in the wilds, in collections of fellow growers with whom he can trade, in greenhouses of dealers who specialize in species but don't list all they have (or even issue catalogs), or he will have to contact specialists in other countries. In exploring the possibilities you may very likely turn up kinds not described in this book, for in a limited volume is is only possible to give examples, not to name every miniature in every genus. Some genera are little-known, and while they may have several desirable species, information may be available on only one or two.

Among the various possible methods of presentation, the best seems to be an alphabetical arrangement. It would be interesting to quote discoverors or authors concerned with naming and studying the species, but space prevents such luxury. Space also prevents listing the many hybrids now available, for that would necessitate excluding interesting species. Moreover, any list of hybrids would soon be out of date as new ones replace those now current, though I illustrate a few hybrids in color just to show some of the possibilities.

Unless otherwise noted, the species that follow can be assumed to be epiphytic and require intermediate temperature conditions and moderate light. The country or countries of origin is given at the end of each species description, followed by the flowering time, where this information was available.

2. Orchids in the Wild Environment

Considering that orchids come from such a variety of habitats, including microclimates within macroclimates, it is remarkable that so many can be grown together in cultivation. Macroclimates are created by season, elevation, and seasonal winds. An example of situations found in many places in the tropics can be seen along the Continental Divide of Costa Rica, where an almost knife-edge crest separates the Atlantic and Pacific slopes. The Atlantic slope is always wetter than the Pacific, and, for the most part, different species grow on the two sides. During the dry season, the Atlantic side still receives rain, and the plants remain lush and green, while across the road on the Pacific slope drought prevails, and the plants are tough and almost crisp. This in itself is not unusual: In the tropics, different climates are often separated by the mere width of a road. In a particular spot, however, a microclimate is created. At a certain hour every afternoon, the wind sweeps up through a canyon on the Atlantic flank pouring a stream of mist over the crest and down on the Pacific side. Plants in its path are wetted; those on either side receive not a drop of moisture. The daily mist creates a microclimatic niche where plants never have to suffer

from drought, and moisture-loving kinds can thrive. When the dry season ends and rains come to the Pacific slope, the nearby drought-stricken orchids perk up and put out new growth.

Every tree has a variety of microclimates. Little sun penetrates close to the ground in a forest, and what few orchids live in the shade are necessarily not light-demanding. Those dwelling in the upper branches receive better light and freer air circulation and so tend to approach dryness part of each day. Some miniatures grow on the tips of the merest twigs; how they manage to germinate, cling, and obtain nourishment there is a continuing mystery. Where a break occurs in the forest—along a stream or road, at the edge of a field or orchard, or at the brink of a canyon—the sun reaches the base of trees and allows light-demanding kinds to grow lower down. Alongside rushing streams and waterfalls, temperatures are usually cooler and the plants damper than in adjacent areas. Steep slopes, even roadbanks, are habitats for some terrestrials, and also for epiphytes that have fallen from trees or germinated amid the ground vegetation. Many in such spots receive brilliant sun, as do those growing in treeless areas of high elevations on exposed, often rocky places. However, in the same spots small plants nestled amid the ground vegetation are well shaded.

Cloud forests are created by mists condensing from moisture-laden air as it rises up the flanks of mountains from the bottom of valleys and canyons. The procession of clouds flowing through the trees, bathing the vegetation, is beautiful to see. Orchids abound in such forests. In addition to the mist, cloud forests also receive a couple of heavy showers a day, but they are not so wet as the rain forests, which receive heavier and more extensive rains; the latter can be at low or high elevations, from warm to cold, but because of the excessive moisture and lesser amount of sun, they harbor fewer orchids.

The temperatures of a plant's native habitat, the prevalence and seasonal distribution of moisture, and the amount of light the plant receives give us clues to its needs in cultivation, but we cannot exactly duplicate the soft, clean air, pure water, and slight differences in light of a native environment. Fortunately, most orchids are somewhat adaptable and, provided the various factors are balanced, will grow and flower under conditions a bit different from those they enjoyed in nature. Once in a while, a plant even does better in cultivation.

For convenience, we can divide orchids into three temperature groups, with emphasis on the more critical night temperatures: "Warm" group, with nights close to 65°F (18°C) in winter, up to 70°F (21°C) in summer; "intermediate," with winter nights close to 60°F (15°C), preferably between 55° and 60°F (13° and 17°C), and a few degrees above in summer; and "cool," with nights of 45° to 50°F (7° to 10°C) in winter, and as little above that as possible in summer. In all cases, day temperatures should rise ten degrees F (six degrees C) higher. Where summer days become excessively hot, it is best to use cooling equipment* or else, as many growers do, put plants outdoors in a shaded area.

Among orchids, there are two types of growth habit: sympodial and monopodial. *Sympodial* plants [Plate 4] have a rhizome from which new growths and roots arise successively, usually seasonally. A plant may make only one new growth a year or two or more at a time, sometimes several times a year. Each new growth is essentially an independent plant, although it obtains some food and water from older parts. The growths may be close together, with the rhizome very short between them, or they may be spaced far apart on a lengthy rhizome. Flowers come from each season's growths, which, with some exceptions, do not bloom again.

Among the sympodials are orchids with thickened stems called pseudobulbs. These act as storage places for water and food and assist the plants in withstanding long or short periods of drought; most have leathery or fleshy leaves coated with wax and stomata sunken in pits—features that retard water loss. Sympodials lacking pseudobulbs do not withstand drying as well, but they may have fleshy, water-storing leaves or may inhabit cool, shady locations. Some pseudobulbless kinds that do live in bright sun or suffer dry spells have exceptionally thick, tough leaves.

Monopodials [Plate 5] have no rhizome and rarely make new growths from the base of the plant. The single stem begins as the seedling develops and grows larger and taller, adding more leaves yearly. Auxiliary stems branch out from the main one, and roots also grow from the stem. Flowers come from successively higher leaf axils. Although most monopodials have fleshy stems and leaves that give some protection from drying, they do not withstand drought as well as plants with pseudobulbs. Some increase in height only slowly, and some tiny ones never become more than a few centimeters tall. Those that grow rapidly end up with a long stem and often green leaves only at the top. Whenever the plant becomes "leggy," the top part can be cut off and restarted, and it will make new roots.

The remarkable leafless orchids are monopodials. Their lack of leaves undoubtedly reduces water loss, but since such plants dwell along with kinds that do have leaves, it is difficult to tie the habit in with evolution. There are also pseudomonopodials such as some dichaeas whose trailing or climbing stems continue to grow in length but which also make new growths from the base. These often root along the stem, making it easy to trim them to a desired size.

Both sympodials and monopodials grow in all tropical and subtropical countries, but a greater proportion of sympodials occurs in the Western Hemisphere. The Eastern Hemisphere—Africa, Malagasy, the

4. Octomeria nana, *a sympodial orchid, in a ceramic pot.*

5. Mystacidium capense, *a dainty African monopodial, at home on a small stick.*

---

*For details on greenhouse management, see my *Home Orchid Growing*, 4th ed. (Englewood Cliffs, N.J., Prentice Hall, 1990).

Orient, southern Asia, India, and the islands of the Pacific—is full of beautiful monopodials.

Terrestrial orchids are mostly of the sympodial type; among them are kinds with and without pseudobulbs. The latter either do not suffer dry seasons or they have underground tubers or fleshy, water-storing roots to sustain them during drought or cold weather. Among them are our native cypripediums, which go through the winter without leaves and make new ones in the spring. Their Asiatic relatives, the paphiopedilums, rarely have to endure drought and do not lose their leaves seasonally.

Another growth habit is found among the deciduous pseudobulbous kinds such as *Catasetum*, *Mormodes*, and others. Many have thin leaves that fall at the end of the growing period, leaving the pseudobulbs naked during the dry season. This is a water-conserving habit, but they, too, grow alongside those that do not shed their leaves.

The roots of epiphytic orchids are covered with velamen, a layer of corky cells that soaks up water and dissolved nutrients and which also holds a great deal of air. The velamen protects the inner water-conducting tissue of the roots and clings to the perch. Some roots hang out in the air, but they have the same structure as those that penetrate the substrate. In nature, the roots have perfect drainage and aeration: They travel along bare bark or through a fluffy mat formed by mosses, lichens, and roots of other plants; the substrate drains quickly after a soaking, and the roots are immediately exposed to air. No orchid can live long in cultivation unless its roots have good drainage and aeration. This is true even of terrestrials, whose roots do not have velamen, but require an open well-aerated medium. A few exceptions are adapted to live in clay soils or bogs.

Orchid flowers are built on one basic, though marvelously varied, pattern. They have three sepals—the outermost parts of the flower that form the bud cover—and three petals. One petal is modified in shape and size and is called the lip or labellum. It can be of the same or a different color from the rest of the flower and is often decorated with fringes or protuberances. In rare cases it is similar in shape to the sepals and petals. The lip is often the most conspicuous part of the flower, but in some kinds the sepals or petals are the showy parts. In the center stands the column, a structure that makes an orchid different from other flowers. In the majority of orchids this fleshy cylinder holds both male and female reproductive organs, the anther at its tip and the stigma just under it. Exceptions are kinds that have separate male and female flowers. The column is continuous with the ovary, and pollen grains deposited on the stigma send their sperm-bearing tubes down through it to fertilize the egg cells and start seed development. The pollen grains are held together in masses called *pollinia*, which are hard and waxy in some kinds, soft and less tightly bound in others.

All orchids have a means of "fastening" pollen to their pollinators, practically forcing them to carry it from one flower to another. Between the anther and the stigma is a structure called the *rostellum*, which varies greatly from genus to genus. In some the rostellum bears a tissue that secretes a sticky substance, which is smeared on the pollinator so that loose pollinia adhere; in others it gives rise to a viscid disc connected by strands to the pollinia, forming an apparatus with the pollinia called a *pollinarium* which sticks to the visitor on contact.

Bees, butterflies, moths, wasps, flies, and less often beetles, as well as various kinds of birds, particularly hummingbirds and other small types, act as pollinators. The flowers lure them with specific scents, sometimes delightful to us but often pleasing only to an insect, or catch their attention by colors, or by tails or lips that sway or bobble in the breeze. The colors, odors, and myriad variations in structure are the features that make orchids so delightful to us, but of the tremendous numbers of species, the pollination of relatively few has been observed. These few, then, are especially interesting, for one can see how they and their pollinators are coordinated. The insect imitators mimic the females of certain species by both scent and structure, causing the males to attempt to copulate with the flowers and so carry pollen from one to another. Some flowers have patches of tissue on the lip that reflect ultraviolet light, forming patterns that we can't see but that are visible and alluring to their pollinators. For the rest, it is fun to guess what might be their special attraction, or how a particular set of bumps or the shape of a lip might act as an aid or lure in pollination.

An orchid seed is very tiny, about the size of a grain of dust, and there may be from a hundred thousand to a million in one seed capsule. As a capsule ripens and splits, the seed spills out, some to settle on surrounding vegetation, the rest to be dispersed by air currents. The embryo is only partially developed, and there is almost no food stored in the seed to nourish it. In nature there is a symbiotic relationship between the seed and certain fungi called *mycorrhiza*, which penetrate the seed coat. The fungi digest nutrients from the humus and the embryo obtains them from the fungi, thus enabling the embryo to complete its development. From the tremendous number of seeds produced, apparently few find just the right environment for germination. In cultivation, seed is germinated without fungi (asymbiotically), in sterile flasks or bottles on an agar jelly to which sugar and nutrient salts have been added. Not all seeds germinate readily, but when they do, thousands of seedlings can be raised in contrast to the few that survive in nature.

3. The Basics of Cultivation

A brief summary of orchid care will get most beginners off to a fair start. Suggestions for handling certain species will be given in their descriptions. For greater detail of all phases of culture, especially in greenhouses, see *Home Orchid Growing*, fourth revised edition (Prentice Hall, 1990), and for growing in the home, see *Orchids as House Plants* (Dover Publications, 1975), both by this author.

Potting and Mounting

The potting of miniatures is no different from that of their larger relatives, and with the materials now in use it is not much different from potting with soil. Many orchids form new roots seasonally, either before or along with new vegetative growth. Disturbing the roots causes some of them to be injured and gives the plant a setback; therefore, the best time to repot is just as new roots start so that they can grow uninjured into fresh medium. Many species make new growth in the spring or summer, others in fall or winter. Spring and summer are considered ideal for repotting, since the days are longer and growth is more rapid, but it is more important to catch the new roots whenever they appear. Therefore, when a plant is outgrowing its pot or when the medium is breaking down (getting soft or mushy), watch for root formation, and repot it no matter what the season. Newly imported plants and plants shipped bare-root obviously must be potted or mounted whenever they arrive. Some take a long time to reroot because their season is past; others may respond with new roots even out of their regular season.

Potting materials

Bark: A favorite growing medium is the bark of white, red, or Douglas fir, chopped and graded according to the diameter of the pieces—fine grade is $\frac{1}{4}$ inch (5 mm) and medium grade $\frac{1}{2}$ inch (1 cm). It may be used alone or mixed with other ingredients. Fine grade is used for smaller plants, for terrestrials such as paphiopedilums, and for kinds needing constant moisture; it can actually be used for all miniatures grown in pots. Sometimes a little redwood bark, either shredded or in chips, is added, for its water-holding, fungus-resisting qualities.

Tree fern: Used widely in countries where tree ferns are native, and by many people in this country, chopped tree fern trunk (called *hapuu*) is another splendid medium. The texture of the fibers of different species varies a bit in toughness, thickness, and water-holding ability. thinner fibers, which become soft when wet, are preferable to the heavy, hard kind. The fine grade, with fibers about an inch (2 cm) long, is best for miniature plants.

Osmunda fiber: The root mass of the osmunda fern, which grows in swampy areas, is an old and once preferred medium. It is scarce now and expensive, sometimes not readily available, but useful for plants that have to be grown in hanging baskets or for those that do not do well in anything else; it is wise to have some on hand.

Soil mixes: Commercial growers offer various mixes for terrestrial orchids such as paphiopedilums and for semi-terrestrials such as cymbidiums. These are usually combinations of loam, sand, fine fir bark, perlite, and other ingredients.

Scoria or other porous volcanic rock: In wet climates where plants are kept outdoors, growers often use scoria instead of bark. Occasionally other growers use it for special purposes; it is graded much like bark.

Perlite: A white, feather-light product of volcanic origin, perlite is a useful addition to almost any medium, especially for tiny plants. It is inert, holds water, does not decay, and serves to keep the medium open. The agricultural grade is best, because its larger pieces do not contain as much powder as the fine grades.

Mounts: Slabs, totem poles, balls, or carved figures of tree fern

6. *A large tree fern stump, or section of trunk, can hold many little plants.*

22

[Plate 6] make good mounts for rambling plants and those that do not do well in pots. Pots made of tree fern are not recommended, because they stay too wet. Fine, close-grained tree fern is better than the coarse, open type, for it holds more water and encourages root growth. Cork bark makes excellent mounts, either just as it is taken from the tree [Plate 7] or in pressed panels used in the building trades. (Never use granulated cork bark as a potting medium: It decays rapidly into a claylike mass.) Small tree branches cut into lengths make natural looking mounts; hardwood is preferable, but many types of wood can be used, even that of sagebrush. Driftwood or wind timber [Plate 8] is most decorative, but any that comes from ocean beaches should be soaked for a long period to remove salt.

Pots: Since the advent of bark as a medium, plastic pots have come into wide use [Plate 9]. They are cheaper and lighter than clay pots, easier to clean, and do not break as readily. Clay pots are still preferred by some growers, however. Drainage holes should be of adequate size to facilitate movement of water out of the pot; glazed pots can be used in place of plastic.

Stakes: Aluminum or steel stakes of various lengths and weights are used for tying up plants and flower stems. Wooden stakes are only temporary, since they rot at the bottom.

Sterilizing equipment: To prevent the spread of disease, particularly of virus, all pots and stakes that have been used must be washed and sterilized before reuse. Tools such as clippers, knives, and razor blades must be sterilized between plants, even if used to cut a single flower or leaf. Metal stakes and tools can be heated in the oven for 20 minutes at 350°F (162°C), or flamed (the best method). Pots can be soaked in Clorox in a 1-10 solution followed by thorough rinsing. Tools can be disinfected by standing them in a saturated solution of TSP (trisodium phosphate).

7. Oncidium variegatum *in flower on cork bark. The other plants are various species of variegata oncidiums.*

8. *Driftwood makes attractive mounts for miniature orchids.*

Potting sympodial plants

Prepare the pot by putting a layer of drainage material (gravel or light weight aggregate) in the bottom. A plant can usually be removed from its old pot by first soaking it and then tapping the pot upside down on the edge of the bench, holding the fingers around the base to catch it. If the roots stick, it may be necessary to run a knife around the inside.

If the plant has merely outgrown its pot and the medium is still good, it can be moved to a larger size without disturbing the root ball; merely place it in a larger pot and fill in with the same kind of material in which it was growing. Firm the medium down around the edges.

If the medium has broken down, tease off the old material and cut off any dead roots. For plants with thick velamen-covered roots such as cattleyas and some epidendrums, it is wise to trim back the roots to stubs of a length to fit neatly in the new pot; these stubs will form branch roots. Healthy thin or wiry roots, especially of kinds grown in con-

9. Maxillaria arbuscula *in a plastic pot.*

stant moisture, need not be trimmed, but dead ones should be removed. The fleshy roots of terrestrials should be disturbed as little as possible. Fine bark or soil mix can be washed off them without injury. Hold the plant in the pot and fill in with the medium, shaking, fingering, and firming it down as you go along.

Small tufted plants usually do not have to be staked but those with slender stems may require support. Push a stake into the medium and tie the stems to it with soft string. Label the plant immediately and add the date of repotting.

Dividing a sympodial means separating it into parts that will maintain themselves as independent plants. With the plant out of the pot and most of the old medium removed, study it to see where the lead growths are, then cut the plant up into sections, each containing a lead growth and several stems behind it. Pot each division as you would a whole plant. The lead growth will continue as before. Parts that are left over, without lead growths, may break dormant buds and develop into active plants.

Potting monopodial plants

As a monopodial plant grows older, it loses leaves from the base and often the roots formed from this older section die off. New roots constantly arise higher on the stem. This habit is more evident on taller-growing kinds, but it is nevertheless true of all. To repot, remove the plant from the pot, break off the older basal section of the stem along with its roots, leaving intact the roots on the younger section. The younger part can then be placed in its own pot, and the forming roots will go into the fresh medium. Plants developing from the sides of the main stem can be removed and potted separately or left in place.

Roots that have grown outside the pot pose a problem: If they are too high to go into the medium, it is best to let them stay outside the new pot; if they come from the stem that is to be set into the medium, they must be trimmed back to stubs. When the plant has been prepared, hold it in the pot and fill in with the medium, firming it down as described above. Stake and label the plant.

Fastening plants to mounts

Plants that require particularly free drainage and aeration and those that ramble or climb are best grown on some sort of mount; most of them take hold best with a little sphagnum moss* under the roots. On a piece of cork bark, tree fern, driftwood, or a little log, secure a layer of damp sphagnum moss with a few laps of nylon fish line [Plate 10]. Then place the plant on the moss, spreading its roots or root stubs naturally, and wind them around with the fish line. Some moss can be placed over the roots in the process. Attach a wire for hanging, and label the plant.

10. *Dendrobium delacourii* on a little log.

*Real sphagnum is a bog moss. Do not use tree or forest moss.

Baskets

Baskets made of redwood slats [Plate 11] are suitable for plants whose flower stems are merely pendent or arching, but, for those whose inflorescences bore down through the medium, open wire containers are better. They can be bought in large sizes, but small ones can be made of chicken wire or wide-mesh hardware cloth. To fill them, use osmunda fiber, wetted and cut into chunks. Fit a few pieces around the roots of the plant to form a ball large enough so that the fiber will be firm when the plant is squeezed into the basket. Check it for uniform firmness by pressing your fingers between the side and the fiber. If it is loose in places, push in another piece or two. A few plants (mentioned later) grow well with sphagnum moss and are handled in the same way, except that the moss cannot be made so firm as the fiber.

11. Neofinetia falcata *in a small hanging tub.*

Handling rootless plants

Most newly imported plants or rootless back divisions of cultivated ones will go ahead nicely when potted or mounted. Occasionally one refuses to reroot or becomes shriveled and needs assistance. It can be helped by enclosing it in a polyethylene bag (check the label to be sure it is polyethylene and not just "plastic") with a little damp bark, tree fern, or sphagnum in the bottom. Plants have been known to remain in such a bag for many months before roots start. It is not usually necessary to add more water, but a bit may be needed after a long period. As soon as developing roots are seen, remove and pot the plant.

Watering and Applying Fertilizers _____

Because orchids do not thrive in a soggy medium, the warning not to overwater should be taken seriously. Perfect drainage keeps water from standing in the pot, but watering too often keeps the medium sopping. When a plant is said to need constant moisture, it means that it can be watered again while still damp. When it is said that the medium should be dry or almost dry between waterings, it means that the surface should be dry, and the medium within the pot, when tested by poking your fingers deep down, should be just barely damp. It is not possible to give rules for frequency of watering; this has to be determined by the grower and will vary according to pot size and seasonal conditions. Plants in baskets and on mounts have to be watered more frequently than those in pots and small pots watered more often than large ones. A daily mist may be required for tiny plants on mounts or in pots.

Fertilizers that are especially formulated for orchids and are completely water-soluble are available from commercial growers who will recommend the proper NPK (nitrogen-phosphorus-potassium) ratio for the medium they suggest. Ratios for use on bark and tree fern run somewhere around 30-30-30 down to 30-10-10, even 10-10-10 depending on

their preferences. Follow directions carefully. A kind made for other plants should be applied at one-half the recommended strength. Since fertilizer should be applied to an already wet medium, a good method is to water first, and then give the fertilizer at every other watering. Watering first has another beneficial action, which is to leach out any accumulated extra salts that are damaging to roots. Most fertilizers contain all the trace elements necessary.

Environmental Conditions

A mild and gentle atmosphere with good air circulation is a must for orchids. Relative humidity between 40 and 60% is sufficient, with a natural rise above that when plants have just been watered or misted. Although plants can tolerate a rise above 85°F (29° to 30°C), a temperature above that is not good for them, and every effort should be made to keep it below. You may read that orchids should not be allowed to stand in a draft; however, it is not harmful for air to blow on the plants. In fact, a current of damp air of moderate temperature is just what we mean by "air circulation." What *is* harmful is a blast of excessively hot, cold, or dry air.

Light must be adjusted to the needs of the kinds of orchids being grown. In artificial light culture, oddly, the intensity need not be so high as in a greenhouse, possibly because artificial light is more uniform: The weather does not change it, and "days" can be as long in winter as in summer. Plants that need shade are satisfied with 1,000 footcandles either in a greenhouse or in a home. With artificial light, this amount can be furnished by two 40-watt fluorescent tubes. Kinds that require medium light need 1,500 to 2,000 footcandles in a greenhouse, around 1,500 footcandles with artificial light, or three 40-watt tubes. Kinds that demand bright light need up to 3,000 footcandles in a greenhouse, which is difficult to furnish artificially. Usually they will adapt themselves to about 2,000 footcandles or four 40-watt tubes. If additional or high-intensity tubes can be used without excessive heat, they would be most beneficial.

A satisfactory artificial light system combines cool white tubes with incandescent bulbs, in a ratio of 100 watts of fluorescent to 25 watts of incandescent. Light intensity falls off with distance from the lamps, and tubes lose efficiency with age. The following table gives the footcandle values of two and four lamps respectively, in relation to distance from the lamps and to their age.

Light-demanding plants can be as close as 4 to 6 inches (10 to 15 cm) below the tubes. Sometimes it is necessary to allow the tips of leaves to almost touch the tubes, but they should be watched for burning. Those that require less light can be placed farther below, according to their needs.

Plants can be grown in windows, either on sills or tiered shelves; in the delightful extended windows now being manufactured that make a miniature greenhouse out of a window; in enclosed cases (once called

TABLE 1. *Illumination in footcandles at various distances from two or four 40-watt standard cool-white fluorescent lamps:*

Distance from lamps (inches)	Two lamps (Used 200 hours)	Four lamps mounted 2 inches apart	
		Used 200 hours	New lamps
	Ft. c.	Ft. c	Ft. c.
1	1,100	1,600	1,800
2	860	1,400	1,600
3	680	1,300	1,400
4	570	1,100	1,300
5	500	940	1,150
6	420	820	1,000
7	360	720	900
8	330	660	830
9	300	600	780
10	280	560	720
11	260	510	660
12	240	480	600
18	130	320	420
24	100	190	260

(From *Yearbook of Agriculture*, U.S. Dept. of Agriculture, 1973.)

Wardian cases) that stand in a window or are equipped with lights; on "light carts" or "light stands" placed either near a window (in which case a little natural light helps with growth and flowering) or away from all natural light; or in a basement room, where greater space and ease in watering make it possible to grow a larger number. Plants in a window will probably have to be shaded when the sun is pouring directly in. This is particularly true for an enclosed case, which can become dreadfully hot in a short time. Extended windows and cases must be well ventilated.

The popularity of terrariums presents the temptation to try them for orchids, but the need for ventilation precludes their being grown in a *closed* terrarium. A large fish tank can substitute for an orchid case, but it must not have a tight lid: It should be uncovered, or the lid should be propped open most of the time. The bottom of the tank may be covered with gravel or bark, or for decorating appeal it may be covered with soil and planted with non-orchidaceous plants, such as small ferns. The orchids should be in their own pots raised up on rocks or logs, on little mounts hung from "trees" or actually planted on them or hung from the sides of the tank. Kinds with trailing stems may be allowed to wander over the bottom material and may even take root in it; this will do no harm, since the main part of the plant will be hanging free. Care must be taken not to allow the air in the tank to become overheated from sun or artificial light

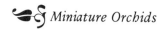

or saturated with humidity. A small fan blowing into it to stir up the air at intervals would be beneficial.

*Problems*_____

Pests and diseases are always with us. A new grower who starts with clean plants is safe for a while, and may think he'll never have to use an insecticide or fungicide. Eventually, however, ordinary garden pests will find his plants, and spores traveling in the air may attack them. High humidity, wet foliage, and lack of air movement favor the spread of bacterial and fungal diseases. Viruses may be present in any plant you acquire; hence the advice to sterilize pots and tools.

Watery spots on leaves are the symptoms of bacterial or fungal diseases. It is difficult to tell them apart so we suggest that if one type of treatment does not work, try another. The spots soon turn brown or black and may ooze droplets containing spores. Isolated spots can be dried up by smearing them with a paste of Tersan 75 (Thiram fungicide), made for golf and lawn turfs but also useful for orchids and not toxic to them in any concentration. Simply mix a bit of the powder with a little water and coat the spot, front and back. To prevent the causal agent from spreading to the rest of the plant, make a weak suspension of Tersan in water and douse the whole plant, then let its foliage remain dry for a week or more. If the disease continues to spread, cut off the involved leaf (along with the stem or pseudobulb if it too is affected), making the cut well down into clean, green tissue, and coat the cut surfaces with the paste. When a pseudobulb is removed, buds along the rhizome will become active and produce new growth. This is also true of lead growths on nonpseudobulbous plants. Bordeaux mixture may also be used but more sparingly than Kocide. (See Appendix.)

A new growth will sometimes rot at the base, perhaps because water standing in it allowed a fungus to develop in the tissues. The growth should be cut out and dry Tersan poured into the wound. Keep the plant dry for a week, and when watering is resumed be careful not to wet the cut area. The growing tip of a monopodial is particularly susceptible to rot, as the leaf bases make a deep cup to hold water. If the top leaf shows a black area, cut it off below the diseased region as quickly as possible and pour dry Tersan into the leaf axil. If caught in time, the growing tip may be saved. If the tip does not survive, a side branch may form from lower down on the stem.

A fairly new fungicide is Banrot, useful in general but especially where root rots are present. Use it at the rate of 1 Tablespoon per gallon of water on individual plants or to treat an infected or threatened group. Bacterial diseases can be treated with Kocide (follow directions carefully). Physan 20 is a useful fungicide. It kills bacteria and fungi on surfaces and can be used without harm ½ to 1½ teaspoons to 1 gallon of water. It can also be used to disinfect benches where diseased plants have stood. It may offer some protection from spread of viruses, as it is also able to kill them on surfaces.

Blackened sheaths should be split down and cut off carefully so as not to injure the buds within; the buds should then be treated with Tersan. Dried sheaths are not a sign of disease, but merely a habit of plants that hold sheaths a long time before flower buds develop (or the plant fails to flower).

In a close, humid atmosphere, flowers may develop a sprinkling of pink or brown spots—*Botrytis* disease of blossoms. Remove all affected flowers immediately to prevent spread, and spray the plants and their neighbors with Banrot. Reduce humidity and increase air circulation.

Viruses attack all orchids, but symptoms vary from one kind to another. One shows up as color break in the flowers—color is patchy, pale in some areas, darker in others—and flowers may be distorted; another causes only subtle light and dark areas. Still another causes necrotic (dead) spots and streaks on flowers, especially easy to see on white blossoms. All can affect the vegetative parts of many species, with dark streaks, pits, or necrotic areas, or—easiest to diagnose—yellow mottling or streaks. Virus diseases cannot be cured, and an infected plant is a menace to others and should be destroyed. Insect injuries sometimes resemble virus diseases, so it is best to have the questionable plant tested by experts. Several laboratories test for virus. See the American Orchid Society Bulletin for their advertisements. Write for their fees and instructions about sending specimens.

The chief pests of orchids are those we battle in the garden—thrips, aphids, scales, mealybugs, mites, slugs, and snails. Malathion is still one of the best means of controlling the first four; Metaldehyde baits kill slugs and snails. Pentac controls mites and false spider mites. Ortho Home and Garden Spray controls aphids on plants and flowers.

Not all ailments are caused by pests or diseases. Too strong a light can burn foliage and blast flowers. A light burn soon dries and does not spread, so it can be differentiated from disease spots. Too great heat can dehydrate and shrivel plants, and can also blast buds. Insufficient light can bring about weak growth and thin flowers and can also prevent flowering. Plants that flower only with short days may not bloom if the lights are left on too long. Except for a few kinds, mainly cattleyas, we do not know what species are day-length sensitive.

The worst environmental enemy is air pollution. Various toxic gases can blast buds and opening flowers. The latter are affected with what is called sepal wilt, where the flower is prematurely aged, the sepals withering first. Flowers can be damaged by the tiniest amount of ethylene, which results from the incomplete combustion of gas, oil, etc., and it is for this reason that greenhouse heaters must be vented to the outside. In the home, a faulty pilot light or break in a flue can bring about the same damage. Sepal wilt of orchids was first studied in cattleyas, but many other kinds are affected as well. Not all orchids are susceptible, however, and in a mixed collection the grower may find some flowers blasted while others are not injured at all. Polluted city air does not always contain ethylene but can nevertheless still cause flower damage.

Encyclopedia of Representative Species

Acostaea

As if to emphasize that not all miniatures are well known, the first alphabetically is the rare, insect-trapping genus *Acostaea*, a relative of *Pleurothallis*; it inhabits the high elevations from Costa Rica to Ecuador.

Acostaea pleurothalloides has paddle-shaped leaves 2 cm tall, tri-lobed at the tip. Flower stems about 4 cm tall, bear two or three minute yellow to red-purple blossoms 6 mm long. A hand lens reveals that the little rounded hood is the dorsal sepal: within it is the broadly winged column, the little upright petals, and the S-curved lip which has a fleshy, hairy crest that overhangs the central portion. The lateral sepals are fused to form a flat tongue that projects outward. The hinged lip is sensitive to touch; the least pressure on the inner part of the crest causes it to spring back between the wings of the column. In this way it traps an insect long enough to ensure its contact with the two pollinia. Other species are *A. colombiana*, *A. trilobata*, and *A. costaricensis*. All are cool growing and like constant moisture. (Colombia and Costa Rica; they flower continuously.)

Ada

The name *Ada* is familiar to most orchid growers because of the large species *A. aurantiaca*. Recently a group of species long included as the section glumaceae of the genus *Brassia* has been transferred to *Ada* due to structures more like *Ada* than *Brassia*, although superficially they strongly resemble the latter. Among them is one miniature, *Ada elegantula*.

Ada elegantula [Plate 12] is a delightful plant with arching grasslike leaves 3 to 20 cm long, one at the top and several from the sides of the small oval, flattened, purple-green pseudobulbs. The flower stems, about as long as the leaves, bear four to five blossoms 3 cm long, yellow-brown or green-brown with darker cross bands [Plate 13]. The sepals are longer than the upward pointing petals; the lip is cream color with a few pinkish spots, a fleshy crest and two hairy keels on its broad basal section, and a pointed tucked-under tip to the mid-lobe. The column is broad, the base of the lip parallel to it. (Colombia, Ecuador, and Peru; flowers in winter.)

13. *A single flower of* Ada elegantula.

Aerangis

Aerangis is but one of the lovely monpodials of the Old World tropics. The genus contains some miniatures and some that are a bit larger. Although many have quite similar sprays of delicate birdlike or star-shaped flowers with graceful spurs, subtle differences make each charming in its own way. A few are completely distinctive: Some have a fan of leaves that stays about the same size through the years, with new leaves coming from the center as older ones die off at the sides; some have an upright stem with alternate leaves. The flowers are usually long-lasting, deliciously fragrant (some more so than others and most only at night), and tend to open in rapid succession so that there is a period when the whole spike is open. All thrive in pots of medium-grade bark but can also be grown on cork or tree fern slabs. The roots tend to ramble and often grow to great lengths.

Aerangis articulata grows to about 15 cm in height and has several pairs of rather broad leaves with bi-lobed tips. Its arching 30 to 40 cm flower stems hold a dozen or more glistening white flowers on pale peach-colored pedicels. The blossoms are 3 to 4 cm across, the arching spurs 15 to 20 cm long. (Malagasy; spring.)

Aerangis biloba is much like *A. articulata* in plant character, but the tips of the leaves have one long sharp point and one rounded one. It has pendent stems of about 12 white flowers, 2 to 4 cm across, arranged close together in a double row. They have rather long, slender parts and pale reddish-tan spurs 4 cm long. (Tropical West Africa; spring.)

Aerangis calanthe is barely 4 cm tall, with several pairs of rather fleshy leaves about 4 cm long. The flower stem is twice as long as the

14. Aerangis clavigera *is pure lace when in flower.*

leaves and bears five or more white flowers 2 cm across, with 4 cm spurs. (Uganda; spring.)

Aerangis citrata gives a remarkable number of flowers for its small size. It grows to 8 to 10 cm tall with three or four pairs of leaves and can have four to ten spikes, each 40 cm long. The crowded double-ranked flowers are white to cream, occasionally yellow, and all face forward. They are 2 to 3 cm across and have short, pale yellow spurs. (Malagasy; late spring to summer.)

Aerangis clavigera [Plate 14] has the plant habit of a small phalaenopsis, with several pairs of broadly oval, horizontal leaves 8 to 10 cm long. Side plantlets form easily. Several 20 to 30 cm long flower stems appear at the same time. The pedicels extend straight out from each side, forming a ladder. The 1 cm flowers with their downward-arching 5 cm spurs are symmetrical and decorative. A plant in bloom has the appearance of pure lace. (Malagasy; autumn).

Aerangis fastuosa is only 4 cm tall, similar to a small phalaenopsis. The several pairs of broad leaves are 8 cm long and closely spaced on the short stem. The few long-spurred 5 cm flowers are sweetly rounded, close together on a short inflorescence, making a lovely bouquet. (Malagasy; late winter to spring.)

Aerangis flabellifolia [Plate 15] has attractive, oddly shaped leaves that form a fan about 15 cm tall. They are leathery with lengthwise ridges on the upper surface formed by accessory veins, and speckled on the back. They are narrow at the base, becoming broader toward the unevenly bi-lobed tip. The plant usually has more than one 20 cm spike of waxy 3 to 4 cm blossoms whose 8 cm spurs extend backward from the flower. (East Africa; fall.)

Aerangis kirkii is a neat plant around 8 to 10 cm tall, eventually consisting of many fans of curiously shaped leaves, narrow at the base, straight sided, and flaring into two deeply rounded lobes at the tip. The white or cream colored flowers, four to five to a stem, are about 4 to 5 cm across and give the impression of a flight of birds. (Kenya; fall.)

Aerangis mystacidii has beautiful leaves, rich green, netted with darker green, wavy on the edges, 10 cm long, and growing in a fan with a 15 cm spread. The 3.2 cm flowers are white with oval parts, the petals bent back like wings, and they are fragrant in the daytime. There is a touch of salmon color at the base of the petals and sepals, and the 10 cm spur turns salmon with age. (Natal, South Africa; summer to fall.)

Aerangis rhodosticta [Plate 16] is one of the prettiest of all orchids. The little plant lies flat or hangs down from its mount of cork (which it prefers); its slender 10 cm shiny green leaves lie close together, all turned face up. The flower spikes extend horizontally and hold 10 to 12 flat, round, 2 cm flowers all facing up with short spurs extending down beneath. They are white to cream color, punctuated in the center by a bright red anther cap. (Camaroons to Kenya; spring and fall.)

15. Aerangis flabellifolia *has distinctive ridged leaves, wider at the bi-lobed tips. It has airy sprays of pure white blossoms.*

16. Aerangis rhodosticta *has sprays of flat flowers all facing up, dotted in the center by a red column tip.*

Aerangis stylosa [Color Plate C-3] is one of the most satisfying of the genus. It has several pairs of light green, slender-oval leaves that make an upright fan 15 cm tall. It usually has several flower stems at once that can reach 40 cm in length. On shorter stems, flowers may all be open at once; on the long ones, flowers may still be opening at the tip when the basal ones have faded. The pure white star-shaped blossoms are 4 cm across, close together on the stem, and their 12 cm spurs arch downward in perfect semicircles. (Malagasy; spring and summer.)

Aerangis verdickii has leaves of metallic green which either form a fan or spread out horizontally and may be ruffled on the edge. The plants vary considerably in size, with a spread of 12 to 40 cm, so that only the smaller ones would qualify as miniatures. The four to eight flowers are cream color, 3 cm in diameter, with petals broader than the sepals and bent back to touch at the tips. The pink 12 cm spurs are gently winding. (South Africa; flowers several times a year.)

Aeranthes

The elfin flowers of this genus are unusual and attractive, and fortunately at least one species is close to the size limit for miniatures and also readily available. There are other available species as well, and any that you may acquire would be worth growing. Most are from Malagasy, a few from the Mascarene Islands.

Aeranthes ramosus has a fan of upright, pale green leaves 10 to 15 cm tall. The long flower stem is like a fine black wire, so thin that one wonders how nutrients get through it; it may be single or branched. Buds come in succession from the extreme tips. The flowers are 4 to 5 cm across, pure apple green, shading into white on the very broad column foot to which the lip is attached. Oddly, the short, chunky spur forms from the tip of the column foot. The petals and sepals are broad at the base and come to an abruptly sharp point. *A. ramosus* var. *orthopoda* [Plate 17] is larger and darker, and is considered by some a separate species, *A. orthopoda*. The plants do well in hanging pots. (Malagasy; from summer through winter.)

17. Aeranthes orthopoda *is a large version of* Aeranthes ramosus, *both of which have green, pixie-like blossoms.*

Aerides

Aerides japonica, See *Sedirea japonica.*

Alamania

Only one species of this Mexican genus is known at present.

Alamania punicea [Color Plate C-4] is a little plant whose fat, 1 cm pseudobulbs are topped by a pair of stiff, fleshy, oval leaves 1 to 1.5

cm long and sharply pointed. The rhizome meanders, branching often and climbing over itself in the process, to create a cushion about 4 cm high. The roots are as thick as the pseudobulbs. Bright-eyed flowers are borne on leafless pseudobulbs that alternate with those that bear leaves. They are red or red-orange, starshaped, 1.2 cm across. A white column and a white or yellow patch at the base of the lip make them most eye-catching. The plants should be mounted and grown in a cool, bright place. They have to be kept dry during the winter, with just a light mist once a day but given abundant water during their growing and flowering season. (Mexico; early summer.)

Amesiella

As far as I know, there is only one species in this genus, *Amesiella philippinensis*; it was formerly *Angraecum philippinensis*. Rudolph Schlechter intended to create a genus with it in honor of Oakes Ames, but died before doing so. Leslie Garay has now carried out Schlechter's intent.

Amesiella philippinensis is another plant of the phalaenopsis habit, with rounded leaves 4 to 5 cm long and a short flower spike holding three or four lovely round, white, fragrant blossoms, 3 cm across. The lip is shorter than the other segments, slightly cupped and yellow in the throat. (Philippines; spring.)

Ancistrochilus

Two delightful species (and perhaps a third) of the genus *Ancistrochilus* spread through tropical West Africa to Uganda. They have conical pseudobulbs shaped like the well-known "chocolate kiss" and rather thin, pleated, stalked, deciduous leaves. They like warm to intermediate temperatures, and should be grown in pots. Give them a dry rest after the leaves fall, and water well during growth and flowering.

Ancistrochilus rothschildianus [Plate 18] forms a single leaf about 8 cm tall on top of the 1 cm tall pseudobulb. The flowering stem is 5 to 7 cm tall, entirely pubescent, as is the ovary, and bears a fragrant, rose and lavender flower (sometimes two) huge for the size of the plant— 5.5 cm across, with oval sepals and narrower petals, all pubescent on the outside. The lip has broad, up-curving side lobes, creamy green, stippled inside with brown. The narrow and pointed front lobe curves down and is decorated with five dark rose ridges that come together on the narrow point. (Sierra Leone to Uganda; winter).

Ancistrochilus thompsonianus is a bit larger in all respects and has two or three leaves to the pseudobulb. The fragrant flowers are 7.5 cm across, with white sepals and petals, green-tinged at the base. The lip has greenish side lobes spotted with purple on the inside. The narrow, green

18. Ancistrochilus rothschildianus *has a large rose and lavender flower on an 8 cm plant.*

35

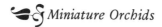

mid-lobe bears five purple lines and is longer and more hooked under than in the *A. rothschildianus.* (Southern Nigeria to Uganda; summer.)

Angraecopsis

The "-opsis" on the end of its name indicates that this genus is similar to *Angraecum*, most famous of all genera from Africa and Malagasy. It has dainty flowers but few species, and its hallmark is a three-lobed lip.

    Angraecopsis amaniensis is a tiny, flat-lying plant that clings to the bark with roots thick for the size of the plant. The barely visible short stem bears three to five thick, leathery, somewhat curving leaves, 3.2 cm long. The 7 cm, slightly zigzag flower stems arise from the woody base of the plant. They can bear up to 25 very fragrant, bright emerald or pale green, star-shaped flowers, 5 to 10 mm long with rather fat, 7 mm long, whitish spurs pointing straight down. The side lobes are needlelike. It sheds its leaves several months before flowering. (Kenya to Malawi; spring.)

    Angraecopsis breviloba has plant characteristics similar to *A. amaniensis*: Its flowers turn upward to form a single row (they are "secund") on the 5 to 6 cm long inflorescence; they are green, 5 mm across, and do not open wide. The forward-pointing spurs end in flattened bulges. It flowers at the cool end of the intermediate temperature range and in heavy shade. (Kenya and Tanzania; summer and fall).

19. Angraecum compactum, *a small plant, has large, serenely lovely flowers.*

Angraecum

A richly varied genus of some 200 species, *Angraecum* spreads throughout Africa to Malagasy and the Comoro Islands and even farther east. The plants have an upright or pendent stem with alternate leaves and pure white or greenish flowers, most of them sweetly fragrant. But this simple description does not do justice to the range of forms among the plants and flowers. They do well a little to the warm or cool side of intermediate temperatures, with generous humidity and medium to high light. More compact plants can be grown in pots; those with pendent or climbing stems on mounts.

    Angraecum chamaeanthus is one of the smallest of the genus, with fleshy leaves 2 cm long and a flower stem 3 cm tall. The tiny, greenish-white flowers are only 2 mm in diameter, with rounded petals, sepals, and lip all pointed at the tip, and a short, chunky spur. It is cool growing or needs a cool spot in the intermediate range. (Northern South Africa to Zambia, Malawi, and Tanzania; spring).

    Angraecum compactum [Plate 19], a serenely lovely species, grows so slowly that a small plant will flower for many years before exceeding 15 cm in height. By then it will probably have made side plantlets that can be removed or left in place to form a many-branched plant. The alternate 5 cm leaves are fleshy and close together. The 4 to 6 cm flowers are huge in proportion, pure white, and waxy. The slender, pointed sepals and petals spread out behind the large, round-oval lip, and the graceful 10 to 12 cm spur curves forward from behind the flower. The ovary has 3 tall wings and 2 small ones. The pedicel flattens to a mere ribbon. (Malagasy; late winter and spring.)

Angraecum cultriforme is a diminutive plant that flowers when very small and grows slowly to 10 to 15 cm in height, giving flowering stems simultaneously from several leaf axils. Its slender 3 to 5 cm leaves are divided into two sharp lobes at the tip and are dull green, spotted on the back. Young roots are shiny green for their whole length, gray when old. The little flower stems are zigzag, 2 to 3 cm long, and bear three or four flowers, one at a time, over a period of months. The 1 cm flower is a tannish-salmon color with pointed petals and sepals, a superior (held uppermost), pointed, scoop-shaped lip. The end of the straight little spur expands into an elongated transparent bulb in which one can see the level of nectar. The plant grows well on cork bark in a shaded spot. (East Africa; summer to winter).

Angraecum distichum [Plate 20] is charmingly "different," with stems of closely spaced triangular leaves reminiscent of a lockhartia plant. The stems branch freely, making quite a bouquet, the tallest reaching 15 cm. Tiny, delicately scented, white flowers come singly from the axils of the newer leaves almost all year round. (West Africa to Uganda; summer, fall, or winter.)

Angraecum equitans is a compact plant from 9 to 10 cm high, with closely packed, fleshy, keeled leaves 3 to 4 cm long. The white flowers, almost 3 cm across, have slender sepals and petals that taper to points and a concave, eliptic, pointed lip. Its 8 cm spur has a large orifice and gradually becomes threadlike. The ovary has 4 keels or wings. (Malagasy; spring.)

Angraecum filicornu has delicate branching stems 10 to 20 cm tall and alternate leaves about the size of short blades of grass. Dainty, single, 2 cm, white flowers come from the leaf axils. The sepals are very slender and pointed, the petals even more so. The lip is fiddle-shaped with a pointed tip, and the spur is filamentous, 9 to 11 cm long. (Malagasy; summer.)

Angraecum germinyanum has beautiful, spidery flowers, so it is lovely to own, even though its strong, leafy stems branch and ramble. The flowers are white, tinged with green or salmon color. The rounded lip, 2 to 4 cm across, is held uppermost, and it and all the other parts taper to tails that curve and zigzag downward about half the distance of the 10 to 14 cm spur. This species is cool growing. (Grande Comore and Malagasy; spring and summer).

Angraecum humile is a lilliputian, barely 5 cm tall, with little, fleshy alternate leaves, 1 cm long. Flower stems are about as tall as the leaves, holding three or four almost microscopic blossoms only 3 mm wide.

20. Angraecum distichum *is a perky little plant with stems clothed with tiny triangular leaves.*

37

21. Anagraecum leonis *has perfectly flat, sickle-shaped leaves and glorious long-spurred, pure white flowers.*

The blossoms are white, with a short green spur constricted in the middle. Grow in heavy shade. (Kenya and Tanzania; spring.)

Angraecum leonis [Plate 21] when past its youth is really larger than "borderline" but is always beautiful. The odd sickle-shaped leaves, laterally flattened, curve alternately from the stem in a flat plane and end in a fine point. The glorious waxen flowers, 10 cm across, are sparkling white, two to four on a stem. They have pointed petals and sepals, a broad, rectangular, almost three-lobed lip, and an S-curved, 7 to 9 cm spur. (Grande Comore; winter.)

Angraecum mauritianum is a branching plant that has slender stems and delicate leaves. A single stem can be over 20 cm long. On a heavily branched plant, the little, single, white, 4 cm flowers resemble Christmas tree ornaments. The petals curve up like little arms, and the lateral sepals curve down beside the lip. The green spur is 8 cm long. (Mascarene Islands; late summer.)

Angraecum minus can be as small as 1 cm and sometimes reaches 4 cm in height. It has a fan of three or four fine, grasslike leaves and a root system large for the plant. Its threadlike flowering stem bears five or six white blossoms 1.5 mm across. (Near the source of the Zambesi River in Northwest Zambia; spring and fall).

Angraecum pseudofilicornu has narrow terete leaves spaced farther apart than in *A. filicornu*, on a slender, upright or pendent stem. The rose-salmon blossoms are shaped somewhat like those of that species except that the lip is wider than long, is cupped, and clasps the column at the base. The spur is 15 cm long, becoming attenuated from a wide orifice. (Malagasy; spring and summer.)

Angraecum pusillum is a trim little plant, about 5 cm tall, with gracefully curved, grasslike leaves closely set in two flat ranks on its short stem. The flower spikes remind one of a pleurothallis, bearing many, 3 to 4 mm, white blossoms with 2 mm spurs. Cool growing. (South Africa; spring.)

Angraecum rutenbergianum, like many others, is about 4 cm tall when young and reaches 12 cm as its stems continue to grow. It has stiff, thick, narrow leaves 2.5 to 5.5 cm long. The dazzlingly white flowers are huge for the plant, 6 to 7 cm long, with slender sepals and petals, a broadly oval lip, pointed at the tip, and a slender spur varying in length from 6 to 14 cm. (Malagasy; midsummer).

Angraecum sacciferum is one of the smallest, 2.5 to 4 cm tall. Its stem bears three to five, slender, up-curving, pointed leaves. Several flower stems 3 to 5 cm long come from the bare lower part of the stem, each holding up to five, minute, yellow to yellow-green blossoms, 5 mm across, which open in succession. They have oval, pointed sepals and petals and a fat, boat-shaped lip with a little, 3 mm, balloonlike spur around which the ovary curls. Grow cool and shaded. (South Africa to Uganda and Congo; autumn.)

Angraecum viguieri has widely spaced, narrow leaves, 12 to 14 cm long on a slender stem, and begins flowering when about 15 cm tall. Older plants are taller but still dainty. The huge satiny flowers, opening one at a time, are 9 cm long not including the 9 to 10 cm spur. The sepals and petals, only 4 to 5 mm wide, taper to a fine point and bend back at the tip. The lip is broadly diamond-shaped and ends in a long, slender point. The color varies from white to greenish-gold. (Malagasy; spring to fall.)

*Anoectochilus*_____

The genus *Anoectochilus* and several other genera are known as the "jewel" orchids and have traditionally been grown for their satiny, colorfully veined foliage. However, their small flowers are also attractive. Most of these terrestrial species require warm temperatures or a warm spot in an intermediate situation, constant humidity without becoming waterlogged, and heavy shade. The potting medium should be a rich, open, fibrous mixture, perhaps shredded osmunda fiber, leaf mold, and perlite. There are some 20 species; the following are only three examples:

Anoectochilus regalis has a rosette of nearly round, velvety leaves, 5 cm long, of rich dark green with an intricate network of gold or reddish veins. The few flowers on the 15 cm stems are white. The sepals are decorated with red hairs on the back, and the lip has two pink spots and a fringe around its edge. (Southern India and Sri Lanka; spring).

Anoectochilus roxburghii [Color Plate C-5], used in Chinese medicine, is much like *A. regalis* in shape and size. The almost iridescent leaves have a suffusion of gold down the center and a network of gold to red-gold veins. The flowers have tawny red petals and sepals and a fantastic lip. The front part consists of two long spatulate lobes with five white fingers projecting from the sides of the basal section. (Himalayas; summer.)

Anoectochilus sikkimensis has smaller leaves, very dark red with gold veins. It has a 20 cm spike of olive-green flowers, whose white lip has green teeth along the edges of the basal section and a pair of wide, flaplike end lobes. Cool to cool-intermediate temperatures. (Sikkim; fall.)

*Ascocentrum*_____

Members of *Ascocentrum* are delightful plants that have long been popular. In recent years they have been hybridized with species of *Vanda* to create small, brightly colored plants that are easy to handle in small areas. The species are like little vandas; one or two are beyond miniature size. All do well in warm or warm-intermediate temperatures.

Ascocentrum curvifolium is rarely more than 12 cm tall, with rather long leaves that could put it in the "borderline" category. The upright flower spike is closely packed with round, cinnabar-red flowers, 2 cm

*22. **Ascocentrum miniatum** has a wealth of cheery yellow-orange blossoms punctuated by a purple column tip.*

in diameter. It requires bright light. (Burma; summer).

Ascocentrum hendersonianum is only 7 cm tall, with leaves 12 cm long. Its 15 cm flower spike bears up to thirty fragrant, brilliant magenta flowers 3 cm in diameter. (Borneo; spring).

Ascocentrum miniatum [Plate 22], which grows a bit taller, has dense spikes of glowing yellow-orange flowers about 2 cm across, punctuated by a purple column tip. (Himalayas, Malay Peninsula, Java, and Borneo; flowers variably.)

Ascocentrum pumilum, about 7 cm tall, has almost needlelike leaves 4 to 6 cm long, and short spikes of rosy-lavender, 2 cm flowers. It needs a shady spot. (Taiwan, winter.)

Barbosella

A modest relative of *Pleurothallis*, *Barbosella* is really quite similar to it. The leaves are paddle-shaped, rising from a creeping rhizome, with papery bracts at their bases. The flowers have joined lateral sepals that form a shallow cup at the base, free dorsal sepal, and petals much smaller than either. The lip lies on the platform of the fused lateral sepals. There are four pollinia. Like *Pleurothallis*, they inhabit the cool cloud forests of tropical America and thrive in cultivation in a cool, somewhat shaded environment, with moisture the year round.

Barbosella australis is a beautiful little creeping plant whose rose-colored flowers are larger than its 2 to 4 cm leaves, but hardly project beyond them. Its lateral sepals, broad at the base, are fused for three-fourths of their length. The smaller dorsal sepal is held forward over the column. The tiny lip is shiny and a darker rose, and the white petals are minute. (Brazil; late summer.)

Barbosella caespitifica is about 6 cm tall, with slender, upright leaves and a single flower on a slim, straight stem of about the same height. The flower is rose color, with its slender dorsal sepal standing straight up and the wider joined laterals straight down. The filamentous petals project forward, their tips slightly thickened. The small lip is green. (Ecuador; late fall.)

Barbosella cucullata [Color Plate C-6] has flower stems more than twice the height of its 4 to 5 cm leaves. The 4 cm long flowers are bright yellow to yellow-green, with a green or reddish lip, and they stand wide open. (Venezuela, Colombia, Ecuador, and Peru; winter.)

Barbosella handroi has greenish flowers quite like those of *B. cucullata* but smaller and very delicate. Its 1 cm leaves are rounded and march along on a creeping rhizome. (Brazil; summer or winter).

Barbosella prorepens is extremely small. If moss grows on the surface of its pot, the 1 cm leaves hardly rise above it, and its flower buds are difficult to distinguish from the moss's spore capsules. The flower stem grows a bit taller with each flower that develops, finally reaching a height of 4 to 5 cm. (Costa Rica; spring.)

Barkeria _____

The members of *Barkeria* are graceful, distinctive plants with pretty flowers in shades of pink and rosy-lavender. In most, sepals and petals are held back from the showy lip. The genus is closely related to *Epidendrum* and for a while was relegated to that genus until it was recently separated again. While *Barkeria* ranges from Mexico to Panama, most known species occur in Mexico, and many new ones are being found there. The plants have slender cylindrical stems, slightly swollen in a few species, and several alternate leaves toward the top. They are deciduous in winter and look like a bunch of dry sticks attached to a tree branch by strong roots. They should be cultivated on a mount, preferably a small log, and hung where they get good light. While leafless they should be kept rather dry and then watered regularly as soon as they begin new growth. Plants range from 2 to 20 cm in height, but even the tallest are slim and dainty. The flower spike comes from the tip of the stem and is often two or three times its length, bearing six to 20 or more flowers.

Barkeria barkeriola is of medium size and has brightly marked 2.5 to 3.5 cm blossoms. The petals and sepals are rosy-lavender. The white lip, narrow at the base, broadens toward the apex where it comes to a sharp point. It is decorated with a patch of dark red on the outer section. There is essentially no callus, just two slightly elevated lines that continue onto the lip. The large column is yellow, heavily speckled with red. (Mexico, the states of Colima, Sinaloa, and Nayarit; late summer and fall.)

Barkeria chinensis [Plate 23] is one of the smallest, with stems up to 8 cm and flowers of about 2 cm. Their color is unusual in the genus, being creamy yellow with a yellow lip marked with red spots and a few red verrucose (warty) veins. The flowers do not open widely; the petals are held forward over the rather long, boat-shaped lip, and the sepals flare outward. Occasionally some of the flowers may self-pollinate. (Mexico to Panama; midwinter.)

Barkeria cyclotella (syn. *scandens*) [Color Plate C-7] is the most brilliantly colored of all, with flowers entirely deep magenta, except for a touch of yellow at the base of the triple lip keels, and a ligher border on the membranous column wings. The blossoms are 3 to 4.5 cm across, with a large rectangular lip. (South Central Mexico; midwinter.)

Barkeria dorotheae is a delightful new species, 3 to 20 cm high, with pink blossoms on a tall stem. They are 2.8 to 3.5 cm in diameter, with rounded, somewhat channeled sepals and petals which curve out evenly like an umbrella over the lip and column and are darker on the back than the front. The dorsal sepal is shorter than the laterals. The lip is

23. **Barkeria chinensis**, *one of the smallest of the genus, has delicate flowers of creamy yellow.*

41

broad at the tip and narrow at the base, and its sides turn down like a saddle. The center of the lip and the broad, winged column are yellow, spotted with purple. Three keels, the center one higher, run the length of the lip and project a bit beyond its end. (Mexico, on the border between Jalisco and Colima at sea level; winter.)

Barkeria elegans (syn. *uniflora*) [Color Plate C-8] bears many eye-catching flowers 5.6 cm across. The sepals and petals are rosy lilac on the front, pale on the back, and all hold themselves horizontally, bringing the dorsal sepal over the lip. The large lip is white with a solid or divided patch of bright magenta on the front, through which run slightly raised veins. The huge, pinkish green column has broad, fleshy wings, wider near the apex, and two dark "eyes" at its tip, sometimes a third "nose" spot, too, giving it the look of a little fish. (Southern Mexico; fall and winter.)

Barkeria halbingeri is another new species, named for Federico Halbinger, who has done most to elucidate the barkerias and describe new species. Its 15 cm stem holds a spike of 4.5 cm, exquisitely shaped, pink flowers. Broad, oval-pointed petals stand out like wings above the skirtlike lip. The basal edges of the lip curl around the base of the column, while its ruffled sides swing down from the very stiff, central, triple keels. The column is a decorative part of the blossom, with its broad green wings and pink central cylinder spotted with red. (Grows only on rocks in Mexico, State of Oaxaca, spring.)

Barkeria lindleyana, perhaps the tallest of the genus, should be considered borderline in size, although some seasonal growths fall within the miniature class. Its stem can be 30 cm tall and the flower spike up to 80 cm. The 5 to 6 cm flowers are entirely rosy-lavender, except for a white patch in the center of the lip and a dark patch at its outer end. The broad petals extend flat like wings, while the sepals are raised up. The lip is almost square; three keels extend nearly to its tip, with the central one raised and thickened at the tip. (Costa Rica; early fall.)

Barkeria lindleyana subspecies *vanneriana* is from Mexico, usually grows on rocks, and differs chiefly in being shorter and having smaller flowers.

Barkeria melanocaulon is pale pinkish-lavender, 3 cm wide. The oval sepals and petals are pointed, the petals far broader. They all curve backward to expose the heart-shaped lip which has three points at the apex where the strong orange, red-spotted keels project beyond its margin. The dark green, densely spotted column has very broad wings, and its tip rises up from the lip. This species grows on rocks and cacti at low elevations and requires the warm end of the intermediate range. (Mexico, state of Oaxaca; winter).

Barkeria naevosa is a small species, with 4 to 8 cm spindle-shaped stems. Its 3.5 cm flowers resemble those of *B. chinensis*, except that they open wider and do not self-pollinate. The pointed sepals, petals, and exterior of the lip are rosy-lavender, while the interior of the boat-shaped lip

is yellow with slightly darker, raised veins. (Oaxaca, Guerrero, and Michoacan; fall and winter.)

Barkeria palmeri, with spindle-shaped stems 2 to 15 cm high,
can have a simple or a branched inflorescence with some hundred densely
packed flowers. Each pale pink blossom is 2 to 3 cm across, with slender
sepals and petals all swept forward. The lip is heart-shaped with a toothed
and rather wavy margin. Three prominent, yellow, verrucose (warty) keels
extend almost to the apex, and from them radiate verrucose lines heavily
marked with dark rose at the base. The plant should not be kept entirely
dry while leafless but should have a weekly misting. (Mexico, states of
Jalisco, Nayarit, and Colima; midwinter.)

Barkeria shoemakeri is a charming new species with diminutive
flowers. Its leaves are erect and fleshy in contrast to the rather thin ones
of other species. A branched stem bears many flowers each only 1.6 cm
across, pale pink with darker veins in the upswept sepals and petals. The
short, rounded lip is narrow at the base and decorated with heavy raised
lines on its ruffled outer section. The tip of the chunky, spotted column
rises up from the lip. It should have some misting while leafless. (Mexico,
state of Michoacan; midwinter.)

Barkeria skinneri [Plate 24], one of the taller and best-known
species, is very lovely. A showy, densely packed stem bears rich cerise
flowers, 2 to 4 cm across. The petals and dorsal sepal are held out at right
angles, and the lateral sepals are sharply reflexed. The lip, rounded through
the center and coming gently to a point, is decorated with five yellow
keels, three large and, in between them, two small ones. (Chiapas, Mexico,
to Guatemala; midwinter.)

24. Barkeria skinneri *is
generous with its rich cerise
flowers decorated with yellow
keels.*

Barkeria spectabilis is rather variable in color, ranging from near
white to lavender. There is also a considerable range in flower size, from
4 to 8 cm, although most are around 5 cm. The petals are turned forward,
the sepals back. The lip is an elongated oval with a white or yellow center
and has a darker patch on the end. Of the three keels, the center one extends to the pointed tip of the lip. The column is deep rose with spotted
wings. (Mexico to Honduras; summer.)

Barkeria strophinx is peach color, has less sharply pointed flower
parts, a yellow patch at the base of the lip, and reddish radiating lines
in its center. The small flowers are densely packed on an unbranched stem.
(Mexico, state of Michoacan; late winter.)

Bolusiella _____

Bolusiella has several diminutive members that are most unusual little
monopodials. The plants are fans of flattened fleshy leaves, and they have
spikes of tiny, white, fragrant flowers. In order to thrive and flower, they
must be mounted and kept damp and in medium light.

43

25. Bolusiella imbricata *is a jewel-like plant with a fan of fleshy, speckled leaves and sprays of tiny flowers.*

26. Bolusiella imbricata. *Detail of the flowers.*

Bolusiella imbricata [Plate 25], for all its height of 3 to 5 cm, is the largest of the genus. The color pattern of the plant is attractive, with pebble-textured leaves dotted with black at their base and attached to overlapping, cream-colored basal sheaths. As they become older, the plants make many side branches and so become bouquets of fans. The 5 to 8 cm flower spikes [Plate 26] bear a double row of pure white blossoms, 3 mm across, which just barely protrude from their bracts and hide their tiny, forward-jutting spurs beneath them. (West Africa through Uganda to Kenya; summer and winter).

Bolusiella iridifolia is a similar plant, with a groove in the upper surface of the more triangular leaves, and without the basal spotting. Its flowers, cradled in boat-shaped bracts, are fewer on the spike and do not open as fully. (Kenya at high elevations, Uganda at lower elevations; irregulary, sometimes twice a year.)

Bolusiella maudae has fewer, broader leaves attached to brown basal sheaths, and a spike of very slender flowers with sharply pointed parts. (Malawi and Natal, South Africa; summer.)

Broughtonia

The few species of this genus, native to the West Indies, are relatives of *Cattleya*, *Laelia*, etc., and have been hybridized with members of that group.

Broughtonia sanguinea, the best known and the only one that can come within the specifications for a miniature, has compressed, oval pseudobulbs, 3 to 5 cm tall, with usually two stiff, fleshy leaves 8 to 13 cm high. Its flower spike is arching, 30 to 60 cm long, bearing a cluster of five to 15, bright rose to scarlet, wide-open blossoms of sparkling, crystalline texture. The sepals are slender, the petals broadly oval, and the lip is round and ruffled. All parts are beautifully veined. A lovely yellow form is *B. sanguinea* 'Carmen Gauntlett.' The species is not easy to grow and is best mounted and hung where there is good light and generous humidity. It should be given a spray of mist once a day. (Jamaica, at low elevations, including the salt flats; spring and summer.)

Bulbophyllum

Of the combined *Bulbophyllum/Cirrhopetalum* "macrogenus," any number we might choose would represent only a fraction of the 2000-odd species. They inhabit both Eastern and Western hemispheres but are far more numerous in the Old World. Sizes range from huge plants weighing 20 lb (about 10 kg), with leaves 5 ft (150 cm) long such as *Bulbophyllum fletcheranum* and *B. macrobulbon*, to some with pseudobulbs the size of the head of a pin. Some flowers are simple in form, others fantastic. Most have ordinary flower stems, while some have a fleshy stalk on which tiny flowers are inserted. A characteristic of both *Bulbophyllum* and *Cirrhopetalum* is a hinged, mobile lip, counterbalanced to flip an insect into the column. For convenience, the two genera will be given separately, although there is actually no consensus as to whether they should be combined or kept distinct.

Bulbophyllum ambrosia [Color Plate C-9] has a creeping, branching rhizome with cylindrical, slightly angular pseudobulbs 2.5 to 4 cm tall, each bearing a single, thick, spatula-shaped leaf 7 cm tall. The plant soon covers a mount of cork bark or tree fern. The remarkable flowers, 2.8 cm long, are produced singly from the base of old and new pseudobulbs. The column has a long foot to which the freely mobile lip is attached. The base of the lip is parallel to the foot of the column, then turns outward and then down, making three right-angle turns. The lateral sepals and the petals are attached to the back of the column foot. The fragrant blossom is light pink with dark rose veins, and the upper surface of the lip is wrinkled and spotted. (Southern China, area of Hong Kong; winter.)

Bulbophyllum barbigerum is one of the strangest of species. From a rather pretty plant 12 cm tall, with perfectly round, flattened pseudobulbs and single leaves, arise spikes of flowers whose foreward jutting, tongue-like lip is a bizarre brush of blood-red hairs. The hairs, the tips of some of which bear knobs, bounce and jiggle in the slightest breeze, while the lips lower and raise themselves like keys on a fairy player piano. The flower itself is 2.5 cm long, with almost invisible petals nestled in the cup formed by the base of the spiky sepals. (Tropical West Africa; spring.)

Bulbophyllum cochleatum has spikes of tiny flowers that form a most beautiful symmetrical pattern on the long arching stem. The 25 cm inflorescence bears a hundred or more 9 mm blossoms, arranged alternately in two compact rows with the lateral sepals toward the center. These curve to form a heart, so that one's eye travels down a double row of miniature hearts. The dorsal sepals stand straight out to the left and right of the ranks. The tongue-shaped lips are purple, fringed with short hairs, and flip over if one lifts the spike. (West Africa to Kenya; all year.)

Bulbophyllum dearei has a striking flower, huge for the size of the plant. The roundish-conical pseudobulbs, 2.5 cm tall, are topped with single, broad, stalked leaves 10 cm tall. The large (7 cm across) fragrant, tawny yellow flowers are long-lasting and of heavy substance; they are produced singly on stems 10 cm tall. The broadly oval dorsal sepal, the largest part of the blossom, has a glandular surface and is decorated with orange lengthwise veins and deep purple crossbars. The narrower lateral sepals are striped with purple and curve up from the "chin" at their base and then bend forward. The strangely shaped lip has broad white side lobes that curve up like a collar, and a mid-lobe consisting of two forward-projecting, purple knobs. It is so delicately hinged that it is in constant motion. The plant needs warm temperatures. (Philippines and Borneo; spring.)

Bulbophyllum falcatum is representative of a group of species

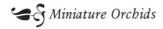

that have a fleshy, flattened rachis (flower stem) on each side of which the flowers are set on the shortest of pedicels. This particular one has pyramidal, deeply angled pseudobulbs 3 cm tall, with two or three leaves 4 to 6 cm long. The inflorescence is 10 cm long, the flower-bearing section accounting for half the length. The 8 mm tall reddish flowers look like tiny animals. The concave dorsal sepal hugs the back of the erect column, the other parts folding around its base. (West Africa to Uganda; winter or summer.)

Bulbophyllum globuliforme is rather rare and may be the smallest of the genus. Its globular pseudobulbs, 1 to 2 mm in diameter, grow along like beads on a string, and the rhizome branches and occasionally forms dense masses. The leaf is a mere pinpoint, 1 to 1.5 mm tall, and the flower stems are 1 to 1.5 cm high. The flowers are 3 mm across, white with a pale yellow lip. (Australia; spring.)

27. Bulbophyllum gravidum *has a red-fringed, hinged lip that jiggles in the slightest air movement.*

Bulbophyllum gravidum [Plate 27] is a delightful relative of *B. cochleatum*, with flowers a full 1 cm long. The plants are 10 to 12 cm tall, with narrow, four-angled, somewhat soft and wrinkled pseudobulbs and paired leaves. The flower stems lengthen over a period of months, opening a dozen or so flowers at a time until a hundred or so have bloomed. They are pale green with a red, fringed, mobile lip. The plant quickly covers a mount, preferring shade and constant moisture. (Malawi; all year.)

Bulbophyllum guttulatum [Color Plate C-10] is one of the prettiest of the genus. The plants are around 10 cm tall, with angled, single-leaved pseudobulbs. The inflorescence is about twice as tall and holds an umbel (fan) of striking flowers, almost iridescent and about 2 cm long. They are yellow with distinct lines of red spots on the petals and sepals, and a bright rose-spotted, bobbling lip. The dorsal sepal is broad at the base, its narrow tip curves forward, the rounded petals stand straight out beside the column, and the large lateral sepals curve down with their upper edge folded inward. (Sikkim Himalayas and Khasia Hills; fall.)

Bulbophyllum macphersonii is a little creeping plant whose 1 to 1.5 mm pseudobulbs bear single channeled leaves the size of a grain of wheat. The shiny red flowers, which are 3 to 5 mm across, are borne singly on stems about 1 cm tall, and they must be examined with a hand lens to see the minute hairs on the petals and lip. This should be grown on a mount. (Australia; fall.)

Bulbophyllum minutissimum, more common than *B. globuliforme*, vies with that species for the title of "smallest." Its 2 to 3 mm pseudobulbs are flattened like the head of a pin, the leaf is 1 mm tall, and the flower stem 2 mm. On tree branches it forms a creeping mass, rather like a mat of moss. The flowers are 4 mm wide, white with red stripes and a red lip. This orchid is difficult to establish, partly because of its very short roots, which are only 5 mm long. It is said, however, that it can be grown on cork bark with only a touch of sphagnum moss beneath it, in a damp, rather bright place. (Australia; spring.)

Bulbophyllum rhynchoglossum [Color Plate C-11] has attrac-

46

tive and peculiar flowers that last barely 24 hours, but it is nevertheless worth having. The 2 to 2.5 cm cherry size pseudobulbs are green at first, ripen to a dull red and become rough in texture. Bearing single, oval, pendent leaves, they soon cover a mount of cork bark or tree fern. The flowers appear one at a time on short peduncles (stems.) Their slender sepals, 3 cm long, are satiny white with red candy-stripes and are reflexed straight back along the ovary, while the impertinent, narrow, red, tongue-shaped lip curves forward. The petals are almost microscopic and the column very tiny. It needs constant moisture and fair shade. (New Guinea; flowers at any time.)

Bulbophyllum sandersonii is a small spectacle with its eye-catching, fleshy, flat ribbonlike, red flower stems curving away from the little fluted, oval pseudobulbs and their paired round leaves. The plant is 6 to 7 cm tall, the flower stems 8 to 10 cm long. The blossoms are 7 mm long, inserted on both sides of the "ribbon," and the conspicuous parts are the spiky dorsal sepal and rounded laterals, which are maroon on the front, green on the back. (Southern and Southeast Africa and Rhodesia; summer.)

Bulbophyllum transarisanense has a flower half as large as the whole plant. The curved, wrinkled, conical pseudobulbs and broad leaves together are 8 to 10 cm high, the flower 4 cm across. It resembles *B. ambrosia* in shape, particularly the lip, but its parts are broader and it is yellow-green with a whitish lip. It requires semishade and a warm spot in intermediate temperatures. (Taiwan; summer.)

Cadetia

Cadetia is a delightful little relative of *Dendrobium*, with most of its 40 species in New Guinea, two in Australia. The plants themselves are bouquets of straight, slim stems, slender, bright green leaves, and single flowers of crystalline texture. They prefer a shady spot with constant moisture. The long-lasting flowers remain fresh for two or three months, and since the plants make a succession of growths throughout the year, they are almost constantly in bloom.

Cadetia chamaephyton is the smallest of the three species described here. Its stems are 1 to 1.5 cm tall, channeled on one side, and bear single leaves of about the same length which end in a sharp point. The flower stems hold the white blossoms at just about leaf level, so that a plant in full bloom is a veritable cushion of them. The delicately fragrant flowers are 8 mm across with wide-spreading, oval sepals, thin petals that point downward, and a small spear-shaped lip. It requires cool temperatures and constant moisture. Each growth flowers several times and the plant is always in bloom.

Cadetia dischorensis [Plates 28 and 29] is 3.5 to 4 cm tall, with dark green leaves. The white flowers are 1.2 cm across, with broad lateral

28. Cadetia dischorensis *is a little cushion of leaves and flowers in a 6 cm pot.*

29. Cadetia dischorensis. *The 1.5 cm blossom has all the dignity of a large flower.*

47

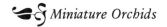

sepals, upward angled petals, and a broad lip, bi-lobed at the outer end and decorated with three raised lines on its crest. Cool temperatures and constant moisture. (New Guinea; always in flower.)

Cadetia taylori is larger and less densely tufted than the preceding two. Its stems are 6 to 7 cm tall, with four flutings, and the leaves are 5 to 6 cm long. The flowers come one at a time from a definite sheath at the juncture of leaf and stem until several have bloomed. They are 1.5 cm across, with broad lateral sepals, a slender dorsal sepal that curves forward, and threadlike petals that arch forward like a pair of antennae. The kidney-shaped lip is pink and covered with velvety hairs. The plants grow natively from sea level to about a 4000 ft elevation (about 1400 m), and thus individual plants may need warm or intermediate temperatures. (Australia; spring to fall.)

Campylocentrum

This monopodial genus contains both leafy and leafless species. The flowers are extremely small, only 1 to 3 mm in length, and most are rather tubular. The charm of the leafy kinds lies in their graceful stems with alternate leaves and tiny "toothbrushes" of minute, white blossoms. They flourish on tree fern or cork bark mounts padded with sphagnum moss and kept damp. The leafless ones are more intriguing but more difficult to grow. They have a minute, bract-covered stem a few milimeters tall, from the base of which grow both roots and flower stems. The tiny blossoms are produced on upright or arching stems, usually several at a time. They usually prefer a clean (not padded) mount in a damp and shaded spot, but with good air circulation and a mist of water once a day. Their roots do not all cling to the mount; many stand out in the air.

Leafy kinds, whose tiny, tubular flowers are distinguished by their spurs:

Campylocentrum brenesii is one of the smaller varieties, growing to 12 cm in height. Its sac-like spur is compressed laterally. (Guatemala and Costa Rica; summer.)

Campylocentrum huebnerii has slender, tapering spurs, more than twice as long as the flowers, making the short spikes quite conspicuous. (Venezuela and Brazil; spring to fall.)

Campylocentrum microphyllum is almost as small as, and quite similar to, *C. brenesii*, except that its club-shaped spur is longer and has an inflated bulb at the end. (Central America).

Campylocentrum rhomboglossum (syn. *aromaticum*) produces more than one spike at its leaf axils, although they are quite short. Its spur turns completely back on itself at the tip. (Brazil; spring to fall.)

Campylocentrum schneeanum is only 6 to 7 cm tall, with a spread of less than 3 cm. The flower spike is as long as the leaves, with flowers 2 mm long, including the fat little spur. (Venezuela; spring.)

C-1. Sophronitis coccinea.

C-2. Lichens, mosses, bromeliads and small orchids on a Drimys tree at 1900 meters elevation, Costa Rica. (Photo by Henry T. Northen.)

C-3. Aerangis stylosa.

C-5. Anoectochilus roxburghii.

C-4. Alamania punicea. (Photo by Raymond McCullough.)

C-7. Barkeria cyclotella (scandens).

C-6. Barbosella cucullata. (Photo by John M. Stewart.)

C-9. Bulbophyllum ambrosia.

C-8. Barkeria elegans (uni-flora). (Photo by William R. Thurston.)

C-10. Bulbophyllum guttulatum.

C-11. Bulbophyllum rhynchoglossum.

C-12. Cattleya luteola × Laelia
Facelis (L. bicolor × L. aclandiae).

C-14. Chondrorhyncha flaveola.

C-13. Cattleya luteola.

C-17. Cleisostoma arietinum.

C-15. Cirrhopetalum lepidum.

C-16. Cirrhopetalum wendlandianum:
detail of top "feathers."

C-18. Constantia cipoensis. (Photo
by John M. Stewart.)

C-19. Dendrobium aurantiroseum.

C-20. Dendrobium dichaeoides.

C-21. Dendrobium dryadum.

C-22. Dendrobium frigidum.

C-23. Dendrobium lichenastrum.

C-24. Dendrobium margaritaceum.

C-25. Dendrobium sophronites.

C-26. Dendrobium subacaule.

C-27. Dendrobium unicum.

C-28. Dendrochilum filiforme.

C-29. Dichaea latifolia.

C-31. Encyclia bractescens. *(Photo by Leon A Wiard.)*

C-32. Encyclia pringlei. *(Photo by Raymond McCullough.)*

C-30. Dracula erythrochaete.

C-33. Gongora cornuta.

C-34. Hintonella mexicana. *(Photo by William R. Thurston.)*

C-35. Isabelia virginalis, 'Fox Den'. *(Photo by Charles Marden Fitch.)*

C-36. Koelensteinia tricolor.

C-37. Laelia crispata.

C-38. Laelia lucasiana.

C-39. Laelia milleri 'Tom Northen'.

C-40. Laelia furfuracea.

C-41. Laelia jongheana.

C-42. Laelia lundii.

C-43. Laelia pumila.

C-44. Laelia rubescens.

C-45. Laelia sincorana.

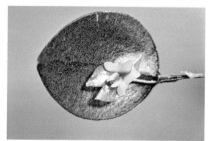

C-46. Lepanthes selenipetala.

C-47. Lepanthes trilobata.

C-48. Lepanthes species. (Photo by
Ronald M. Hawley.)

C-49. Lepanthopsis floripecten.

C-51. Masdevallia erinacea.

C-50. Masdevallia caudata.

C-53. Masdevallia saltatrix.

C-52. Masdevallia rosea.

C-54. Masdevallia strobelii.

C-56. Meiracyllium trinasutum.

C-55. Maxillaria reichenheimiana.

C-57. Meiracyllium wendlandi.
(Photo by Leon A. Wiard.)

C-58. Mexicoa ghiesbreghtiana.

C-59. Miltoniopsis roezlii.

C-60. Mystacidium caffrum.

C-61. Nageliella angustifolia.

C-62. Macroclinium xiphorius.

C-63. Odontoglossum cervantesii.

C-64. Odontoglossum krameri.

C-65. Oncidium cornigerum

C-67. Oncidium hookeri.

C-68. Oncidium morenoi.

C-66. Oncidium dayanum.

C-69. Oncidium pulchellum.

C-70. Oncidium triquetrum.

C-71. Oncidium uniflorum.

C-72. Ornithochilus fuscus. *(Photo by Lee Kuhn.)*

C-73. Paphiopedilum charlesworthii.

C-74. Phalaenopsis equestris.

C-75. Phalaenopsis lueddemanniana.

C-76. Phalaenopsis pulchra.

C-77. Pleurothallis schiedii.

C-78. Pleurothallis sonderana. *(Photo by John M. Stewart.)*

C-79. Pleurothallis talpinaria.

C-80. Polystachya latilabris.

C-81. Promenaea xanthina.

C-84. Sarcochilus segawii.

C-87. Epiphronitis Pat, *an intergeneric hybrid of* Epidendrum pyriforme *and* Sophronitis coccinea.

C-91. Tuberolabium kotoense.

C-82. Psygmorchis pusillam.

C-85. Scaphosepalum lima. *(Photo by George C. Kennedy.)*

C-88. Sophronitis cernua 'mineira'.

C-83. Sarcochilus segawii.

C-86. Sigmatostalix crescentilabia.

C-89. Sophronitis wittigiana.

C-90. Telipogon costaricensis.

C-92. Zygostates lunata.

Campylocentrum sellowii has fleshy, nearly cylindrical, channeled leaves, and it, too, gives more than one spike at an axil. Its spur makes a near right-angle turn. (Brazil; fall to spring.)

Campylocentrum ulaei is unusual in that the flower stems are longer than the leaves, making a showier plant than most. Its spur is shaped like a fat sock. It is a dainty, branched climber. (Brazil and Peru; winter to summer.)

Leafless kinds:

Campylocentrum burchelii is one of the prettiest, because it has a tremendous number of feathery flower spikes 5 to 6 cm long, each holding 30 or more 2.5 mm blossoms. The flower has a very fat ovary and a triangular spur. (Brazil; winter to summer.)

Campylocentrum fasciola comes a close second for number of spikes. Its green spur is distinguished by having three ridges curving around its center and sides. (Central America and South America to Peru and Brazil; summer.)

Campylocentrum hirtellum has fewer flower stems, but it makes two or three tiny leaves that soon fall. (Brazil; summer.)

Campylocentrum minutum has yellow flowers on a fuzzy stem only 2.3 cm long. Its spur is twice the length of the flowers, which makes them a total of 3 mm. (Peru.)

Campylocentrum pachyrrhizum has flat, ribbonlike roots. The cream-colored flowers do not stand out from the stem; rather, the base of each is closely surrounded by a ruffled bract. (Florida, West Indies, Trinidad, Venezuela, and French Guiana; late winter and spring.)

Campylocentrum porrectum (*Harrisella porrecta*) has shiny green flowers and a short, bulbous spur. There are few to the stem. (Mexico, Florida, El Salvador, and West Indies; summer).

Campylocentrum pubirhachis has flower spikes rather more open than some, with little blossoms standing out farther and the curved, fat spur better shown off. (Brazil; summer.)

Capanemia _____

Twelve species compose this genus of lovely little plants with tiny pseudobulbs, grasslike or needlelike leaves, and minute, white flowers. They prefer warm to intermediate temperatures and damp conditions.

Capanemia australis is a diminutive pincushion of terete (cylindrical) leaves 1.3 cm tall, arising from rounded pseudobulbs 3 mm high. The 4 mm flowers [Plate 30] with orange speckles on the thickened lip crest, are borne three to four on a stem about as long as the leaves. (Brazil; summer.)

Capanemia brachycion is said to be the showiest of the genus, with leaves like small blades of grass and masses of roundish flowers. (Brazil; summer to fall.)

30. Capanemia australis *gives sprays of three or four of these 4 mm white flowers speckled with orange.*

Capanemia carinata hides its flowers among terete leaves 2.7 cm high. The pseudobulbs are more slender than in other species. (Brazil; winter to spring.)

Capanemia micromera is much like *C. australis* in size and characteristics, with flowers somewhat globe-shaped. (Brazil; winter or summer.)

Capanemia thereziae is tall for the genus, with leaves 5 to 6 cm high, broad and tapering to a point. Yellow-green flowers are borne two or three to a stem that is shorter than the leaves. (Brazil; spring and summer.)

Capanemia uliginosa is another showy plant, about 4 to 6 cm tall, with rather stiff, curved, grassy leaves and ridged pseudobulbs. Its flower stems are densely packed with 1 cm blossoms with a yellow crest and a touch of pink at the base of the column. (Brazil; spring.)

Cattleya

Some of the bifoliate sections of *Cattleya* are quite small, two coming under the 15 cm limit, a few just over it. Both groups are delightful in every way, and even the borderline ones are petite compared to some of their towering relatives. Their small size is apparently dominant, since they make exquisite little hybrids when crossed with larger species [Color Plate C-12]. The potting medium should be allowed to approach dryness before watering.

Cattleya aclandiae [Plate 31] is 10 cm tall, including the slender pseudobulbs and pair of rounded leaves, 4 to 5 cm long, that spread horizontally. The wide-open flowers are fragrant, heavily waxen, and 6 to 8 cm across, almost as large as the plant itself. They usually come in pairs. The sepals and slightly wavy petals are slender, their tips curved forward, yellow-green, boldly marked with deep brown spots. In complete contrast is the large lip with its bright pink mid-lobe and white side lobes that flare out beside the fat, dark rose-colored column. Since the plant makes only three or so roots per year, it is especially important not to overwater and also to let the plant have a somewhat dry period during the winter. (Brazil; early summer.)

Cattleya forbesii grows to about 20 cm or a bit more. It is dainty with slender parts and gives four or more sweetly colored, 8 to 10 cm flowers [Plate 32]. Pale shades of green, tan, and pinkish-yellow are combined in the sepals and petals, while the lip is creamy pink on the outside, yellow marked with orange veins and some pink on the inside. (Brazil; fall to spring.)

Cattleya luteola [Color Plate C-13] averages about 15 cm tall, occasionally a bit over that, with narrow oval, flattened, ridged pseudobulbs and oval leaves. The diminutive flowers are pale yellow with a bright yellow center to the lip. One form has pink in the throat. The flowers,

31. Cattleya aclandiae, *itself only 10 cm tall, has brightly colored flowers 6 to 8 cm across. The white and rose lip makes a sharp contrast to the green, brown-barred sepals and petals.*

32. Cattleya forbesii *is sweetly colored in tones of pink, cream, tan, and green.*

four to six to a spike, are 5 cm across, with slender sepals and petals and a tubular lip with a flared mid-lobe. It does well on a mount in good light. (Brazil; summer to fall.)

Cattleya schillerana is rather like *C. aclandiae* in growth habit, 20 to 30 cm tall, and the flowers have the same color combination. The sepals and petals do not curve as much, and the side lobes of the lip enfold the column. The mid-lobe of the lip is pale pink with deep rose veins. (Brazil; summer to fall.)

Cattleya walkerana has an odd growth habit and the largest flowers of this group [Plate 33]. The plant, which reaches 20 to 25 cm in height, makes pseudobulbs with single leaves during spring and summer, but does not bloom from these. The flower spike arises from the base of a pseudobulb in late fall, to bloom in midwinter. The base of the spike is somewhat thickened and remains as a stub after the flowers have faded and been cut. Therefore, as the rhizome travels along, it bears regular pseudobulbs alternating with the stubs of flower spikes. The heavy, deliciously fragrant, velvety blossoms are 9 to 12 cm across, entirely rose-violet except for a touch of yellow on the crest. The sepals are slender oval, the petals much broader. The lip has a flaring mid-lobe and rounded side lobes that spread outward beside the fat column. There is a white form. (Brazil; fall to spring.)

33. Cattleya walkeriana *has large, fragrant, velvety blossoms of rich rose-violet.*

Cattleyopsis

This is quite similar to *Broughtonia* and one of its three members comes within the miniature class.

Cattleyopsis lindeni is 15 cm tall and has small, thick pseudobulbs and a pair of thick, stiff leaves with toothed edges. The 90 cm arching flower spike bears up to 12 flowers at its tip. They are 3 to 4 cm across, pale rose with a darker lip. (Bahamas and Cuba; late winter and early spring.)

Cattleyopsis ortgiesiana is smaller than the preceding, but its flower stem holds more blossoms, and they open over a longer period. The petals and sepals are pale rose to magenta, and the lip is darker with yellow and purple veins. (Bahamas and Cuba; late winter and spring.)

Centroglossa

This is a little genus related to *Ornithocephalus*.

Centroglossa tripollinica is about 4 cm tall, with round pseudobulbs each bearing a single, slender, pointed leaf. The flower spike, 4 to 6 cm tall, bears tiny round flowers with a funnel-shaped lip that hangs straight down beneath the column. It should be grown on a mount with moss, constantly damp and quite warm. (Brazil; fall to spring.)

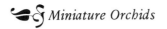

Ceratostylis _____

The plants in this genus consist of a wandering rhizome along which in-dividual leaves are produced from very short basal stems. The latter are covered with papery bracts that hide the juncture between leaf and rhizome. Flowers come from the joint between leaf and stem.

Ceratostylis retisquama is the most attractive of the genus. The leaves are semi-terete, channeled and curved, 12 cm long. The flowers are bright brick-red with an enameled surface, about 2.5 cm across. The oval pointed petals and sepals are similar and the lip very tiny, so that the appearance is of a five-pointed star. They occur singly or in pairs on short peduncles. (Philippines; flowers several times a year.)

Chamaeangis _____

The genus spreads from East and Central Africa to Malagasy and associ-ated islands. The species are monopodials with very short stems, two to six oval leaves with uneven tips, and dense spikes of minute flowers with short little inflated spurs.

Chamaeangis divitiflora has two to four leaves 3.5 to 5 cm long and flower spikes 6 cm tall densely covered with white flowers less than 2 mm long and having a 2 mm spur. (Malagasy; spring).

Chamaeangis hariotiana grows 4 to 5 cm tall, with four to seven leaves, and flower spikes reaching 20 cm in height. The tiny 3 to 4 mm blossoms are only 1 mm apart on the stem. (Grande Comore; spring).

Chamaeangis oligantha is 5 to 6 cm tall, with four to seven leaves, and flowers spikes 10 cm long. It bears fewer flowers than the above two species, only eight to 15 to the stem, and they are just as small. (Mad-agascar; winter.)

Cheiradenia _____

Two small species compose the genus *Cheiradenia*. They have egg-shaped pseudobulbs 1 cm tall hidden by the leaf bases and tiny flowers backed by tufts of bracts.

Cheiradenia cuspidata has two or three oval, tapering leaves 3 to 6 cm tall and an upright flower stem bearing a large tuft of bracts, almost like the seed heads of some grasses. The round, greenish-yellow flowers have pointed sepals and petals and a perfectly round lip, and open four or five at a time. (Brazil; winter).

Cheiradenia imthurnii grows on either trees or rocks. It has five oval leaves 5 to 7 cm tall, and a flower stem 7 to 8 cm high. The pretty globe-shaped flowers are 7 mm across, with rounded parts that are white speckled with dark purple. The scoop-shaped lip has a callus with four teeth over which a fifth tooth projects. (Venezuela, British Guiana, and Brazil.)

Chiloschista _____

Not all of the leafless orchids have flowers as small as those previously described, and a few have truly large ones. Those of the genus *Chiloschista* come in between. Of the few species, one is particularly pretty:

Chiloschista lunifera has round, flat flowers 1.2 cm in diameter. They are yellow with large purple spots, especially eye-catching as they are widely spaced on a 7 to 30 cm stem springing from the mass of bare roots. The lip is shaped like a cup, with large side lobes that curve upward from the very small mid-lobe. Intermediate or warm. (Sikkim to Burma; fall or winter.)

Chondrorhyncha _____

Most members of this genus are too large to be included here, but some delightful ones come just within or slightly beyond our stated limit. The plants lack pseudobulbs and have a fan of thin, prominently veined leaves that last for some years. The flowers come singly on stems shorter than the leaves. They should be kept damp at all times and grown in good light.

Chondrorhyncha chestertonii reaches just 15 cm. Its fragrant, waxy flowers are 8 cm across and present a charming aspect with their greenish-white sepals and petals all flaring upward to allow the yellow-green short-fringed lip to stand alone. (Colombia; summer.)

Chondrorhyncha fimbriata is about the size of the preceding species. Its creamy yellow sepals and petals are not held upward but instead are evenly spread. The lip is quite fantastic, with a small shield-shaped central part edged with long fringe. (Colombia; summer to fall.)

Chondrorhyncha flaveola [Color Plate C-14] is a dainty plant, although it grows to some 20 cm in height. It is always in flower, which is an attribute not all plants possess. The 5 cm, yellowish flowers are tinged with pink and have a large, much ruffled, fringed lip decorated with red-orange spots in the center. It is cool growing. (Colombia; flowers continually.)

Chytroglossa _____

One of the many relatives of *Ornithocephalus*, *Chytroglossa* has a fan of slender, keeled leaves 3 to 4 cm long and pendent stems of numerous, small flowers. Apparently, there are only about three species:

Chytroglossa aurata is said to be the prettiest, with flowers 1.3

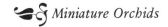

cm across. The green dorsal sepal and petals form a little umbrella over the yellow, heart-shaped lip, which is brightly dotted with red. All the flower parts have finely toothed edges. (Brazil; winter).

Chytroglossa marileonae has slightly smaller flowers and fewer on the stem, but they are very decorative little blossoms. The dorsal sepal and petals stand upright, the latter curving forward at their tips. The lip has pointed side lobes and a pointed tip that turns up. (Brazil; spring).

Chytroglossa paulensis also has fewer flowers of about the same size as the preceding. They are not quite so decorative as either of the others, but delightful, nevertheless. (Brazil; spring.)

Cirrhopetalum

Though often combined with the genus *Bulbophyllum*, *Cirrhopetalum* is distinguished by having filaments or feathery appendages on the tips of the petals and often more prominently on the dorsal sepal, as well. Their long lateral sepals are often joined to form a platformlike structure, or they may have their edges folded together.

Cirrhopetalum amesianum and *C. cummingii*: see *C. lepidum*.

Cirrhopetalum fascinator is a small plant with very long flowers. The pseudobulbs are 5 cm tall and the roundish leaf is of equal height. The whole flower is 15 to 20 cm long. The 3 cm, greenish, long-triangular dorsal sepal and smaller petals have fuzzy edges and are spotted with red. The brown lateral sepals trail off into long, slender tails to make up the rest of the total length. (Vietnam and Laos; fall). Some others with excessively long tails are *C. longissimum*, *C. putidum*, *C. flaviflorum*, *C. medusae*, and *C. surigaense*. *C. medusae* is well known for its "mop-head" or tassel of white or cream-colored flowers, but it is too large to be called a miniature.

Cirrhopetalum gracillimum has a half-umbel (half-wheel) of striking red flowers. It has moderately long tails which separate from the infolded part of the lateral sepals at a point about a third of their length, giving the impression of a slender swallowtail. (Thailand through Malaya and New Guinea to Fiji.) Other species with this characteristic are *C. lishanensis* and *C. uraiensis*, both yellow with red markings.

Cirrhopetalum lepidum [Color Plate C-15] has small, conical pseudobulbs and rounded oval leaves. It gives a perfect wheel of flat, pink, 2 cm flowers whose lateral sepals come together to form a broad tongue. The dorsal sepal and petals are trimmed with "whiskers," and the former stands over the little red, bobbling lip. Apparently synonymous with this species are *C. amesianum* and *C. cummingii*, and quite similar to it are *C. roxburghii* and *C. sikkimensis*. (Thailand, throughout southeast Asia, Malaya, and the Philippines; summer to winter.)

Cirrhopetalum makoyanum is structurally similar to the *lepidum* group, but its slender lateral sepals fold so tightly as to resemble the

spokes of a wheel. The fragrant flowers are yellowish, with red spots on the dorsal sepal and petals. (Singapore; winter.)

Cirrhopetalum ornatissimum belongs to a group with fantastically decorated sepals and petals. This particular one has cilia around the dorsal sepal and bunches of minuscule "carrots" at the ends of the petals. The lateral sepals are long and tapering but not filamentous. The whole flower is about 10 cm long, yellow, spotted and veined with red. (India and Himalayas; winter).

Cirrhopetalum wendlandianum [Plate 34 and Color Plate C-16] and a few like it have the most bizarre decorations of the genus. The dorsal sepal and petals of this species are not only ciliated but bear tufts of irregularly shaped "feathers" that jiggle with the least air movement. The red flowers are 15 cm long, the "feathers" darker red, and the long lateral sepals striped with the darker tone. They occur four to a stem, and their tops are close together on short peduncles so that they form a pyramid. (Burma and Thailand; spring.) Of similar appearance and size are *C. rothschildianum* and *C. fimbriantum*.

34. Cirrhopetalum wendlandianum *doesn't show its wild decorations unless looked at close up.*

Cischweinfia

The odd name of this new genus was coined from the abbreviation "C. Schweinf." used by Charles Schweinfurth to designate his authority in naming new species. Pronounced Cee-schweinfia, the genus was created in his honor for his years of work at the Orchid Herbarium of Oakes Ames. It contains several species that had been variously put in—*Aspasia, Miltonia,* and *Trichopilia*—but did not really fit. Finally they proved to be structurally alike and deserving of a genus of their own. Several new species have been added since the genus was founded. The plants are delicate-looking, with oval, flattened pseudobulbs 12 to 15 cm tall which bear a single thin, slender leaf from the top and one or two from the sides. The rather pretty flowers are small and wide open, with plain, slender-oval sepals and petals. They are characterized by a fuzzy anther cap and a pair of short arms from below the stigma; a tube (nectary) between the ovary and the base of the flower parts; and a lip attached to the base of the column by the edges of its "claw" (the narrow basal section), with small side lobes that turn tightly against the column.

Cischweinfia colombiana, a new species, is larger than the others, reaching 20 cm in height. It has flowers 2.8 cm across, with sepals and petals green, vaguely barred with brown, a round lip bordered with white, and brown spots within the tube and on the side lobes. (Colombia, spring.)

Cischweinfia dasyandra (formerly *Trichopilia*) has pale green or greenish yellow sepals and petals, a cream lip with pink spots, and is yellow or brownish yellow in the throat. (Costa Rica, Panama, and Colombia; summer.)

Cischweinfia platychila, a new species, has yellow and green

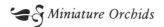

sepals and petals, and a long flat lip which is white with an orange crest. (Ecuador and Colombia; spring.)

Cischweinfia pusilla has a flower 2 to 2.5 cm across, with brown and yellow sepals and petals, and a creamy white lip. (Panama and perhaps Colombia; spring.)

Cischweinfia rostrata, also a new species, has flowers 2 cm across, with pale green sepals and petals, and a cream lip with faint pink spots. (Ecuador and Colombia.)

Cischweinfia, sp. nov., a new species not yet named or described officially, has brown flowers 1.3 cm across. The white lip is hardly longer than the column and has bright red patches in the center. The long column hood conceals the bright rose, fuzzy anther from the side. (Peru; flowers several times a year.)

Cleisostoma

This is a large genus of monopodials, and many species from other genera have been moved to it. The chief characteristic differentiating it from others is the presence of a callus on the inside back wall of the spur that forms a partition above the nectary.

Cleisostoma arietinum [Plate 35]; formerly *Sarcanthus recurvum*) is one of the most delightful of species. The plant has a ladder-like form, with alternate fleshy leaves curving down from the central stem. It grows slowly and for a long time remains below 10 cm in height. Branch stems come from both lower and upper portions of the stem. The flower spike, 6 to 8 cm long, is completely surrounded by 30 to 50 tiny, waxen, pink and white, birdlike blossoms 5 to 6 mm across [Color Plate C-17]. The sepals and petals stand back from the large pink-tipped column, and the lip is attached at its base. The front lobe of the lip with its upstanding side lobes is pink, while the fat bilobed spur is white. Prefers shade and constant moisture. (Thailand; late summer.)

Cleisostoma brachybotrya (formerly *Pomatocalpa brachybotrya*) has few slender, flat leaves up to 10 cm long and tightly whorled clusters of fleshy, yellow flowers of somewhat the same shape as the preceding species. Likes warmth and shade. (Taiwan; spring.)

Cleisostoma subulata (formerly *Sarcanthus pugioniforme*) may approach borderline size. It has small, long-lasting, yellow flowers striped with red-brown on branched flower stems. (Thailand; early winter.)

35. Cleisostoma arietinum, *a ladder of fleshy leaves with a spray of cream and pink flowers.*

Cochlioda

Cochlioda is related to *Odontoglossum*, *Oncidium* and *Miltonia* and has been hybridized with them to give beautiful showy flowers.

Cochlioda vulcanica has oval, compressed pseudobulbs 2.5 to 6 cm tall and two leaves 7 to 15 cm long. The flower stem is 20 cm in length and arches horizontally, bearing six to 12, wide-open, rose-purple flowers, each 4 cm across. The dorsal sepal and the petals are similar, the lateral sepals longer and a bit wavy. The beautiful lip has wide-spreading lateral lobes that form a perfect heart, along the center of which the column lies flat. The little, heart-shaped mid-lobe curves under this portion. Cool growing. (Peru; fall and winter.)

Coelogyne

Best known of the hundred or more species in the genus *Coelogyne* are the large plants. One so lovely and fragrant that it must be mentioned is *C. nitida*, sometimes confused with *C. ochracea*, another delightful species. There are probably many small species that are not written about or offered in catalogs but which a fancier may be able to locate. All grow easily and soon become bouquets of growths and flowers.

Coelogyne corymbosa has chunky, 3 to 4 cm pseudobulbs that are rather four-angled, shiny when young and wrinkled after the first year, bearing two leaves 12 cm tall. The flower stem comes from the top of the developing growth and carries four or five sparkling white, star-shaped flowers with brightly "painted" lip markings [Plate 36]. The inside of the long side lobes that enfold the column has a yellow area outlined and veined with dark sienna; the front lobe has two bright orange eye spots also outlined in sienna. (Himalayas; spring.)

36. Coelogyne corymbosa *has pure white flowers with unusual "painted" orange lip markings outlined in dark sienna.*

Coelogyne fimbriata is a bit rambling, with neat, oval pseudobulbs 2 to 3 cm tall, spaced about 3 cm apart, and bearing a pair of oval, pointed leaves 4 to 5 cm tall. The flower stem, arising from the top of the mature pseudobulb, is about the same height as the leaf. It bears a pair of greenish-tan flowers 3 to 4 cm across that have oval sepals and almost filamentous petals. The large, three-lobed lip is veined with red-brown, and has two wavy keels down the center, and a finely fringed edge. Cool to intermediate, needs a short rest in midwinter. (China, India, Thailand, and Vietnam; autumn.)

Coelogyne fuliginosa is much like the preceding but may be just a bit taller and a little more generous with flowers. The flowers also are similar, one slight difference being the larger side lobes to the lip and fringe around only the mid-lobe. (Himalayas; winter).

Coelogyne odoratissima has rounded pseudobulbs and a pair of leaves totaling about 12 cm height. The flowering stem comes from the top of the young developing growth and bears several fragrant, white, waxy blossoms about 6 cm across. The lip has small side lobes and a rather large oval mid-lobe decorated with a yellow stripe down the middle. (Sri Lanka and southern India; spring and summer.)

37. Comparettia falcata *livens up the hedges and small trees of tropical America with its stems of 2 cm bright rose flowers.*

Comparettia

The few species in this genus are all brightly colored and have a beautiful, large, spreading lip. One of their characteristics is a double spur from the lip hidden inside a spur formed by the lateral sepals. The plants are all small, with tiny pseudobulbs and single leaves 7 to 12 cm tall. They give generous numbers of flowers. They may be grown either in a pot or on a mount.

Comparettia coccinea carries stems of six to eight flowers 2 cm long, which have an almost square lip with wavy edges. It ranges from pale to bright scarlet. (Brazil; fall.)

Comparettia falcata, the most widespread of the genus, has 2 cm, bright rose-colored flowers veined with darker rose [Plate 37]. The petals and dorsal sepal form a hood over the column. The rounded lip is bilobed and the spur short and straight. (Mexico to northern South America; spring.)

Comparettia macroplectron, whose name means "large lip," has pink flowers 4 cm long, densely spotted with rose-violet, the sepals and petals more so than the lip. A young plant may produce only a few flowers, an older one long stems of blossoms. (Colombia; midwinter).

Comparettia speciosa has flowers of intense orange, the petals and sepals veined with a darker tone and the lip faintly veined. The spur is slender and pointed, sometimes hooked at the end. (Colombia; fall.)

Constantia

These beautiful little plants have 6 to 10 mm pseudobulbs, massed together so tightly that they acquire flattened sides where they meet, and tiny, paired, rounded leaves, all of a fluorescent green.

Constantia cipoensis [Color Plate C-18] has a creamy white flower 2 cm across on a short peduncle. Its broadly oval sepals and narrower petals are held slightly forward, and its somewhat diamond-shaped lip has an orange patch at the base. The yellow-green pollinia at the tip of the column add to the color scheme. It is difficult to keep in cultivation but worth bearing in mind for the time when the secret of its needs is revealed. (Brazil; spring.)

Corybas

This is a genus of odd little terrestrials, widespread from the Himalayas through Malaysia, New Guinea, Australia, and New Zealand. They have tiny tubers about the size of a small bean, round or heart-shaped leaves the size of a nickel or quarter that hug the ground at first and later stand 2 cm or more above it, and little elfin flowers. In their damp woods, they sometimes grow up under the leaf mold, and the flowers barely peek through. They make runners, at the end of which the tubers are formed. The old plant dies at the end of the season, and the tubers sprout new plants. When grown in cultivation, some of the tubers may go too deep into the soil (a sandy loam with leaf mold) so that they have to be located and repotted. It's quite a job going through the soil by the teaspoonful searching for the light brown tubers which are shiny when wet, for they are only 2 to 6 mm in diameter. They may be put in fresh soil about 2 cm below the surface, either in pots or flats. If they have not already sprouted, keep them a little dry for a few weeks; if sprouted, keep the pots damp.

Corybas pruinosus is typical of the Australian species. Its gray-green dorsal sepal forms a hood over the column and encloses the very small petals and lateral sepals. The green lip is a broad, shallow funnel with purple fringe around the edge. It has two "back door" openings at its base, through which a pollinating insect may leave the flower. The 2 to 2.5 cm blossom comes from the juncture of leaf and stem, and thus appears on top of the leaf. Cool growing. (New South Wales, Australia; spring and summer.)

Corybas trilobus [Plates 38 and 39] is a New Zealand type, whose sepals and petals are needlelike and stand out like antennae. The dorsal sepal forms a hood over the fringed funnel of the 1 cm wide lip, while the petals stand up, and the lateral sepals spread sideways. The green flowers come from the base of the plant, at first crowded under the leaf and then emerging beside it. As they age, both leaf and flower stems grow taller. (New Zealand; winter.)

38. *Penny-size leaves and tiny green Mars-man flowers belong to* Corybas trilobus.

39. Corybas trilobus. *A single flower.*

Cryptarrhena

Of two delightful species in this genus, the better known *Cryptarrhena lunata* is too large, but the other is suitable for a miniature collection.

Cryptarrhena guatemalensis grows to about 8 cm, rarely up to 15 cm in height. It has oval, compressed pseudobulbs 1.3 cm tall and a tuft of slender leaves, two from the top and several from the sides of the pseudobulb. The 15 cm flower stem bears many pale green flowers 1.3 cm across, with widespread sepals and petals and a four-lobed, fanciful lip. The lip has a triangular central portion from which extensions dangle at the front edge and two slender, erect side lobes. (Guatemala to Colombia and British Guiana; summer.)

Cryptocentrum

The more interesting species of this genus have flowers rather resembling a starfish, specifically a brittle star. They are not colorful, but a dull, green-

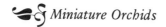

ish tan, purple, or olive color. The plants are almost monopodial, with upright stems that bear an increasing number of leaves through the years, eventually leaving a naked, woody base. The flower stalks come from the lower part of the stem and bear one blossom each. The long sepals are slender and stiff, the petals are shorter and stand out stiffly to each side of the column, and the much shorter, triangular lip hangs out like a little tongue. The column sits in a depression made by the base of the other parts.

Cryptocentrum calcaratum is 6 to 8 cm tall, with an olive-tan flower about 4 cm long. (Costa Rica; fall.)

Cryptocentrum peruvianum is only 2.5 cm high, with a purple flower barely 1 cm long. (Peru.)

Cryptocentrum pseudobulbosum is an exception, in that it has a small pseudobulb with a pair of leaves, the whole plant being but 4 to 5 cm tall. The flower differs slightly, also, with the petals as long as the sepals, or longer. (Peru.)

Cryptophoranthus

The members of this genus, relatives of *Pleurothallis*, are called "window" orchids because the tips of the sepals are united, enclosing the other flower parts and allowing only a slit on each side for an insect to enter. The tufted stems have funnel-shaped bracts and bear oval leaves. From one to six flowers on short pedicels come from the base of the leaf, often appearing to grow out of the topmost bract. They have two pollinia.

Cryptophoranthus atropurpureum is 7 to 14 cm tall and has a tight cluster of deep crimson flowers about 2 cm long. (Cuba and Jamaica; fall and winter.)

Cryptophoranthus lepidotus is 5 to 17 cm tall, with a cluster of several dull purple blossoms on rather long peduncles. (Panama; summer.)

Cryptophoranthus sarcophyllus is 2.5 to 4 cm tall, with leaves striped purple on the back. The one or two downy flowers are purple with darker spots. (Venezuela.)

Cyrtorchis

This is a genus of lovely African monopodials that have fragrant, star-shaped, long-spurred flowers.

Cyrtorchis crassifolia, surely the tiniest of the genus, is 3 cm high. Succulent bluish gray leaves extend straight right and left of the stem, reminiscent of a crassula plant. The fleshy leaves are 4 cm long, folded in a deep V at the mid-rib. Two spikes almost always appear at once, each holding four to six shining white blossoms nearly 2 cm across, with a spur 2.8 cm long. Does best with high humidity but should not be kept overwet. (Zaire, Tanzania, Rhodesia, and Angola; generally summer.)

Cyrtorchis praetermissa has five or six pairs of closely set alternate leaves 7 cm long. Roots come from the bare part of the stem, so a portion of this must be retained if the plant is cut and restarted. Flower spikes 6 to 8 cm long come from the lower leaf axils and bear 15 to 20 waxy, white blossoms, which are 1.2 to 1.3 cm across, with pointed parts, and slender spurs 2.6 cm long. (Uganda to Transvaal; summer). A variety *zuluensis* has flat leaves and slightly larger flowers. (Northern Zululand; winter.)

Dendrobium

A huge genus of 1600 species, *Dendrobium* ranges from Japan down through Asia to India, on to Taiwan, Malaysia, Indonesia, Australia, and New Zealand, with the greatest concentration in New Guinea. There are many species with canes (the name used for their slender, jointed stems) 2 to 5 ft tall, several giants up to 18 ft (one of which is *D. violaceoflavens*), and some only a centimeter in height. Flowers range from 15 cm to 5 mm, but some small plants have flowers larger than those of the big ones, and some of the miniatures (indeed, some of the larger ones, too) have flowers that last on the plant for from five to nine months.

Dendrobium aberrans has peculiar stems seen in a number of species: the lower part is a thin, woody stalk; the upper part swollen into a spindle shape. The total height, including a pair of small oval, flat-spreading leaves, is 5 to 12 cm. The round, wide-open, creamy white flowers are 1.5 cm across, produced year after year from old and new growths, in short-stemmed clusters of five or six. The broad sepals extend flat, the much more slender petals curl back between them, and the lip is suspended from the column foot. It has large, down-curving side lobes, between which are the two slender divisions of the mid-lobe. The very fat, globular spur is formed by the base of the lateral sepals. (New Guinea; winter, spring, and fall.)

Dendrobium aggregatum, a popular species, soon covers a slab with its 5 cm, corrugated pseudobulbs and their single 5 cm leaves. The 15 cm flower stems form a cascade of yellow-orange blossoms 4 cm across, with small, oval sepals and petals and a large round lip that is deep orange in the center and finely fringed on the edge. The variety *jenkinsii* is only 7 cm tall and has 2 cm flowers with kidney-shaped lips. Both need a cool, dry spell after the growths mature in order to encourage flowering. (South China to Burma, Thailand, and Laos; fall or spring.)

Dendrobium atroviolaceum has long-lasting flowers the texture of soft leather. The plants are 20 cm tall, with stalked, spindle-shaped pseudobulbs and paired leaves. Both old and new pseudobulbs flower over and over, producing paired flowers on short stems. The blossoms are 6 cm across, cream color shading to green at the base of the parts. The sepals

are broad at the base with rolled-back edges and sharply pointed tips, densely spotted on the outside with purple. These spots show through on the front surface. The petals are broader at the tips, spotted at the base. The lip has rounded, erect side lobes striped with brilliant violet and a boat-shaped outer lobe less brightly striped. The ovary is stippled with purple. (New Guinea; flowers most of the year.)

Dendrobium aurantiroseum [Color Plate C-19] is a charming new species. It has rounded pseudobulbs 2 cm tall that taper upward to a thin stem 2 cm long, from which arises a pair of oval leaves 4 to 8 cm long. The leaves fall at the end of the growing season, and from the tip of the pseudobulbs come tight clusters of exquisite pink and white flowers whose red-orange lips are tipped with pink. The rounded sepals and petals form an open fan, with the vertical, pointed lip inserted in its center and continuous with the straight spur formed by the base of the lateral sepals. When this species has covered a mount and is in bloom, the blossoms form an uninterrupted mass. Cool growing with constant moisture. (New Guinea; winter.)

Dendrobium beckleri has little terete leaves 5 cm long that grow directly from a creeping rhizome. It can be very small, with the leaves close together, perfectly at home on a small stick, but there are individuals whose leaves are spaced farther apart and become dangling. The upside down flowers, 2.5 to 3.5 cm across, come singly on short stems and hold themselves vertically with the lip uppermost. The slender sepals and narrower petals are yellow-tan, and the sharply curving, narrow lip is white and much ruffled. The lateral sepals form a short chin. The back of the flower is beautifully striped with red. Cool growing with constant moisture. (Australia; spring and summer.)

Dendrobium bellatulum is a marvelous little species with a flower huge for the size of the plant. The pseudobulbs are chunky, 5 to 8 cm tall, and bear three or four slender leaves 4 cm long. The leaf sheaths clasping the stem are covered with short black hairs, giving the impression that the stem is hairy. Short flower spikes from the upper nodes bear one or two white flowers with a brilliant lip. The blossoms are 4.5 cm across, with triangular sepals and petals spreading wide. The lip is three-lobed, the erect side lobes are tinged with pale red on the upper part, brilliant crimson at the base and across the throat of the lip. Five red verrucose (warty) keels lie in the throat, three of which end in a papillose cushion on the mid-lobe. The mid-lobe is broad, down-turned, and divided at the tip, entirely bright yellow-orange. (Thailand; late winter.)

Dendrobium capillipes has rather fat, spindle-shaped pseudobulbs that carry four or five thin leaves, for a total height of 10 to 12 cm. The pseudobulbs become yellow after the leaves fall. The round flowers are 3 cm across, two or three to a stem, and a rich yellow, as is the column. The center of the lip is a deeper tone and has a few red stripes in the throat. (India and Thailand; spring.)

Dendrobium coerulescens [Plate 40] has a pointed lip centered

40. Dendrobium coerulescens *has almost needle-shaped leaves and little blue-gray flowers with rose colored lips.*

in the flat fan formed by the sepals and petals. It has tiny pseudobulbs with leaves like pine needles 6 to 8 cm long. The flowers are 2.5 to 3 cm long to the tip of the spur and nestle in pairs among the leaf bases [Plate 41]. They are a most extraordinary combination of colors—blue-gray sepals and petals, a rose-colored lip tipped with scarlet, and a rose-colored spur. Grows cool, damp, and shady. (New Guinea; flowers open in spring, fade in fall.)

Dendrobium cucumerinum has bumpy little, cucumber-like leaves 1.5 to 3.5 cm long, spaced at short intervals on a wandering rhizome. The 1.5 cm long flowers have slender, wispy petals and dorsal sepal, broader lateral sepals which make a pointed chin, and a small, crisped lip. They are cream color or greenish-yellow with red stripes on the base of the parts and red keels and spots on the lip. (Southeast Australia; spring.)

Dendrobium cyanocentrum has the basic structure of *D. coerulescens*, except that the sepals and petals are reflexed (folded back) away from the lip, leaving the lip projecting forward and giving the flower the appearance of the blossom of a shooting star. The coloring is distinctive, too: petals and sepals are striped with blue-violet on a white ground, the lip is brownish with purple stripes, and the column is bluish. The flower is about 1.5 cm long. The little pseudobulbs near a pair of slender, rough-textured, somewhat twisted leaves, and the whole plant is some 5 cm tall. Cool and shady, constantly damp. (New Guinea; late winter and spring.)

Dendrobium delacourii [see Plate 10] is another example of a species having both small and large individuals; various authors give different sizes. A small plant measures 5 to 6 cm in height, including the plump little pseudobulbs and pair of oval leaves. The flower stems come from the upper leaf axils and hold six or more charming, fleshy, greenish-white flowers 1.5 to 2 cm across [Plate 42]. They have broadly oval sepals, little oar-shaped petals, and a somewhat boat-shaped yellow lip striped with bright red inside and edged with orange fingers. (Small varieties may be native to Thailand, larger ones to Burma and Siam; summer to fall.)

Dendrobium denudans can flower with stems of 6 cm but may reach 12 to 15 cm in height. The delicate stems are slender and the narrow leaves thin. Three or four nodding flower stems come from the upper leaf axils, bearing a feathery array of creamy green blossoms 1.5 cm long. They have narrow, pointed parts and a little curved, crisped, red-striped lip with toothed side lobes. (India and Sikkim; late summer and early fall.)

Dendrobium dichaeoides [Color Plate C-20] resembles a dichaea plant, with its pendent stems and tiny, closely set alternate leaves. The stems reach 8 to 12 cm in length, and the broad, pointed leaves are 1 to 1.3 cm long, all turned face up and clasping the stem with their bases. The flowers occur in a dense cluster at the stem tip. They resemble those of *D. aurantiroseum* but are narrower and solid bright rose, with a bit of white on the column. (New Guinea; fall.)

Dendrobium dryadum [Color Plate C-21] grows up to 15 cm in height, and its leaves, although narrow, are not needlelike. The fan-shaped

41. Dendrobium coerulescens. *The flowers come in pairs, facing in opposite directions. Note the short spur formed by the broad lateral sepals, into which the base of the lip fits.*

42. Dendrobium delacourii *has fleshy 1.5 to 2 cm flowers that are white with an orange and red lip whose edge is trimmed with little fat fingers.*

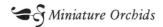

flowers are 4 cm long, of light to dark pink, with a brownish-green lip tipped with dark orange. The ovary has five tall and four low keels. Cool, shade, and constant moisture. (New Guinea; flowers last from spring to the following winter.)

Dendrobium frigidum [Color Plate C-22], another with fan-shaped flowers, is a perfect jewel, only 4 to 6 cm tall, with oval pseudobulbs and oval leaves. The flowers just reach the tip of the leaves and are 2.5 cm long, ice green, with a deep green lip tipped with orange. They usually come in pairs facing in opposite directions. Cool, damp, shady. (New Guinea; flowers last for several months, beginning in fall or winter.)

Dendrobium lamellatum has an intriguing plant form: its stems are broad and flat, measuring 12 cm in length, 3 cm in width, and are cardboard thin. The two or three leaves spread horizontally from the top joints of the stem and are broadly oval, 7.5 cm long. Three or four greenish-white flowers shaped like a wide-mouthed funnel appear on a short stem from the tip of the pseudobulb. (Sumatra, Java, and Malaya; summer.)

Dendrobium leonis looks like a fleshy lockhartia plant, with succulent, triangular, overlapping leaves clothing its 10 to 25 cm stems. The fragrant, chunky flowers arise from the upper leaf axils. They are 1.5 cm across, pale green flushed with purple, with broad sepals and narrow petals forming a cup from which the tongue-shaped lip juts out. (Borneo, Sumatra, and Malaya; winter).

Dendrobium lichenastrum [Color Plate C-23] looks like a succulent, with its tiny, balloon-shaped, 1 to 1.5 cm leaves crowded together on a creeping rhizome. It quickly becomes a solid mat. The cup-shaped 5 mm flowers on short pedicels are cream-yellow with an orange lip. Slightly larger is the variety *prenticei*. Cool, damp, bright light. (Australia; flowers at any time.)

Dendrobium linguiforme [Plate 43] grows like the preceding but is much larger and has tough, thick leaves that are ribbed, 2 to 3 cm long. Flower stems 10 cm long bear a wealth of fragrant, waxy white blossoms 2 cm long, faintly striped with pink, whose long, slender parts create a feathery appearance. Cool, damp, moderate light. (Australia; fall to winter.)

Dendrobium margaritaceum [Color Plate C-24] is a near twin to *D. bellatulum*. The plants are perhaps a bit more slender and the flowers not quite so voluptuous, although they are the same general size. The inside floor of the lip is brilliant red, as are the lower parts of the side lobes. The prominent keels end in a fat, yellow cushion on the outer lobe, which is white, tinged with yellow in the center but not all yellow as in *D. bellatulum*. (Thailand; summer and fall.)

Dendrobium monophyllum, nicknamed "lily of the valley" for its sweet fragrance, is said to be one of the loveliest of Australian orchids, yet difficult to cultivate. Its conical pseudobulbs are 1.5 to 3 cm tall and usually bear a single, oval leaf 5 to 12 cm long. The 20 or so cup-shaped, 1 cm flowers nod, all facing the lower side of the 7 to 17 cm stem, and are

43. Dendrobium linguiforme is a mass of white feathers.

yellow with a darker lip. It is suggested that it be grown on a mount in a damp, warm place with good light. (Australia; flowers at any time.)

Dendrobium moorei [Plate 44] is a lovely but variable species. It can be as short as 12 cm but may grow taller some years. Its slender stems bear three or four leaves, and sprays of pure white flowers [Plate 45] about 2 cm long, with slender parts, a fairly long spur, and a sweet fragrance. (Lord Howe Island off the coast of Australia; winter.)

Epigeneum nakaharai is a small mat plant with pseudobulbs 3 cm tall and leaves 4 cm long. Its star-shaped flowers [Plate 46] are quite showy, 2.5 cm across, greenish-yellow, with a smooth, waxy, almost square lip of brilliant orange. (Taiwan; fall or winter.)

Dendrobium porphyrochilum is a charming little species with cylindrical pseudobulbs 1 to 2 cm tall bearing one to three linear-oval leaves 2 to 6 cm long. A stem slightly exceeding the leaves bears six to ten nodding flowers 6 mm long. The sepals and petals are pale green with red veins, and the lip is brown-purple edged with green. The column is white spotted with purple. (Sikkim; spring.)

Dendrobium pseudofrigidum is twice the size of *D. frigidum*, with larger but otherwise nearly identical flowers. They are about 3 cm long, greenish-white or cream color, with a lighter green lip, and they, too, last for months. While they usually occur in pairs, they can also come in triplets. Cool, damp, shady. (New Guinea; fall to spring.)

Dendrobium pugioniforme is a trailing plant with flat, spear-shaped leaves 2 to 3 cm long. They arise at long intervals on a branching rhizome that roots at the nodes. The pale green, 2 to 2.5 cm flowers are much like those of *D. beckleri*. Damp, shady. (Australia; spring.)

Dendrobium pygmaeum has globose pseudobulbs 1.5 cm tall and a pair of leaves 1.5 to 3.5 cm long. A cluster of 1 cm flowers on a short stem arises from the tip of the pseudobulb after the leaves have fallen. The flowers are white except for the amethyst anther and the lip, which is tan veined with brown and has an amethyst front lobe. Intermediate temperature during growing period, cool for flowering. (Sikkim; spring.)

Dendrobium rigidum is similar to *D. linguiforme* in growth habit. The 1 to 1.5 cm, fleshy, cup-shaped flowers are very decorative, yellow with bright red sides to the lip and column. Grows on the warm side of intermediate temperatures. (Australia; flowers any time.)

Dendrobium sanseiense is a mat plant, 4 cm tall, including the 1.5 cm pseudobulbs. Its flowers are lovely, elongated, pink and white, upright bells, with out-curving, pointed parts. Each stands on its own stem, just above the plant. Warm spot in intermediate situation. (Taiwan; summer.)

Dendrobium senile is a humorous-looking plant, with curly, fat, 8 cm pseudobulbs covered with white hairs. The flowers are a delicate lemon-yellow and are lemon scented, wide open, on long pedicels, two or three together, 6 cm across. The three-lobed lip has a green blotch on each

44. *The sweetly fragrant flowers of* Dendrobium moorei *are pure white bells with little spurs.*

45. Dendrobium moorei. *Detail of the flowers.*

46. *The square, orange lip is the distinctive feature of* Epigeneum nakaharai, *a flower 2.5 cm across.*

side of an orange-yellow disc. (Burma, Thailand, and Laos; spring and summer.)

Dendrobium cuthbertsonii [Color Plate C-25] defies credibility. It is a tiny plant, barely 3 cm tall, including the small, oval pseudobulbs and pair of extremely rough, papillose leaves which are dark green on top, purple underneath. The flowers, shaped like a wide-mouthed funnel, are as long as or longer than the plant. They stand on short pedicels just above the leaves, so that they dwarf the vegetative parts. They are brilliant scarlet, red-orange, or deep red, and their rounded sepals and petals spread wide to a diameter of 2 to 2.5 cm. The lip is small but conspicuous: a little pointed funnel, veined with dark red. The flowers usually last eight to nine months and can last longer, one year's flowers fading as the next season's buds appear. Cool, damp, fairly shady. (New Guinea; spring through following winter.)

Dendrobium subacaule [Color Plate C-26] is a perfect gem. It is only 1.5 cm tall, including the minuscule, purple-red pseudobulbs and pair of oval, pointed leaves that are green on top, purple underneath. The 1 cm tall flowers face each other in pairs at the tip of the leafless pseudobulbs and are brilliant red with an orange lip. The same pseudobulb flowers at least two years in succession. Cool, damp, good light. (New Guinea; the flowers last from spring to fall.)

Dendrobium tetragonum [see Plate 3] grows small in the cooler areas of Australia, larger in the tropical parts. The former reach a length of 7 to 12 cm when continued in cool cultivation. Their stems consist of a long, thin, basal woody section and a four-angled, swollen upper part, topped by three pointed leaves. The flowers are shaped like a brassia, 8 to 10 cm long, with long tails to the sepals and petals, and a shorter lip, broad at the base, pointed at the tip. They are greenish-brown with brown edging and brown veins and spots in the lip. Cool, damp, and a bit shady. (Australia; fall or spring.)

Dendrobium theionanthum is a tiny species, 2.5 to 3 cm tall, with needlelike leaves. Its long-lasting 1 cm fan-shaped flowers are light yellow with an orange-tipped lip. Cool, damp, shady. (New Guinea; fall).

Dendrobium toressae has leaves like grains of wheat alternating on either side of a creeping rhizome. They are deeply channeled on top, rounded underneath, and covered with pinprick-size dimples. The flowers are the size of the head of a safety match, globular, tannish-pink with a yellow lip. Cool, damp, shady. (Australia; spring).

Dendrobium uncatum is a beautiful plant, with bright green leaves 6 or 7 mm wide and about 7 cm tall, arising from a somewhat swollen stem. The flowers are of the fan type, similar in shape to those of *D. dryadum* and *D. frigidum*. They are bright rosy orange with a pure orange tip to the brownish, very slender lip, and stand upright singly or in pairs. (New Guinea; fall.)

Dendrobium unicum [Color Plate C-27], long mistakenly called *D. arachnites*, is certainly unique, as its name implies. It is 7 to 9 cm tall, with a few small leaves that fall the second year. Before or after leaf fall, several stems of bright orange, weirdly shaped flowers appear. They are huge for the plant, 5 cm long, with slender sepals and petals that curl around each other, allowing the impertinent, tonguelike lip to project straight forward. The flower holds itself so that the lip faces down, and one must turn it over to see its beautifully veined surface. (Burma; summer to winter.)

Dendrochilum

The few, well-known species of this genus are, with one exception, larger than our present limit, and even this can slightly exceed it with its dainty proportions.

Dendrochilum filiforme [Color Plate C-28], the "golden chain" orchid, is a perfect fountain of tiny flowers. Slender pseudobulbs 3 cm tall bear single, slender leaves 12 to 15 cm long. To give an idea of its delicate form, as many as 60 pseudobulbs can be easily contained in a 10 cm (4-in.) pot. The threadlike flower stems come from the top of the developing pseudobulbs, rise straight up for 20 to 25 cm, and then turn down at the point where the flowers begin, arching under the weight of a hundred or more little blossoms. The round, flat, sparkling golden flowers 5 mm in diameter are borne in two ranks on the stem, and they last for a month or more [Plate 47]. Grow in good light, and water well the year around. (Philippines; summer.)

47. Dendrochilum filiforme. *There are a hundred or more of these tiny, round, crystalline blossoms to each golden "chain."*

Dendrophylax

This genus of leafless orchids may produce a tiny leaf or two in the seedling stage but none when mature. The plants give large, attractive flowers.

Dendrophylax barrettiae has short thin roots up to 12 cm long. Several flowers appear at the same time, each on a 2.5 cm stem. They are light green, becoming yellow with age. The sepals and petals are slender, 5 to 6 mm long, the spur 2.5 cm, and the lip 2.5 cm across, oval and pointed. Grows in a warm spot within intermediate temperatures, well shaded. (Jamaica; late summer.)

Dendrophylax fawcettii [Plate 48] has much larger, exquisitely fragrant flowers and thicker, longer roots. The blossoms come singly or in pairs on a stem 5 to 8 cm long. They have a velvety texture and are 5 to 7 cm long, not counting the 15 cm spur. The oval sepals and somewhat narrower petals are green, as is the base of the long lip, which is concave with a raised keel down the center. The outer part is white and divides into a pair of pantaloon-shaped lobes. Grow in shade, constantly damp. (Grand Cayman; summer.)

48. *Deliciously fragrant, green and white, the large blossom of the leafless orchid* Dendrophylax fawcettii *makes an almost miraculous appearance from the bare roots.*

Dendrophylax funalis is similar to the preceding but said to have an unpleasant odor which, however, does not deter people from growing it. Its sepals and petals are green at first, becoming paler after a few days. The lip is white, the outer portion rounded, and the spur is 5 cm long. Grows in rather bright light. (Jamaica; early fall.)

Dendrophylax varius has flat, grayish, dark-spotted roots and a much taller, sometimes branched flower stem that bears up to eight blossoms. The all-white flowers are only 1.5 cm long, with tiny sepals and petals and a rounded lip with a spot of bright yellow in the center. (Cuba and Hispaniola; spring.)

Diaphananthe

The genus *Diaphananthe* is monopodial, with sprays of small, transparent, deliciously fragrant flowers. They should be grown on a slab with constant moisture.

Diaphananthe pulchella grows to a height of 10 cm and has alternate strap-shaped leaves 10 to 12 cm long. The 9 cm flower stems come from the leaf axils, many at a time, each holding ten to 12 greenish-white flowers 1.5 cm across, arranged in a spiral. The sepals and petals are triangular, the lip round, three-lobed, and frilled on the edge, and the spur is 2.5 to 3 cm long. Cool to intermediate temperatures. (Malawi, Tanzania, and Zambia; winter).

Diaphananthe rutila is smaller, with longer flower sprays densely covered with pinkish, transparent flowers. Their pervading perfume makes up for their unostentatious appearance. They are 8 mm across, with a rounded, fan-shaped lip finely toothed on the edge, and a curved spur 5 to 7 mm long. (Kenya, Tanzania, and Uganda to West Africa; summer.)

Dichaea

49. *The lacy stems of* Dichaea ciliolata *make a beautiful little pot plant and give rise to 7 mm green and maroon blossoms.*

This genus of some 40 dainty species is pseudomonopodial. Its stems continue to grow in length, forming branch stems and roots from their sides, while new stems come from the base. They are graceful, almost fernlike, and while some are small and never take up much room, others grow into considerable masses and make a lovely background for small potted plants. The prettiest ones are those that retain their leaves, that is, whose leaves are not articulated to the leaf sheaths along the stem and therefore do not fall. All those described here are of this type. The flowers are globose and come on short pedicels on the newer part of the stem, and they have an anchor-shaped lip. The long trailing species are best grown on a slab or "tree" padded with osmunda fiber or sphagnum moss. Little ones can be grown in pots. All grow luxuriantly with constant moisture and shade.

Dichaea ciliolata [Plate 49] is a diminutive species whose details require a hand lens. Its leaves are only 2.5 to 3 mm long, finely toothed or ciliated on the edges and ending in a spiky point. The relatively large flowers, about 7 mm across, are minutely warty on the back. The points of the lip's "anchor" are particularly long, arching back to touch the base of the column. The blossom is pale green with fine maroon spots arranged more or less in lines. The ovary is covered with minuscule green "fingers." (Costa Rica and Panama; spring to fall.)

Dichaea latifolia [Plate 50] has longer leaves, 1 to 1.5 cm, which point forward on the stem and are smooth on the edges, and the stems grow to a greater length. The flower [Color Plate C-29] is crystalline white with pink spots, and the lip is somewhat cupped between the upright side lobes. (Brazil; summer.)

Dichaea muricata [Plate 51] is variable in size; the leaves of some individuals are half as large as those of others. The larger type can make pendulous stems 30 to 60 cm long, perhaps longer through the years. A young plant is small for a while but branches freely and soon forms quite a mass of stems; older stems can be cut off and restarted at any time. The broadly triangular leaves are 1 to 2 cm long, twisted at the base so that they all face up on the stem. The flower is 1 to 1.5 cm across, cream color or pale bluish-lavender, heavily blotched with deep purple, and warty on the outside. The cupped outer end of the lip is less spotted but is edged with light violet. In Guatemala it is said that the plant is crushed and used as a poultice for snakebite. (Mexico to Brazil and the Lesser Antilles; generally spring.)

Dichaea neglecta [Plate 52] is sometimes considered a variety of *D. muricata* but more often a separate species. Both plant and flowers are smaller, and the leaf sheaths are densely spotted with dark green. The flower is a rich green spotted with red, and the parts are warty on the outside. (Mexico, Guatemala, and Nicaragua; fall.)

Dinema

The single species of this genus has been removed from *Epidendrum* and *Encyclia* and put back in the genus created for it in 1826.

Dinema polybulbon is a creeping plant with little pseudobulbs 1.3 cm tall topped by a pair of leaves 4.5 cm long. The wide-open flowers are 3 cm across and have slender, light tan sepals and petals suffused with reddish-brown down the midline. The white lip spreads into a rounded, ruffled outer lobe. The column is raised up from the lip and has two slender horns projecting from either side of its tip, features that distinguish it from members of the two genera mentioned above. (Mexico to Honduras, Cuba, and Jamaica; winter.)

50. Dichaea latifolia, *shown here as a newly collected plant, will branch and spread.*

51. *The globe-shaped flower of* Dichaea muricata *is cream color, spotted with bluish purple.*

52. Dichaea neglecta *demonstrates how plants of this genus spread and branch to form a pendent mass of greenery.*

Diplocentrum

There are only two species in this genus. They are monopodials with narrow, fleshy leaves rounded on the bottom, channeled on top, and quite limber. The long-lasting flowers are round and waxy, with a sac-like lip that has a short double chin or spur.

Diplocentrum congestum is the smaller of the two, with two to four leaves 2 to 7 cm long, and a 9 cm flower stem that holds a number of blossoms 5 to 7 mm across. The sepals and petals are pale pink or pinkish-brown with a median stripe of pink, and the lip varies from white to pink. (Southern India; spring and summer.)

Diplocentrum recurvum retains five or six leaves at a time, which are 7 to 9 cm long, and has a flower stem 10 to 20 cm long. The pink and white flowers are 1 to 1.5 cm across, many on the stem. (Southern India; summer.)

Dipteranthus

The few species of this genus, related to *Ornithocephalus*, have a unique column structure. There is a staminode (a shield-shaped structure) on each side of the anther. The plants have minute pseudobulbs 3 to 4 mm high and single leaves about 4 cm tall. Both species given here require a damp, shady location at the warm end of intermediate temperatures.

Dipteranthus pellucidus has a pendent flower stem 4 to 5 cm long holding some 20 tiny, white, transparent blossoms 5 mm in diameter. (Brazil; winter.)

Dipteranthus planifolius has 3 mm pseudobulbs and fairly fleshy, rigid leaves 4 cm tall. The flowers are about 8 mm across, yellow-brown, eight or nine to a stem. They have the additional peculiarity of an asymmetrical lip and column; both are twisted to one side instead of being precisely centered. (Venezuela; anytime of year.)

Domingoa

There are two species known in this genus, with a possible third being investigated.

Domingoa hymenoides has stiff, stemlike pseudobulbs that carry single leaves 3 to 4 cm long. The plant soon becomes a bouquet of growths. The delicate arching flower stem is 15 cm long and bears several blossoms toward the end. They are 2 cm across, with widespread sepals, and forward-held petals, yellow to yellow-green, striped with red. The long, rectangular, reddish lip has a pair of upright keels on the crest and a thickened keel down the center. The species has been crossed with members of the cattleya group. Warm-intermediate. (Cuba, Hispaniola, and Puerto Rico; summer.)

Dracula

This picturesque name, which means "little dragon," has been given by Dr. Carlyle A. Luer to a new genus he has created for some 60 species he recently removed from *Masdevallia*. Formerly called the "chimaera group," some of them are truly ferocious or monster-like in appearance, being large, hairy, and possessed of long tails. Even the small species are furry and odd looking. The plants differ from *Masdevallia* in having thin, keeled leaves that fold together at the base. Technical differences that mark the flowers are petals that have divided tips or end in knobs, and a two-part, often mobile lip consisting of an outer portion (epichile) fastened to a basal section (hypochile) that is in turn hinged to the foot of the column. The plants do best at intermediate temperatures.

Dracula astuta is 6 to 12 cm tall with leaves of thin substance that widen gradually toward the top and have almost parallel sides. The delightful pendulous flowers are grayish-tan bells 2 cm long, with dark brown tails 4 to 5 cm long. The interior of the flower is covered with short gray hairs, and the thick, rounded spoon-shaped lip bobbles like a bell clapper. (Costa Rica; flowers repeatedly from the same stems through the summer.)

Dracula chestertoni is charming and distinctive. The plant is 7 to 10 cm tall; the pendulous flower stem is 7 to 10 cm long. It flowers again and again. The flowers [Plate 53] are about 7 cm across, gray-green, warty, and speckled with purple. The narrow dorsal sepal has its sides folded back a bit, and the laterals are broad and flat. Their almost black tails are 2 cm long. The lip is huge for the type, in fact, for the genus, 2 cm across, shallowly concave with its rim turned up all around and the sides rising high. It is white with raised red veins, solid red at the base. The nubbin-like petals stand beside the column. (Colombia; spring.)

Dracula erythrocheate [Color Plate C-30], whose name means "red bristles," is 12 to 14 cm tall with an 18 to 24 cm flower stem that arches out from the plant. The wide, shallow sepaline cup, 2 to 3 cm across, has a cream background and is thickly lined with short rose-colored hairs. The red-purple tails are 5 cm long. It flowers two or three times from the same stems. (Guatemala to Costa Rica; spring through fall.) Some other small species in this group are *D. houtteana* and *D. velutina*.

53. Dracula chestertonii *has the look of a "monster" typical of all the one time chimaera group; what look like eyes are the tiny petals.*

Dryadella

A group of utterly charming little species has also been removed from

Masdevallia and made into a separate genus by Dr. Luer. He named this new genus *Dryadella* after the dryads, mythological nymphs of trees and forests. The plants differ from masdevallias in having narrow, channeled, fleshy leaves. The flowers also differ; the lateral sepals have a transverse callus or thickened fold near the base, below which they are joined to form a chin or mentum below the column foot, and the lip is long and tongue-like.

Dryadella edwallii [Plate 54] has rather sharply pointed, quite fleshy leaves, 2 to 3 cm long and only 5 mm wide. Its flowers, 2.5 to 3 cm long, hide among the leaves or barely show above them. Their "protective" coloring and their buds shaped like birds' heads, give this species and its cousins the nickname "partridge in the grass." The sepals form an open cup, from which their broad bases spread wide. All terminate in a long, slender tail. The blossoms have a cream background, on which the dorsal sepal is banded with red, the lateral sepals heavily spotted. (Brazil; summer and also at other times.)

Dryadella lilliputana has succulent leaves, deeply channeled and ending in a point. The flowers stand on a bit longer stems and show themselves better than do those of *D. edwallii* and more especially of *D. simula*. Their color is pale cream, lightly dotted with red. The sepals are oval at the base narrowing to slender tails that curve apart toward their tips. (Brazil; winter.)

Dryadella simula [Plate 55] quickly spreads into a cushion of leaves. Plants may vary in size from those with leaves 3 mm wide and 5 cm long to some with leaves 6 mm wide and 8 cm long. The short-stemmed, hidden flowers are 1.5 to 2 cm long, with a very broad dorsal sepal heavily banded with red, and lateral sepals that flare apart and are only lightly spotted. The tails are much shorter than in the other two species described. (Brazil; spring.) There are many species similar to these three, among them *D. o'brieniana* and *D. zebrina*.

Drymoda

In a plant family with so many forms, *Drymoda* is a curiosity among curiosities. The flattened, disc-shaped pseudobulbs, 2 cm wide are covered with papillae encrusted with calcium carbonate. As they age they lose this covering and are left a shiny green. A tiny leaf appears on each pseudobulb and is quickly deciduous. Plants must be grown on a slab.

Drymoda picta has a threadlike flower stem 4 cm tall which carries one flower 2 cm across. A winged column with an extremely long foot has the dorsal sepal and petals attached toward its top and the broad, pointed lateral sepals and lip attached to the bottom. The sepals and petals are yellow-green striped with purple, and the lip is dark violet. (Burma; summer.)

Drymoda siamensis is similar vegetatively, as are the flowers. The latter are yellowish, suffused with red-brown, with a larger lip and narrower petals toothed on the edges. (Thailand; spring.)

54. Dryadella edwallii *has fleshy little leaves and tiny flowers that peek out from among them. The blossoms are protectively colored in a way, being speckled with red on a cream background.*

55. Dryadella simula *hides its tiny flowers in a mass of fleshy little leaves.*

Drymoanthus

Two minute monopodials make up this genus, one in Australia, given here, and one in New Zealand for which information was not available.

Drymoanthus minutus has several 2 cm leaves from a stem only 1 to 2 cm tall. It can flower when much smaller than this, however. The flower stem is shorter than the leaves and bears half a dozen green flowers 2 to 2.5 mm in diameter which do not open widely. (Australia; summer.)

Encheiridion

This is a genus of a single, tiny, leafless species.

Encheiridion macrorrhynchum, whose specific name means "large beak," has a beaklike rostellum similar to that of *Ornithocephalus*, although it is not in any way related to that genus. The sparkling white flowers, a few millimeters in diameter, have a hooded dorsal sepal, a long bi-lobed lip, and a curved spur with a rather humpy tip. Warm growing. (West Africa; spring and summer.)

Encyclia

Perhaps a thousand species make up the partnership or "macrogenus" formed by *Encyclia* and *Epidendrum*. *Encyclia* almost always has pseudo-bulbs; the column is never entirely fused to the lip; the clinandrum (anther bed) is three-lobed on its upper edge; and the rostellum is similar to that of *Cattleya*. There are only a few real miniatures in *Encyclia*. Some others are small enough on the average to be included, but they can occasionally make taller growths.

Encyclia asperula is a charming little plant with pseudobulbs 1.5 to 3 cm tall topped by a single, very narrow, rigid leaf. The short, warty flowering stem bears two to nine blossoms 2.3 to 3 cm across, pale green with a white lip, the sepals narrow, the petals even more so. The mid-lobe of the lip is round with a wavy edge, the sides turned down slightly. The side lobes embrace the column; their tips turn up and out like points of a collar, and they are decorated with a few purple stripes at their base. The column has wings that sweep down and curve over the isthmus of the lip. (Mexico, Chiapas, and Oaxaca; midwinter.)

Encyclia boothiana, called the "little dollar orchid" in Florida, has flattened, almost perfectly round pseudobulbs 2 to 3 cm across and two or three fairly broad leaves. The stiff, waxy, tiger-striped flowers are 2 cm across, one to five on a stem that is 5 to 10 cm tall. Sepals and petals are slender-oval, and the fleshy, cream-colored lip is short and stubby, with the lateral lobes turned down. (Southern Florida, Mexico, British Honduras, to Bahamas and Cuba; winter.)

73

Encyclia bractescens [Color Plate C-31] has conical pseudobulbs 1.5 to 3 cm tall and grasslike leaves that are normally 10 to 12 cm long; even if longer, they droop and take up little room. On a willowy stem are produced five to 12 bright, showy flowers 5 to 6 cm across, with narrow, brownish-green sepals and petals, and a white lip veined with pink. The base of the lip is narrow, and the column adheres to it for one-third its length. The side lobes turn up, facing front beside the anther and add a perky note. (Mexico to Honduras and the Bahamas; spring.)

Encyclia ghiesbreghtiana has ovoid pseudobulbs up to 6.5 cm tall and leaves 6 to 20 cm long. The delightful flowers, 4 cm across and three or more to a short stem, have greenish-brown sepals and petals and a skirt-shaped, white lip with a few purple veins at the base. A striking note is its chubby green column spotted with bright red. (Mexico; spring.)

Encyclia mariae is a most beautiful species. The plant is of modest size, with gray-green leaves. The flowers [Plate 56] are voluptuous, about 6 cm wide, with green sepals and petals. The huge white lip, 4 to 7 cm long, is broad and ruffled, decorated with green lines in the throat, and enfolds the column with its side lobes. (Northeast Mexico; late spring and early summer.)

Encyclia microbulbon is much like *E. bractescens* in both plant and flower characteristics and is two-thirds its size. The lip is decorated with scattered pink spots instead of veins, and the side lobes of the lip flare outward instead of turning up. The sepals and petals are pure apple green, sometimes veined with brown. (Mexico; late spring.)

Encyclia pringlei [Color Plate C-32] has ovoid pseudobulbs 1.5 to 3.5 cm tall and leaves 4.5 to 9.5 cm long. Its 2.5 cm flowers are among the most attractive of the group. The yellow-green sepals stand up as if clipped together at the tips, while the petals curve down around the perfectly shield-shaped lip. The lip is translucent white lined with opaque, snow-white lines; the column is suffused with rose, giving a focal point to the blossom. (Mexico; spring.)

Encyclia pygmaea is a pretty plant with insignificant flowers. It has slender oval pseudobulbs 1.8 to 3 cm tall, spaced along a creeping rhizome, and paired leaves 2.5 to 5 cm long. Three or four flowers 0.5 to 1 cm across nestle between the leaves. They have green sepals and petals and a white lip whose mid-lobe is a mere point and whose side lobes are almost square and enfold the tip of the column. (Southern Florida, Mexico, West Indies, and Central America south to Peru; fall.)

Encyclia subulatifolia is an extraordinary plant with threadlike leaves borne on equally threadlike stems, arising from very fat, rough, pink-tipped roots. The stems are 1 to 8 cm tall and the leaves 2.5 cm long, occasionally reaching 12 cm. The flower stems are even thinner, up to 30 cm long and often branched. The lovely little flowers are incredibly fragrant for their size, 1 to 1.5 cm in diameter. They are shaped like little cattleyas, with sepals and petals that are greenish brown, or green with

56. Encyclia mariae *has voluptuous green and white flowers on a modest plant. (From a Kodachrome by John M. Stewart.)*

reddish veins, a white lip huge for the flower and much ruffled, and a red-tipped column. (Mexico; spring.)

Encyclia tenuissima is a dainty plant with clustered, oval, brownish-green pseudobulbs 0.7 to 1.6 cm tall, bearing single, very narrow leaves 3.5 to 8.5 cm long. The inflorescence is simple or may have a branch or two and holds two to 12 nodding, but showy, bright yellow or yellow-orange flowers, each about 1.3 cm long. The petals and sepals are slender and pointed, held forward at about a 45° angle over the lip. The narrow base of the lip is attached to the underside of the column for three-fourths its length. The outer lobe is broad and arrowhead-shaped, with two short keels at its base and several raised veins on the expanded portion, of which the central two are warty, the others wavy. (Southwestern Mexico; spring.)

Encyclia tripunctata loses its leaves in the winter, starts new growth in the spring, and flowers from the leafless pseudobulbs as new growth progresses. The oval pseudobulbs are small and light yellow-green, and with the strap-shaped leaves the plant reaches some 12 to 15 cm in height. The flower stem is much shorter and bears one to five bright blossoms 3 to 4 cm across. The yellow-green sepals and petals are offset by a white lip and a dark purple column, the end of which shows three yellow spots, the yellow teeth of the column tips. (Western Mexico; spring and summer.)

Encyclia vagans is a small member of the "cochleata" or "cockle-shell" group, the species that have an upside down, striped, shell-shaped lip. Its slim pseudobulbs and two or three slender leaves give it an average height of 16 to 18 cm, but its pseudobulbs are widely spaced on the creeping rhizome so that it needs a good-sized mount to spread over. It flowers generously, having four to eight or more blossoms to the upright stem [Plate 57]. They are 4 cm long, white, with pointed sepals and petals having a short purple stripe near the base, and the shell-shaped lip is striped with purple. (Mexico to Costa Rica; summer.) Similar species are *E. abbreviata*, *E. calamaria*, and *E. neurosa*. The more familiar species are larger.

57. Encyclia vagans *is a small member of the "cockle-shell" group, with white blossoms striped with purple*

Epidendrum

The distinctive characteristics of *Epidendrum* are a slender, leafy stem, except for a few that form a pseudobulb; a column completely united with the lip; the column narrow, the hood over the anther sometimes fringed; and the rostellum a thin plate more or less parallel to the axis of the column, deeply slit, forming a vicidium (viscid disc) connected to the pollinia. Some miniatures have delightfully odd plant forms.

Epidendrum boothii, see *Nidema boothii*.

Epidendrum fimbriatum has fernlike, rambling, branching stems clothed with slender alternate leaves 3 to 6 cm long. It is constantly in

58. Epidendrum longipetalum *is a curious flower whose narrow ribbon-like petals twist around behind the lateral sepals to dangle like tails. In the newly opening flower, upper left, it can be seen that the petals are short at first, eventually lengthening as in the other flower.*

59. Epidendrum miserum *is a true lilliputian. Vegetative growth is formed from summer into fall.*

flower. The delicate stems at the tips of the growths continue to form one bud after another for a year or more, with three or four blossoms open at once. The exquisite little, round flowers are 1 cm across, white or pink, spotted with violet. The scoop-shaped lip is fringed. Since the stems root where they branch, new plants can easily be started. Cool growing. (Venezuela, Colombia, Ecuador, and Peru; always in bloom.)

Epidendrum geminiflorum derives its name from that fact that its flowers come in pairs, forming at the tips of the short stems. The plant starts with a stem only 5 to 6 cm tall, with five or six little, oval leaves, forming new stems both from the base and sides of the mature stems. It also roots from the nodes. The flowers are greenish, 1.5 cm across, with slender sepals and petals and a heart-shaped, three-lobed lip. Grows either in a pot or on a slab. (Colombia, Ecuador, and Peru; fall.)

Epidendrum laceratum has slender stems about 4.5 cm tall, with several leaves. The white, star-shaped flowers come on short pedicels in clusters of four or five. They are about 1 cm across, with a pointed lip irregularly fringed around the edge. (Peru.)

Epidendrum lockhartioides has beautiful stems similar to a lockhartia plant, with little flat, triangular, closely set leaves. It rarely grows taller than 15 cm. The minute green flowers, 1.5 cm across, come from the last few leaf axils and open with their sepals and petals pressed back against the leaves. The tiny lip secretes a drop of fluid at its base. The plants are shade loving and need constant moisture. (Costa Rica and Panama; summer.)

Epidendrum longipetalum is a charming and humorous species. From a 5 cm stem bearing a pair of rather stiff, oval leaves, there comes a long flower stem in late winter. In March the first flower opens [Plate 58] and buds continue to form for the rest of the year. Sometimes two flowers are open at once, sometimes there is an interval between them. Therefore, do not cut off a flower stem until you are sure no more blossoms will appear. The flower is transparent green, with oval sepals, and narrow ribbonlike petals that hang down behind the lateral sepals and grow longer as the flower ages, reaching 4 to 5 cm. They are sometimes straight, sometimes twisted. The somewhat heart-shaped lip is so shiny that it looks wet. (Mexico; from March on.)

Epidendrum manarae, a diminutive, creeping plant, has round, wrinkled pseudobulbs about 8 mm tall, bearing two to four, oval pointed leaves 1.5 cm long. Tiny globular flowers 4 mm across arise on short pedicels, two to five together. The triangular sepals are pale green, the slender petals white, and the stiff spoon-shaped lip is cream-green spotted with maroon. (Venezuela; spring.)

Epidendrum microcharis, a rare deciduous lilliputian, consists of a mat of tiny pseudobulbs 1.5 to 2 cm tall, each bearing two or three slender, thin leaves, purple tinged on the back. From the tip of the mature pseudobulb, and before the leaves drop, come several flowers on short pedicels. They are 1.5 cm across, fleshy, with spreading sepals and petals, yellowish with many purple spots, or green tinged with lilac. The mid-lobe of the lip flares from its attachment at the end of the column into a squarish central section, toothed around the edge, and it has two small divergent lobes at its outer end. Cool growing, drier in the winter. (Guatemala and Mexico; late summer and fall.)

Epidendrum miserum has a growth habit similar to the preceding. Its pseudobulbs are rounder and gray-green, and while they can bear one or two leaves, three is the normal number [Plate 59]. Leaves fall just as buds form. Flowers are 1.2 cm long, in clusters of two to six [Plate 60]. They are creamy green suffused or finely stippled with red, and have tiny sepals and petals, and a flat, four-lobed lip. (Mexico; mid-winter.)

Epidendrum nanum is a little, branching, leafy plant much like *E. geminiflorum*. Its flowers also come in pairs and are green with pointed parts and a three-lobed lip. (Peru.)

Epidendrum polybulbon: see *Dinema polybulbon*.

Epidendrum porpax: see *Neolehmannia porpax*.

Epidendrum repens is a lacy, creeping, pendent plant, with slender stems clothed with rounded leaves 1 cm long. It has such inconspicuous flowers that it has to be grown solely for its own beauty. As with *Dichaea*, the stems branch and elongate so that it covers a slab and some stems hang free. The green-brown, translucent blossoms, 1.5 cm long, come singly at the ends of the stem and are delicate little stars. (Mexico to Venezuela and the West Indies; summer.)

Epidendrum serpens, one of the oddities, has irregular oval pseudobulbs 1.5 cm tall, flat on top, with a squared-off shoulder. The broad, flat leaf, 6 cm long, stands straight up from one side of the flat area. The cluster of flowers on short pedicels comes from the top of the developing growth. The star-shaped blossoms are fleshy, brownish-pink, 1.5 cm across, with an arrow-shaped lip toothed on the edge. (Venezuela, Colombia, Ecuador, and Peru; spring.)

Epidendrum tortipetalum is the near twin of *E. longipetalum*. The plant is a good bit larger, reaching 15 cm in height, and has a longer, more woody flower stem. The latter makes additional branches in succeeding years. The flowers are also a little larger but have the same general form [Plate 61], with spirally twisted petals that hang down behind the lateral sepals. The sepals are not as pointed as in *E. longipetalum*, and the lip is more rhomboid and blunter at the end. (Mexico; flowers continuously.)

Eria

Like its near relative *Dendrobium*, *Eria* is a large genus with a variety of types. Typically, they are "wooly," that is, some parts are clothed with hairs, but this is not true of all. Most are large plants, but there are also miniatures, more than can be given here. The flowers all have eight pollinia and a chin formed by the attachment of the lateral sepals to the column

60. Epidendrum miserum. *Leaves drop in late fall, and soon the flower buds appear, to open in winter.*

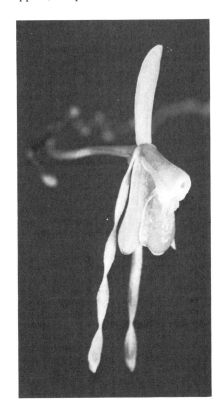

61. Epidendrum tortipetalum *is a near twin to* E. longipetalum. *The lip is shaped differently, and the lip crest has taller keels. In both, the flower stem keeps making blossoms for over a year.*

foot. The lip is also attached to the column foot and usually curves up and then turns outward. They are best grown on a slab.

Eria clavata reaches a height of about 11 cm, including the cylindrical, 4 cm tall pseudobulbs and slender leaves. On a stem 4 cm tall are held about eight prettily colored flowers 8 mm long, with white sepals and petals tipped with pink, and a pale pink lip with deep purple side lobes and keels and a fuzzy place in the center. (Penang Island.)

Eria cylindrostachya is more generous with its flowers. It has rather tapering, curved pseudobulbs 6 cm tall and a pair of oval leaves 10 cm long. The arching, 15 cm flower stem comes from the side of the pseudobulb and is densely covered with greenish-white, waxy blossoms, each 5 mm across. (Philippines; midwinter.)

Eria dalzellii has curious little disc-shaped, reticulate veined pseudobulbs about the diameter of a penny, flattened to the branch and overlapping each other. The 3 to 9 cm flower spike comes from the tip of the new growth, between the pair of oval leaves which are 3 to 7 cm long and warty on the edges. The tubular flowers, all facing one side of the stem, are 6 to 8 mm long, the pointed sepals and petals creamy yellow, edged with minute papillae. The little lip is orange. Warm growing. (Southern India; midwinter).

Eria exilis is another species with tiny circular pseudobulbs 0.3 to 1.2 cm across; each bears two or three leaves 0.2 to 2.5 cm long. The flower stem, which comes from between the leaves, is 1 to 4 cm tall and bears a dozen minuscule flowers 2 mm long opening one or two at a time. They are translucent greenish-white, with an olive-green lip. (India, Sri Lanka, and Thailand; spring.)

Eria extinctoria, an extremely tiny plant, has flowers large for its size. Its somewhat flattened pseudobulbs are 5 mm in diameter, the single leaf about 1 cm tall. The 4 cm flower stem comes from the top of the pseudobulb after the leaf has fallen and bears one flower 1.5 cm long, white flushed with pink. The lip has three orange papillose ridges. (Burma; spring.)

Eria maingayi is a pretty species with 3 cm stems bearing two or three narrow, fleshy leaves 8 cm long. A 5 cm flower stem holds six to eight wide-open blossoms, 1 to 2 cm across, that are white except for the lip, which is green with a purple patch at the base. (Penang Island.)

Eria microchilos is similar to, but even smaller than *E. dalzellii*, with a filamentous flower stem 2.5 to 8 cm tall and six or so wide-open, star-shaped pale yellow blossoms. The spreading sepals and petals are 7 to 8 mm long, narrow and pointed, the lip tiny and pointed, 4 mm long. (Southern India; summer.)

Eria muscicola is surely the tiniest of the genus. The whole plant, from the flattened pseudobulb to the tip of the three oval leaves, is 1.5 cm high. The flower spike, only 1 cm tall, bears a pair of green flowers 3 mm long, with slender, pointed parts that do not open widely. (India, Sri Lanka, Burma, Assam, and Thailand.)

Eria raptans is called the "peanut wooly orchid" in Taiwan, where there is a nickname for every species. Its pseudobulbs are like little round peanuts, 1.5 to 2 cm tall, bearing a pair of slender oval leaves 5 to 8 cm long. The wooly flower stem, 4 cm tall, comes with the young leaves, and the one to three wide-open flowers it holds have pointed white sepals and petals and a broad yellow lip. Grow cool and shady. (Taiwan; spring).

Eria reticosa is another species with disc-shaped pseudobulbs, 0.7 to 1.5 cm across. The paired 2 to 7 cm leaves and the flower spike come at the same time from the underside of the pseudobulb. The fragrant white flowers are 2 to 3.7 cm long, almost as large as the plant, with slender, triangular sepals and petals sometimes suffused with pink, and a three-lobed lip, orange in the center, the side lobes edged with red. (Southern India; spring and summer.)

Erycina

Two small oncidium-like species make up the genus *Erycina*. The flowers of both are almost all lip and look like birds in flight. They grow on twigs or small branches, and only a few of their thin roots cling to the bark, the rest forming a sort of "nest" in the air. Both should be grown on small slabs or sections of branches.

Erycina diaphana is the smaller of the two, with round, slightly compressed pseudobulbs 2 cm tall and a single short leaf from the top and several smaller ones from the sides. The rather delicate flower stem holds six or more waxy yellow blossoms 1 cm across. The insignificant sepals and petals fold back behind the column. The tip of the column is bent sharply backward, but the long rostellum, the "beak," is seen from a top view. The fan-shaped side lobes of the lip are the "wings" and the mid-lobe the "tail." The lip is decorated with a raised, fleshy, three-lobed crest. Should have a short dry period in midwinter. (Mexico; January to April.)

Erycina echinata [Plate 62] has more definitely compressed pseudobulbs 3 cm tall, and the top leaf can be a mere prick. The leaves that come from the side of the pseudobulb are tough and veined with brown. The flowers are more numerous on an often branched inflorescence and are about 2 cm across. They are fancier, too [Plate 63]: the side lobes of the lip are wide fans, slightly ruffled on the edges, and the mid-lobe is kidney-shaped from a narrow isthmus. Two upright, square keels are centered on the crest. It needs a longer dry period, with an occasional misting. Occasionally an exceptionally large plant is found, twice the size vegetatively and with branched flower stems 15 to 20 cm long, opening numerous flowers over a period of months. (Mexico; January to April.)

62. Erycina echinata *makes a nest of roots. Note the aborted leaf on the top of the pseudobulb. The branched flower stem holds a number of yellow birdlike blossoms.*

63. Erycina echinata. *A single flower, showing the big side lobes of the lip. The little shiny point at the top of the flower is the viscid disc of the column. (From a Kodachrome by Leon A. Wiard.)*

*Fernandezia*_____

A handful of species makes up this genus of pseudobulbless plants whose rather thick stems bear a ladder of tiny alternate leaves and numerous bright flowers on short stems. They come from the high Andes and therefore are cool growing and need constant moisture. They have recently been removed from a genus called *Centropetalum*, a name descriptive of a petal-like extension of the partition between the anther and the stigma that forms a hood around the upper part of the column.

Fernandezia hartwegii is up to 20 cm tall but dainty, its stems clothed with leaves 2.3 cm long. The bright orange-red flowers are somewhat bell-shaped with pointed sepals, petals, and lip, the latter having a slight chin at its base. (Peru and Colombia; summer and winter.)

Fernandezia sanguinea is 10 to 12 cm tall, slender, with fleshy leaves 1.5 cm long. Numerous single flowers of rich pink come from the leaf axils and barely extend beyond the leaf tips. They are 1 cm across, somewhat cupped, with slender pointed sepals and petals and a longer, out-turned lip. (Colombia, Ecuador, Peru, and Venezuela; all year.)

Fernandezia subbiflora is about 12 cm tall, with slender fleshy leaves 0.7 to 1.5 cm long, close together on the stem. The 1.7 cm flowers are yellow, orange, purple, or scarlet, on fairly long pedicels so that they stand away from the stem more than in some of the other species. The slender dorsal sepal and wider petals are pointed, the lateral sepals are united at the base, and the large lip is rounded and spreading. (Ecuador and Peru.)

*Gastrochilus*_____

The "gastro-" in the name of several genera means literally "stomach" and is particularly descriptive of the genus *Gastrochilus*, which has a stomach-like or bellylike lip. The lip of *Gastrochilus* is further characterized by an extended rim on the outer edge, a "shelf" or "front porch," that is sometimes fringed. These are monopodial orchids, some with few leaves and an abbreviated stem, others with a leafy stem that may be short or fairly long.

Gastrochilus dalzellianus has a pair of rabbit-ear leaves 3 to 9 cm long and a horizontal flower stem holding a roundish head of charming, fleshy, greenish-white blossoms 1.5 cm across. The sepals and petals are broader at the outer end, wide-spreading and curved forward at the tips. The distinctive feature of the flower is the downward curving, almost skirtlike "shelf" on the lip. (Bombay; winter.)

Gastrochilus formosanum has leafy stems reminiscent of *Dichaea*, albeit the leaves are more fleshy and deeply channeled. Singly or in groups of two or three along the stem appear the little round flowers, 1.2 cm across, yellow with bright red spots. The lip "shelf" is white with a deep brown blotch in the center. Warm growing with medium light. (Taiwan; spring).

Gastrochilus fuscopunctatus is an intriguing little plant with gray-green fleshy leaves spotted with purple and kinky roots from the leaf axils. The stems, growing to about 9 cm, are covered with closely set leaves, 1.5 cm long. The plant makes many branches and soon becomes a thick bunch of stems and roots. The 5 mm flowers are fleshy, cream-colored, spotted with rose, and come on the underside of the stem at every leaf axil. It's not too easy to get it to flower, however, but it seems to prefer medium light and constant moisture. (Taiwan; flowers at any time.)

Gastrochilus japonicus (syn. *somai*) has several pairs of fleshy leaves 5 to 8 cm long. Several short-stemmed flower clusters appear at the same time, forming a dense nosegay of round, green or yellow blossoms with a carmine blotch at the base of the lip and white fingers on its outer edge. Warm-intermediate. (Taiwan; fall.)

Gastrochilus maculatus has two or three narrow leaves 4 to 8 cm long, dark grayish-green with purple spots. The horizontal flower stem, twice the length of the leaves, bears several flowers about 1 cm across of pure yellow or yellow with purple spots. (Bombay area; winter.)

Gastrochilus platycalcaratus is a rather short, chunky little plant with a few leathery leaves 5 cm long. The six to nine flowers are 1.5 cm across, waxy, and fragrant. The sepals and petals are yellow spotted with brown, and the laterally compressed lip is white, the surface of its "shelf" finely papillose. (Burma; late winter and spring.)

Gastrochilus rontabunensis, a very tiny plant, has a few pairs of leaves 1.5 cm long, fleshy and purple spotted. The flower cluster is about the height of the leaves. The 8 mm flowers are dull yellow with a white lip whose "shelf" is fringed. (Taiwan; summer.)

Genyorchis

The genus *Genyorchis* has only a few species, including the exquisite little jewel described below.

Genyorchis pumila [Plate 64] is about 3 cm tall with little, four-angled pseudobulbs and paired roundish leaves on a creeping rhizome. A delicate flower stem 6 cm tall holds six or seven 4.5 mm long ivory-colored flowers with a rose-tipped column [Plate 65]. The blossoms hold themselves upside down with the lateral sepals spreading apart to reveal the rest of the flower as in *Polystachya*. (West Africa to Uganda; mid-winter.)

64. *The threadlike flower spikes of* Genyorchis pumila *are really large for the minute plant. The plant spreads into a small mat.*

65. *Detail of the 4.5 mm flowers of* Genyorchis pumila. *The rose-tipped column can be clearly seen.*

Gongora _____

This genus of oddly formed flowers is related to *Stanhopea* but distinctly different. The flowers are held upside down so that a bee clinging to the overhead lip brushes against the column beneath it, touching the viscid disc, and goes off with the pollinia stuck to its hind end. The flower stems are thin, limber, and pendulous, and come successively for many months.

Gongora cornuta [Color Plate C-33] is borderline for size, being just to one side or the other of 20 cm in height. It has conical, ridged pseudobulbs and paired thin, pleated leaves. The 2 cm flowers, which look like a conference of bees, are held on down-curving, flaring pedicels, all facing inward. They are orange-gold finely stippled with red. The broad, rounded sepals extend backward, exposing the column and lip. The latter, which is pure wax, has an animal-like form. The minuscule petals are attached to the sides of the column. It can be grown in a pot or on a small log so that the flower stems hang free. (Costa Rica, Nicaragua, and Panama; fall.) Two closely related species are *G. armeniaca* and *G. horichiana.*

Goodyera _____

This is another genus of "jewel orchids" with beautifully veined or marbled foliage. The genus *Goodyera* occurs in most parts of the world but apparently not in Africa. Those from the tropics are easier to cultivate than those from temperate regions. The leaves form a basal rosette 8 to 10 cm tall, from which there arises a slender stem densely covered on its upper portion with small flowers. All should be grown in a rich, porous compost, possibly containing some sharp sand, actually a compost similar to that in which paphiopedilums thrive.

Goodyera daibuzanensis is an example of species with marbled leaves. Here they are spear-shaped, rich green, 5 cm long, with light gray-green patches large in the central areas, becoming smaller toward the edges. The little flowers are white. (Taiwan.)

Goodyera hemsleyana has narrower leaves, 2 to 4 cm long which come to a slender point, beautifully veined with metallic green [Plate 66]. The fuzzy little blossoms are 1 to 1.2 cm long, white tipped with pink. Cool growing. (Sikkim and Darjeeling Himalayas; summer.)

Goodyera rontabunensis has tesselated leaves, that is, the colors are clearly marked off from each other. In this species, the dark green occurs in uneven rectangular patches contained within cream-green borders. The leaves are shaped like a broad spearhead. The flowers are small and white. (Taiwan; summer.)

66. Goodyera hemsleyana,
one of the "jewel orchids"
with beautiful foliage.

Haraëlla

The only known species of this genus has long been a favorite.

Haraëlla odorata [Plate 67] is a small monopodial that slowly advances from two or three pairs of leaves to eight or ten, reaching a length of 6 to 7 cm after a number of years. The plants branch rather freely. Two or three delightful flowers come on short stems, opening one at a time. They are 2 cm long, creamy green, the oval sepals and petals composing the top half of the flower, the rather long, fiddle-shaped, beautifully fringed lip the lower half. On the lip there is a "picture" of a reddish beetle, which suggests that the pollinator may be a beetle that performs pseudocopulation. The roots do not seem to cling well, but the plant thrives on a mount such as a piece of driftwood, or in a pot. (Taiwan; spring through fall.)

67. Haraëlla odorata
mounted on a piece of driftwood.

Hexadesmia

A difference in number of pollinia technically separates *Hexadesmia*, which has six, from *Scaphyglottis* with four, and both are somewhat related to members of the Epidendrum complex. All have the odd habit of building new pseudobulbs on top of old ones, although some do it more freely than others. They also make new growths from the rhizome. The upper pseudobulbs make their own roots and can be removed and started over. Plants can be grown either in pots or on mounts, the latter probably being preferable.

Hexadesmia crurigera is an exquisite species [Plate 68]. The spindle-shaped pseudobulb has a thin, woody basal section and bears paired, grasslike leaves. Plants are 10 to 15 cm tall. The delicate flower stems, about 5 to 10 cm long, hold several unusual little blossoms 1.5 cm long [Plate 69], pure white except for the dark green, purple, or red-black column that looks out from the depths of the flower. The dorsal sepal is hooded over the column. The long broad lip is slightly bi-lobed at the tip. (Mexico to Costa Rica; summer.)

Hexadesmia micrantha [Plate 70] is unusual in that it produces flower stems densely covered with blossoms. The pseudobulbs do not have a tapering base, and they have less tendency to form on top of each other.

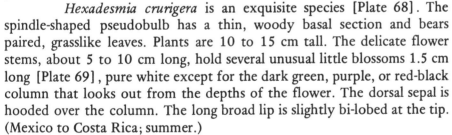

68. A plant of Hexadesmia
crurigera. *The 1.5 cm flowers are as showy on this plant as are the flowers of much larger kinds.*

69. Hexadesmia crurigera. *A single flower, with its dark column peering over the beautiful, full-lip.*

83

70. Hexadesmia micrantha *has many tiny blossoms on each spray.*

71. *The minute flowers of* Hexadesmia micrantha *are 4 mm across.*

The leaves are wider than in the preceding species but still grasslike. Plant height is about 12 to 15 cm. The minute flowers [Plate 71] are 4 mm across, round and wide open, with a short lip whose side lobes clasp the column. They are usually pure white but may sometimes be faintly tinged with lavender or green. (Costa Rica, Nicaragua, and Guatemala; spring and summer.)

Hexadesmia tenuis (syn. *sessilis*) has little oval pseudobulbs about 2 cm tall and a single grasslike leaf. The three or four flowers come on a filamentous stem, at wide intervals. They are 2 to 3 mm across, cup-shaped, with broad, dark green concave sepals and petals whose points turn out, and a rounded, dark purple lip. The column is almost black with a white anther. (Mexico, Venezuela, Colombia, and Brazil; summer.)

Hexisea

For a touch of bright red, the members of *Hexisea* are desirable plants. Two species are well known, and both make pseudobulbs on top of each other. They can be kept small by removing the top ones and resetting them.

Hexisea bidentata has pseudobulbs up to 10 cm tall, deeply grooved, and brownish purple, with a pair of short stiff leaves. The flowers are 3 cm across, bright orange-red, with a patch of dark maroon on the lip. The pointed parts form an open star. (Mexico south to Peru; flowers at intervals during the year.)

Hexisea imbricata has smaller pseudobulbs that are smooth when young and clothed with sheathing bracts. New pseudobulbs come freely from lower leaf axils. The flowers are 2 cm across in shades of orange-red to salmon but do not have the maroon patch on the lip. They also do not open so widely as the preceding species. (Mexico south to Peru; midwinter.)

Hintonella

The single species of this genus is a charming little plant, related to *Ornithocephalus.*

Hintonella mexicana [Color Plate C-34] has a minuscule pseudobulb from whose top and base come little curved, semi-terete leaves 1.5 to 3 cm long. The delicate flower stem extends to just about the same length and carries three or four lovely flowers which are surprisingly long-lasting. They are somewhat bell-shaped, 8 mm across, translucent white with a crystalline texture. The sepals and petals are narrow and pointed, the lip broad and bowl-shaped with the outer portion turned down. Just at the point where the lip curves down, there is a semicircular ridge edged with papillae, and, leading from it to the base of the lip, there is a linear papillose ridge. The crest and side lobes are striped and spotted with light brown. Best grown on a slab of cork bark. (Mexico; winter.)

Hofmeisterella

Another relative of *Ornithocephalus*, this genus also has only one member.

Hofmeisterella eumicroscopica has a tiny fan of narrow, fleshy leaves 2.5 cm tall, while the flowering stem is three times that height. Several delightful flowers, large for the size of the plant, open one or two at a time. They are 1.2 cm long, with narrow yellow sepals and petals all flared upward, and a long, pointed, arrowhead-shaped lip that is yellow with rosy-purple in the center. Cool growing. (Colombia, Ecuador, Peru, and Venezuela; anytime of year.)

Holcoglossum

This genus contains but few species.

Holcoglossum quasipinifolium is one whose name is fun to translate: it means "rather pine-needle-like foliage," and it is indeed a tuft of rounded, needlelike leaves about 6 cm long. One to several white flowers, large for the plant, are produced on 10 to 12 cm stems. They are wide open, with wavy spatula-shaped sepals and petals, and a squarish lip leading into a broad, funnel-shaped spur. The side lobes of the lip are yellow. (Taiwan; late winter to spring.)

Homalopetalum

The genus has but few species, all tiny plants with rounded pseudobulbs on a creeping, branching rhizome, bearing single, fleshy, oval, pointed leaves. The flowers are large for the plant and come singly on stems somewhat longer than the leaves.

Homalopetalum pachyphyllum has rounded pseudobulbs that become red and wrinkled with age, spaced about 1 cm apart on the rhizome, and leaves 3 to 5 cm long. The short flower stem holds the 1.5 cm, yellow-green blossoms close to the base of the leaves. The petals and dorsal sepal form a hood over the column, while the broad, pointed lateral sepals extend outward beside the lip. The lip is squarish, with a raised, semicircular crest. (Mexico; summer.)

Homalopetalum pumilio is a rock dweller, sending its branching, creeping rhizome over lichen-and-moss-covered surfaces. The little, oval, green pseudobulbs are 5 to 7 mm tall, the tiny mule-ear leaves 2 to 3 cm. The slender flower stem comes from the top of the pseudobulb and holds a single, spidery, brownish-green blossom 4 to 6 cm long [Plate 72]. The

72. *The spidery flower of* Homalopetalum pumilio *is almost twice the length of the tiny 3 to 4 cm plant from which it comes. The flower looks delicate but is quite long-lasting.*

sepals and forward-curving petals are narrow and tapering. The narrow, diamond-shaped lip has a pair of out-turned cushion-shaped keels at its base. Best grown on a slab with constant moisture. (Mexico; summer.)

Homalopetalum vomeriforme is very much like the preceding, except that its pseudobulbs stand on stalklike, 5 mm stems, its sepals and petals are not so much attenuated, and the lip is completely smooth. (Jamaica; late winter to spring.)

Ione (Sunipia)

Fewer than a dozen epiphytic species, some of them lovely miniatures, make up the genus *Ione* (*Sunipia*, according to Dressler). They have one-leaved globose or conical pseudobulbs. The structure of the rostellum and caudicles of the pollinia are worth noting. There are four pollinia, separated into two pairs. Each pair is attached to a long caudicle ending in a mass of sticky material or a distinct, viscid disc, except that in one species, *I. intermedia*, the two caudicles share a viscid disc. The rostellum in all species has two projections on which the caudicles lie.

Ione (Sunipia) andersoni has fat, little pseudobulbs 7 mm tall, close together on the rhizome, and each bears a leaf 2 to 2.5 cm tall. The single flower arises on a 7 mm stem and is 8 mm in diameter, with yellow sepals and petals, and a purple lip. Its broad sepals curl back. The petals are broad and ciliated on the edges of their membranous base, while the tips are fleshy and pointed. The lip has a rounded, tooth-edged base and a fleshy pointed mid-lobe. (Sikkim; spring.)

Ione (Sunipia) bicolor is 7 to 9 cm tall, including pseudobulb and leaf. The slender flowers, six or seven to an upright spike, are 2.2 cm long. The sepals and petals are translucent with claret-colored veins, and the lip is pure claret. The latter is fiddle-shaped, with deeply toothed, squared sides, and a white "lump" in the center near the tip. Cool end of intermediate temperatures. (Sikkim; late fall.)

Ione (Sunipia) bifurcatoflorens is 3 to 5 cm tall, with pale green, globular pseudobulbs close together on the rhizome. A pair of round, 2 cm flowers arise on a short stem. The broad sepals are green, the narrow pointed petals and lip yellow. (Taiwan; summer).

Ione (Sunipia) intermedia has semitransparent ovoid pseudobulbs 1 cm tall, with a leaf 6 to 10 cm long. The flower stalk is barely taller than the pseudobulbs and bears a single, slender, pale green flower 1 cm long. (Sikkim.)

Ionopsis

Two species in this genus are well known, one particularly so, and both have a wide geographical range. They should be mounted on a slab and not kept too wet.

Ionopsis satyrioides is a small plant with a fan of dark green terete channeled leaves 4 to 6 cm tall. The delicate, slightly branching inflorescence, about 7 cm long, produces about 20 dainty flowers 6 to 8 mm long. They are white striped with pink. The sepals are united at the base, preventing the full opening of the flower. Their ends are turned out, as are those of the petals, and the somewhat oblong lip projects beyond them. The old flower stem sometimes gives a second crop of blossoms. (West Indies, Colombia, Peru, and Venezuela; spring to fall.)

Ionopsis utricularioides, the larger, better known plant, has two or three flat, tough leaves per growth, 7 to 15 cm tall, with a tiny, leafless pseudobulb in the middle. The flower spray can be 20 to 30 cm long, even longer at times, and is many branched, densely covered with charming and distinctive flowers [Plate 73]. They are 1.5 to 2 cm long, with a platform-like lip, bilobed at the tip, projecting from a small hood formed by the sepals and petals. Colors range from white veined with pink, to light or dark lavender with darker veins. (Florida, West Indies, and from Mexico to Peru; winter into summer.)

73. *Two flowers from the many held on the sprays of* Ionopsis utricularioides. *The pink and white blossoms are almost all lip. (Photo by Thomas H. Northen.)*

Isabelia

Two delightful species are contained in this genus, both with slim, terete leaves from small pseudobulbs covered with loose, threadlike bracts.

Isabelia pulchella has a branching rhizome that soon covers a slab or totem pole and sends branches out into the air. The pseudobulbs are about 1 cm tall, 2 to 3 cm apart on the slender rhizome, and the leaves, like stiff narrow blades of grass, are 6 cm long. Single bright magenta flowers are borne on stems about as long as the leaves. The waxy sepals are joined at the base to form a rounded spur which covers an inner spur formed by the attachment of the lip to the column foot. From where they become free, the sepals flare out, as do the petals, forming a circle 2 cm in diameter. The lip has a perfectly circular outer lobe that is papillose on the surface and toothed around the edge and a narrow, fleshy, white basal section. (Brazil; fall to winter.)

Isabelia virginalis [Color Plate C-35] has a most unusual appearance: The pseudobulbs are completely covered with a network of fibers that looks exactly like baskets. Pseudobulbs are set close together on the rhizome and from each arises a needlelike leaf. The exquisite little, cattleya-like flowers come singly from the top of the pseudobulbs. They are 1 cm wide, white with a rose flush, a cream-colored, velvety lip in the center of which can be seen the entrance to the spur, and a rose-tipped column. (Brazil; late fall.)

Jaquiniella _____

The genus *Jaquiniella* consists of a few species that have alternate fleshy leaves on a slender stem. Some have such inconspicuous flowers that you hardly know when they are in bloom, and some are self-pollinating, which results in the initiation of seed capsules almost before the flowers are evident. At least one species is rather attractive and worth growing.

Jaquiniella cernua ranges in height from 5 to 10 cm and has stems that bear alternate thick, fleshy, channeled leaves 2.5 cm long. From the upper leaf axils come single orange flowers with broad sepals that form a three-pointed star, within which are centered the smaller petals and the slightly boat-shaped lip. (Mexico; spring.)

Jumellea _____

74. Jumellea confusa *has a slow-growing leafy stem, and from its leaf axils come single, pure white flowers.*

Fanciers of angrecoid orchids will want to have a species or two of *Jumellea*. The literature does not always reveal at what size a species begins to flower, and it is difficult to tell whether the given height is the maximum attained or the height at which the plant matures. The fragrant flowers are white, sometimes slightly tinged with green, and in some species yellow. In all, the dorsal sepal stands straight up or bends slightly backward, the petals are horizontal or slanted down a bit, and the lateral sepals extend sideways at an angle. The lip is long, more or less oval, and the spur is of various lengths.

Jumellea comorensis is a dainty rambling plant whose slender, branching stems are clothed with narrow, 3 to 4 cm leaves. The single flowers are showy, 4 cm long, with a filamentous, almost straight spur 12 cm long. (Grande Comore; flowers all year around.)

Jumellea confusa is said to reach 60 cm in height, but the plant illustrated [Plate 74], a division of an older plant, has taken several years to reach 9 cm and is already starting its own branches from near the base. The latter can be retained if the older section becomes too tall. The species is said to be extremely variable. The one illustrated, a flower 3 cm long, has a shorter spur than is apparently true in some other cases. (Malagasy; late summer and early fall.)

Jumellea filicornoides is definitely prettier when young. Its rather stiffly upright stems bear leaves 4 to 7 cm long, and the lower leaves fall as the stems grow taller. Stems can flower when only 10 to 15 cm tall, at which time they are leafy, but as they approach their ultimate height of 30 cm the basal parts are bare. The plants branch from near the base, so there are always some young stems coming along. The flowers, 2.5 to 3 cm long with a short spur, are distinctive, because the petals and lateral sepals all sweep in a downward curve. (Rhodesia, Malawi, and Natal, South Africa; fall.)

Jumellea henryi is a diminutive version of *J. comorensis*, with stems 7 to 11 cm long covered with tiny leaves of 1 to 1.5 cm. The flowers are 2.5 cm long with spurs three times that length. (Malagasy; spring.)

Jumellea linearipetala remains short, with a stem only 2 cm tall, and four or five thick leaves 4 to 7 cm long. The flowers are nearly 3 cm long and come from below the leaves. They have very slender parts and a short spur. (Malagasy; summer.)

Jumellea ophioplectron also has a short stem and a few leaves. The flower is large for the plant, 5 cm long, with triangular parts, yellow-green with a white lip, and a yellowish spur 10 cm long. (Malagasy; winter and summer.)

Kalopternix _____

This is a genus created to contain a few species removed from *Epidendrum* because of differences in column structure.

Kalopternix deltoglossum is a tiny creeping plant with rounded or oval leaves 2 to 4 cm long attached singly to the merest hint of a pseudobulb and close together on the rhizome. The leaves are purplish on the back and tend to be tinged with brown or purple on the face when old. The 1.5 cm, star-shaped flowers are greenish-brown suffused with purple and are produced close under the leaf, more than one at a time or in succession. The front part of the lip is triangular and finely toothed. (Venezuela; spring.)

Kalopternix sophronitis, the best known of the new genus, might more appropriately have been named *stapelioides* because the flowers have a similar starfish appearance. The leaves are blue-green with silvery bloom on them, and they are attached in twos or threes to pseudobulbs barely 2 cm tall on a creeping rhizome. The 3.5 to 4 cm flowers are gray-green flecked with dull red, produced two or more at a time, or in succession. The broad, flat column is colored like the flower, and the anther appears on its upper end like a small button. The lip is papillose, juicy-looking, and blackish red, with a circular base from which extends a narrow, pointed strap. The flowers turn red when old. Cool growing, constant dampness. (Ecuador; flowers several times a year.)

Kefersteinia _____

Related to *Zygopetalum*, the species of *Kefersteinia* are 12 to 20 cm tall, without pseudobulbs, and have a fan of slender leaves of thin substance. The flowers are much alike and rather translucent. They have spreading, slender sepals and petals of about the same length, and a lip that spreads skirtlike from a semicircular, up-curving basal section. A bilobed crest is a conspicuous addition to the basal part. The blossoms come singly, and some are pendent. Plants can be grown on slabs or in pots and kept damp

75. Keffersteinia graminea
*has green sepals and petals
and a large fringed lip
heavily spotted with red
on a cream background.*

and shaded. Although plants are given certain dimensions in the literature, many remain smaller, and for that reason will be included here.

Kefersteinia graminea, a bit over 20 cm tall, has flowers 4 to 4.5 cm across [Plate 75], with green sepals and petals, and a finely fringed lip, cream-colored and densely spotted with red. (Venezuela, Colombia, and Ecuador; summer and fall.)

Kefersteinia lojae is one of the smaller species, 12 cm tall; its flowers are 2.5 cm across. Sepals and petals are whitish with red spots that increase in density toward their tips. The rounded, fringed lip is so densely spotted at the outer edge that it appears to be solid maroon. (Peru; summer.)

Kefersteinia sanguinolenta, 20 cm tall, holds its flowers on short, upright stems. They are 2 cm across, with pale green sepals and petals spotted with purple at the base. The lip curves up parallel to the column, and its front section then bends sharply down. It is white, much ruffled and toothed around the edge, velvety on the surface, and covered with large, irregular blotches of purple. (Venezuela and Ecuador; spring to fall.)

Kefersteinia tolimensis to 18 cm tall. The 3.5 cm flowers have green sepals and petals with purple spots that begin toward the outer ends and increase in density toward the base. The heavily ruffled, deeply toothed, sometimes actually fringed lip is almost solid dark wine-purple. (Colombia, Ecuador, Venezuela; fall.)

Kegeliella

There are two known species of *Kegeliella,* plants that have ribbed, conical pseudobulbs and fairly broad pleated leaves; in fact, they look like small members of *Gongora.*

Kegeliella houtteana is 12 to 15 cm tall, including the pseudobulbs and the three leaves they bear. The inflorescence is pendulous, 10 cm long, covered with reddish, glandular hairs that continue over the backs of the sepals. The few, 2.5 cm flowers are pale yellow and of thin substance. Sepals and petals are slender and pointed, the latter barred with red. The lip has a short, pointed mid-lobe and squarish, erect side lobes. (Panama, Jamaica, Trinidad, and Surinam; summer and winter.)

Kegeliella kupperi has 2 to 3 cm pseudobulbs that bear a pair of leaves 4 to 8 cm tall. The 9 to 12 cm flower stem is pendulous, and, as in the preceding species, it and the outside of the sepals are covered with glandular hairs. The flowers are 3 cm long, with a fleshy lip whose side lobes are rounded; the mid-lobe small and somewhat heart-shaped. (Costa Rica and Panama; summer.)

Kingidium

The few species in this genus have been variously included in *Doritis* and *Phalaenopsis* but have recently been returned to this earlier genus:

Kingidium decumbens has two or three oval leaves about 12 cm long, wavy-edged and of rather thin substance. The inflorescence is about the length of the leaves and bears at its end a succession of eight or more waxy flowers 2 cm across, wide open, with white, oval sepals and petals spotted with purple at the base. The strongly three-lobed purple lip forms a small chin at the base, its large, oval, striped side lobes standing erect; its diamond-shaped mid-lobe spreading from a narrow isthmus and decorated with a forked callus. Warm–intermediate. (Widespread from southern India and Sri Lanka throughout southeast Asia and Malaysia to the Philippines; flowers several times a year.)

Koellensteinia

This is a close relative of *Kefersteinia* but has fleshy flowers, several to the stem.

Koellensteinia graminea is normally about 10 cm tall but can occasionally make taller leaves. The leaves are narrow and tapering, only 6 to 9 mm wide. The flower stalk can be either upright or pendent, about 8 to 9 cm long, and bears several round, waxy blossoms 2 cm across. The broadly oval sepals and petals are cream color tinted with green and pink. The lip is white grading to yellow in the center and has a kidney-shaped mid-lobe and erect side lobes. All parts are lightly striped with purple. (Colombia to Bolivia and Venezuela; spring).

Koellensteinia tricolor [Color Plate C-36], a smaller plant, is more generous with its flowers. There are 15 or more fragrant, waxy, beautifully colored, 1 cm blossoms to the stem. The broad sepals and petals are lime green barred with red-brown. The white lip is cupped at its base and has an extended outer rim and tall side lobes. The inner surface of the latter and the tufts of hairs on the lip crest are bright rose, and the base of the column is also marked with rose. (Guianas and Brazil; fall.)

Laelia

The genus *Laelia* is closely related to *Cattleya*, the chief morphological difference being that it has eight pollinia while *Cattleya* has four. A few species look like the ordinary cattleyas, but the rest are quite distinct. Plants range from large to small, from slender to chunky. Most are native to Brazil. Among them are some 40 particularly charming species with star-shaped, usually brightly colored flowers, including such familiar kinds as *L. flava* and *L. cinnabarina*, too tall to be included here, but also some

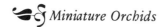

much smaller species that have flowers large for their size. Entirely different are a few of modest size with cattleya-like flowers, some native to Brazil, some from other areas. For convenience, they will be presented in two groups, those with star-shaped flowers and those with cattleya-like ones.

Species of Laelia *with star-shaped flowers*

Because they live in rocky places in the mountains, they are given the name rupicolous, which means "rock dwelling." It is interesting that they have such similar plant and flower forms. In fact, some are so much alike that they must be compared by means of anatomical drawings to determine their species. They have cylindrical or conical pseudobulbs, some shorter than others, and exceedingly tough, thick leaves, more or less folded at the mid-vein. The flowers have more or less equal sepals and petals, while the lip has long side lobes that enfold the column and an extended mid-lobe with ruffled edges.

Their habitats give clues to their cultural needs. Growing on rock faces or in crevices, they have perfect drainage. Most grow in full sun, although the smaller ones may be shaded by ground vegetation. They need a dry rest, or at least less water, after flowering and until new growth starts; they benefit from a humid atmosphere, however, and an occasional misting. They seem to thrive with intermediate temperatures, but may have cooler nights natively. If some don't flower, the cooler nights might be tried.

Laelia bradei has pseudobulbs 3 to 4 cm tall with only a slight swelling at the base, topped by a stiff, scoop-shaped leaf of the same length. The sturdy inflorescence, about 6 cm tall, bears three or four round, brilliant yellow blossoms 2 cm across. The sepals and petals are broadly oval. The shorter lip has long, broad side lobes, and the ruffled mid-lobe is wider at the tip than at its base. (Brazil; fall.)

Laelia briegeri varies from 10 to 17 cm in height. Its pseudobulbs and leaves are nearly the same length, the leaves a bit flatter than in the preceding species. The 27 to 30 cm flower spike holds four or five flowers 4 cm across. They have rather spatula-shaped sepals and petals, the latter a bit wavy on the edges, and a short lip whose mid-lobe is round when spread out. There are two color phases, one a brilliant yellow, the other creamy yellow tinged with pink. (Brazil; summer.)

Laelia crispata (syn. *rupestris*) [Color Plate C-37] varies from 15 to 40 cm in height, and plants in each size range maintain their height. The flower spike is always much taller than the leaves. The 4 to 5 cm flowers are beautifully colored: The sepals and petals a rich rose with white along the mid-vein. The lip is distinctive, its side lobes pale, ruffled with deep rose on their front edges. The yellow mid-lobe, sharply divided from the side lobes, is edged with a dark rose ruffle. (Brazil; midwinter.)

Laelia esalqueana has fat, slightly curved pseudobulbs 2.5 to 3 cm tall, crowded together on the rhizome, with a fleshy leaf 5 cm long, tipped backward from the apex of the pseudobulb. The flower stalk is 4.5 cm tall and holds four golden yellow blossoms 3 cm across, with unusually broad sepals and petals. The lip is short, but the tips of the side lobes, when spread out, extend as far as the mid-lobe. A distinctive feature, shared only with *L. ghillanyi*, is that the column is broader at the base than at the apex. (Brazil; summer.)

Laelia ghillanyi has fat, greenish-purple pseudobulbs 3 cm tall and unlike the others, may have single or paired leaves 3 cm long. Flowers vary from light cream to deep rose and are borne eight or nine on a short spike. They are 3.5 cm across, the petals wavy on the edges. The side lobes of the lip are white below, shading to purple on top, ruffled on the forward edges. The round mid-lobe is widely separated from the side lobes, yellow inside, with a broad, rather fleshy ruffle around its edge. The column is broader at the base than at the apex. (Brazil; spring.)

Laelia itambana has pseudobulbs only 2.5 to 3.5 cm tall and leaves of the same length. The rich yellow flowers are 4.5 cm across, borne in pairs on a stem barely as tall as the leaves. The lip is rather more plain than some, entirely yellow, with a small front lobe and two smooth keels on the crest. (Brazil; spring and summer.)

Laelia lilliputana [Plate 76], tiniest of the group, has pseudobulbs only 1 to 1.5 cm tall and a little reddish, extremely stiff leaf 1 to 2.5 cm long. A stem 3 cm long holds the single flower, which is 3 cm across. It is whitish, tinged with lavender and rose and has a sparkling texture. In sharp contrast, the ruffled mid-lobe of the lip is deep orange. (Brazil; late spring).

Laelia longipes has slightly conical pseudobulbs topped by a fleshy leaf. The flowers are yellow or white with a yellow lip, several to a moderately tall stem, and are 5.7 cm across, with slender, flat-spreading parts. (Brazil; fall.)

Laelia lucasiana (syn. *ostermeyeri*) [Color Plate C-38] has thick, sometimes globose pseudobulbs 3 cm tall and rather wide leaves 4 to 8 cm long. The bright rose-pink flowers, 4.5 cm in diameter, have a long, narrow, entirely deep gold lip, with dark brown "eyes" in the throat. (Brazil; late summer). A species called *L. fournieri* is actually a white form of this species with yellow lip.

Laelia mantiqueirae (syn. *crispilabia*) reaches 12 cm in height, including the slim, conical pseudobulbs and fairly narrow leaves. The 4.5 cm flowers, several to a rather short inflorescence, are rich rose color. The rather spatula-shaped sepals and petals tend to curve backward. The lip is perhaps the most beautiful in this group and was responsible for the alternate name *crispilabia*. The long side lobes are veined with dark violet, their outer ends ruffled and finely fringed in dark violet. The mid-lobe is white in the center, edged all around with the same fringed dark violet ruffle. (Brazil; winter to spring.)

Laelia milleri [Color Plate C-39] created a sensation when it

76. *Tiniest of the genus,* Laelia lilliputana *is one of the rupicolous or rock-dwelling species. Its 3 cm blossom is white, tinged with lavender and rose, and has a deep orange lip.*

was discovered not too many years ago, because of its long-lasting, brilliant red to red-orange flowers. The species was avidly collected, and what was left of it was destroyed by mining operations in its restricted habitat. The only plants now known are in cultivation, but it is hoped that it may one day be rediscovered in nature. It is a small plant, 12 to 15 cm high, with flower stalks 30 to 50 cm tall, bearing six to 15 blossoms. They have slender, pointed sepals and petals, and a long, narrow lip that is yellow inside veined with red, ruffled on the outer edge. They are 4 to 5 cm across, individually long-lasting, and since buds open successively over a long period, the plant stays in bloom for three months or more. (Brazil; spring to fall.)

Species of Laelia *with cattleya-like flowers*

This group has a variety of plant types and includes sizes from very small to 15 cm tall. They range from Mexico to Brazil.

Laelia albida resembles a small bifoliate cattleya in plant form. The somewhat arching inflorescence, 30 cm or more long, bears four to eight lovely, 4.5 cm blossoms that are basically white tinged with pink, especially the outer portion of the lip. The sepals are slender and pointed, quite straight, the petals are broad and pointed, somewhat wavy, and the lip is fiddle-shaped with three yellow keels on the crest. The base of the column is often deep rose, lending an attractive accent. (Mexico; fall to winter.)

Laelia furfuracea [Color Plate C-40] has plump pseudobulbs slightly fluted and tapering at the top and a single, rather thick, rigid leaf. The arching inflorescence bears three to five beautiful satiny flowers 8 cm across, shaped in general like those of *L. albida*, but with broader petals. The sepals are pale pink, the petals and lip a darker tone. (Mexico; midwinter.)

Laelia jongheana, a rupicolous species, is among the loveliest of the genus [Color Plate C-41]. It has almost egg-shaped pseudobulbs and broad, thick single leaves. The flowers come on short stems, usually in pairs, and are 10 cm across, but not very long-lasting. They are pink-lavender, some plants having darker flowers than others, with slender sepals and broad, pointed petals. The side lobes of the lip enfold the column, and the long, spreading, ruffled mid-lobe, cream-yellow inside, has seven golden keels very much ruffled where they emerge onto the outer portion. Grows easily, making many leads. (Brazil; midwinter.)

Laelia lundii, also a rupicolous kind, has pencil-thin pseudobulbs and quill-like leaves [Plate 77]. The exquisite little 4 cm flowers [Color Plate C-42] arise in pairs from the developing growths just as the leaves begin to emerge. They are perfect miniaturized cattleyas, with white or pale lilac flowers, richly veined with purple in the ruffled lip. (Brazil; midwinter.)

Laelia pumila [Color Plate C-43] is a modest plant 10 to 15 cm

77. Laelia lundii *is a veritable bouquet of little cattleya-like flowers.*

94

tall with large, fragrant, rich violet flowers about 8 cm across. Sepals, oval petals, and the tube of the lip are rosy-violet, while the spreading mid-lobe is a much darker shade. There is a bit of yellow in the throat. (Brazil; fall.)

Laelia rubescens [Color Plate C-44] is questionably included, for although some plants remain small, many grow to a fairly large size. They are distinctive for their circular, compressed pseudobulbs 4 to 5 cm across, with a slight ridge on each side. They are shiny green when new, wrinkled and often reddish when old. The paired leaves are about 8 cm long, widely divergent. The flowers, about eight to a stem, range from white with yellow and red in the throat to various shades of pink and lavender. Sepals are slender, petals and lip fairly wide. Best grown on a slab or little log and given a dry rest in winter. (Mexico to Panama; fall.)

Laelia sincorana [Color Plate C-45] was discovered over 70 years ago and had not been seen again until it was refound in 1975. Its tiny, round pseudobulbs, no larger than marbles, are surely the extreme of the rupicolous type, as are the short, fat leaves. The huge, rose-colored flower dwarfs the plant. It is 7 cm across, wide open and flat, with oval petals twice the width of the sepals and a cattleya-like lip that rolls around the column and spreads its mid-lobe wide. The base and interior of the lip are light cream, while the outer section and front edges of the side lobes are rich violet. Five raised keels line the crest. (Brazil; winter.)

Lanium

If one uses a hand lens to look at the flowers of this genus, their relationship to *Epidendrum* becomes clear; otherwise, the cloud of tiny blossoms looks more like a flight of mosquitoes. The dainty, creeping plants have leafy stems 5 to 7 cm tall or tiny pseudobulbs a few centimeters high, with two or three tiny leaves. The flower stems, pedicels, and often the back of the sepals are covered with fine wool, which suggested its generic name, *Lanium*, from the Latin word *lana* meaning "wool."

Lanium avicula has pseudobulbs 2 cm tall and leaves the same length. The branched flower stem bears many blossoms, creamy white or yellowish white, 1.2 cm across. They have slender, pointed sepals and petals and a little, pointed, scoop-shaped lip. (Brazil and Peru; fall).

Lanium microphyllum covers a slab with its creeping rhizome and graceful, leafy stems. The little flowers hold their pointed sepals and petals almost straight back from the column and pointed lip. They are pale yellow, slightly tinged with pink, 1 cm long. (Colombia, Ecuador, Peru, Venezuela, Surinam, and Guyana; winter.)

78. Lankesterella ceracifolia
is a tiny plant with soft
green leaves.

79. *The little fuzzy*
flowers of Lankesterella
ceracifolia.

Lankesterella

The genus was named in honor of the late Charles H. Lankester of Costa Rica, an illustrious amateur orchidist whose garden has been preserved for future generations of orchid lovers. The ten species are epiphytic, although one might expect from their appearance that they were terrestrial. They have rosettes of soft, tender leaves and produce flower stems and flowers covered with fine white hairs. New rosettes come from the old each year, and, at the same time, additional ones form so that the plant becomes a cushion of leaf whorls. A flower stalk bearing a few blossoms comes from the center of each whorl. The flowers of different species are much alike, and any would be a delight to grow. They prefer shade and constant moisture, and do well in a small pot.

Lankesterella ceracifolia [Plate 78] has oval, pointed leaves 1 to 2 cm long, seven or so in a rosette. The flower stalk with several blossoms is 5 cm tall [Plate 79]. The tiny green-veined white blossoms resemble penstemons in general shape. They are about 1.5 cm long, somewhat tubular, with the ends of the petals and the dorsal sepal turned up, the large lip spread downward, and the lateral sepals forming a short spur with their united bases. (Brazil; fall.)

Lankesterella orthantha is similar in plant habit. Its flowers are green and white, more tubular than the preceding, and backed by a large floral bract. The lateral sepals form a blunt chin. Cool growing. (Costa Rica, Venezuela, and Ecuador; spring.)

Leochilus

Small relatives of *Oncidium*, the members of *Leochilus* have small pseudobulbs and leaves and give a half dozen flowers with long, oval lips and small sepals and petals. In all, the large anther looks like the head of an animal.

Leochilus ampliflorus [Plate 80] is large for the genus, with triangular, ridged pseudobulbs 2.5 cm tall and leaves some 7 cm long. The pendent, willowy flower stem holds five or six creamy green, 2.5 cm flowers with a white lip. The dorsal sepal forms a hood over the column, and the petals stand slightly forward; all are striped with red-brown. The lip broadens toward the outer end and has a pair of wide, fleshy keels on the crest. (Mexico; summer.)

Leochilus carinatus has a much flattened oval pseudobulb 1.2 cm tall, a 7 cm leaf from its top, and a shorter one from the base. The erect branching flower stem reaches 15 cm in length and bears many flowers. It makes plantlets after the blooming period. The blossoms are 2 cm long, distinctive for the fingerlike processes on the lip crest. They are yellow-green, the sepals flushed with brown, and the forward-held petals striped with brown. The basal half of the lip is broad, the end narrower, and the crest is spotted with brown. (Mexico; late summer.)

Leochilus labiatus has bright shiny green pseudobulbs 1 cm tall, with a single leaf at the top and three from the sides, 3 to 5 cm long. The erect flower stalk holds a few fleshy flowers 1.2 cm long. Sepals and petals are broad and pointed, the laterals united to about the middle. The petals stand erect beside the column. The lip has a pair of rounded protuberances at its base, between which are a few hairs. Farther along, it has a broad, backward pointing flap, and it makes a right-angle bend just where the two types of decorations meet. The front end is spatula-shaped, pointed or slightly bilobed at the very tip. (Guatemala to Panama, West Indies, Trinidad, and Venezuela; summer to autumn.)

Leochilus oncidioides has conical, compressed pseudobulbs and a single leaf whose mid-vein is extended in a sharp point. The arching to pendent inflorescence holds six or seven blossoms 1 cm long, grayish, with a line of dull red spots on the sepals and petals. The lip has one large blotch in the center with a few scattered ones surrounding it. The lip is slightly wider toward the outer end and has a double-ridged fuzzy callus with a depression at its base that is smooth inside. (Mexico, Guatemala, and Honduras; late fall.)

Leochilus scriptus is much like the preceding, except that the lateral sepals are not united and the lip is slightly bilobed at the tip. A cuplike depression at the base is filled with silky hairs. (Mexico to Panama and Colombia; spring.)

80. Leochilus ampliflorus *is one of the largest of its genus, with blossoms 2.5 cm long, creamy green, striped with red-brown. (From a Kodachrome by Leon A. Wiard.)*

Lepanthes

With the exception of a few tallish species, the genus *Lepanthes* is made up of jewel-like miniatures that range from Mexico through Central America and the Caribbean Islands, south to Peru and Brazil. The number recorded has at least doubled in the past decade or two, with possibly 175 now known, and new ones being found all the time. The genus is related to *Pleurothallis* and likes the same cool, damp, shady conditions enjoyed by those high-elevation plants. The clustered stems have funnel-shaped bracts, ciliated on their edges, and single, round or oval leaves. The minute flowers, most only a few millimeters long, come on herringbone or ladder-like inflorescences at the junction of leaf and stem and usually open one at a time over a long period. Additional inflorescences come from the same leaf. The sepals are triangular, somewhat joined at their bases. The hallmark of the genus is the structure of the fleshy petals, which are bilobed and attached somewhere toward the middle rather than by one end as in other flowers. The side lobes of the lip usually hug the column, while the tiny mid-lobe protrudes from beneath its tip. They have two pollinia.

I do not mean to give short shrift to this lovely genus, but to try to describe more than a few species would be futile, as anything but a detailed, scientific description plus anatomical drawings would fail to

81. *In* Lepanthes angustisepala *the long slim parts are the sepals; the petals are the crescent-shaped "swellings" above the column; and the lip is the dark lobes that hug the column.*

82. *In* Lepanthes obtusa *the sepals are broad triangles, the petals are the two large, somewhat boomerang-shaped parts, and the smaller and similarly shaped parts next to the column are lobes of the lip.*

identify them. Any of the tiny, glowing, colorful species that might come into your possession would be a treasure to own. Many that are being brought in now have not yet been identified.

Lepanthes angustisepala is about 7 cm tall, with slender, pointed leaves toothed on the edges. The flower [Plate 81] has unusually long sepals of golden yellow that give the blossom a length of 1.2 to 2 cm. The minute petals, column, and lip are rose-red. (Dominican Republic; early summer.) (There is another species, whose name I do not know, that is just the opposite, with unusually long, thin petals, each shaped like a broad U and attached at the bottom of the curve.)

Lepanthes obtusa and the species immediately below, are what might be called typical, yet they give an idea of the subtle differences between species. *L. obtusa*, a plant 10 to 12 cm tall, with leaves small for its height, has shiny ruby-red flowers 3 to 4 mm long [Plate 82]. The sepals are broad, united for a good portion of their length. The petals are widest in the middle and the lip has side lobes elongated front and back. (Jamaica; winter.)

Lepanthes selenipetala [Color Plate C-46] has narrower parts, petals pinched in the middle and broader at the upper end, and smaller side lobes to the lip. The flower has green-gold sepals, and the petals are yellow on the edges, red toward the center. The column is also red. (Dominican Republic; spring.)

Lepanthes trilobata [Color Plate C-47] is a very tiny plant but striking for the proportionate size of its flowers [Plate 83], which are all of 3 mm long, and for their unusually large lip. The sepals are pinkish yellow, the rest of the flower bright yellow tinged with red. The lip does not hug the column as in other species, thus letting one see how small the mid-lobe is in comparison to the side lobes. This large lip balances the large, fishtail petals. (Dominican Republic; spring.)

Lepanthes species, unidentified [Color Plate C-48] is but one of the new types coming from the Andes, with fantastic flowers, some of them furry, in tones of green, purple, gold, and red. (Ecuador; summer.)

Lepanthopsis

Tiny cousins of *Lepanthes*, the plants of *Lepanthopsis* have the same form and the same ciliated, funnel-shaped bracts. The minute flowers are born in two neat ranks, back to back on the stem. There are but few species known as yet. They have two pollinia. They require the same culture as *Lepanthes*.

Lepanthopsis floripecten [Color Plate C-49] is a charming plant, 3 cm tall, with an inflorescence about the same length. The nearly transparent blossoms could be made of glass. The coloring is subtle, yellow-green, faintly tinged with pink. The blossoms are 4 to 6 mm long, with their lateral sepals united for two-thirds their length, slightly divergent at the tips. What appears to be two broad ears on the column are actually separate stigmas. (Honduras, Costa Rica, Colombia, Venezuela, and Brazil; spring.)

Leptotes

A member of the *Cattleya/Epidendrum* complex, the small genus *Leptotes* has some six species, two of which are very popular. They have terete leaves attached to insignificant, cylindrical pseudobulbs. Slabs of cork bark or tree fern suit them well.

Leptotes bicolor is the larger, more vigorous of the two. Its leaves are 10 to 15 cm long, and from their base come short stems bearing several fragrant flowers [Plate 84]. The blossoms are 4 to 5 cm across, their slender sepals and petals white, and the long narrow lip rich magenta with a white tip and side lobes. The column is brownish with two bright "eyes" beside the anther. (Brazil and Paraguay; spring and fall.)

Leptotes unicolor [Plate 85] is half the size of the preceding, both in plant and in flower. The sepals are pale pink, the petals darker, and the lip solid magenta. (Brazil; winter.)

Liparis

With over 350 species of epiphytes, lithophytes, and terrestrials in many parts of the world, *Liparis* ranks as one of the larger genera. Many are large plants that give a profusion of very small flowers. Some are tiny plants whose flowers are proportionate to their size. Some have handsome foliage and dense spikes of stunning little flowers. All can be grown in pots of fine bark and perlite, but the terrestrials may also be grown in a soil mix and the epiphytes on small logs or pieces of cork bark.

Liparis coelogynoides is a beautiful little spreading epiphyte with leaves the size and texture of grass and globose pseudobulbs 1 cm high. Eight to 20 delicate flowers come on long, arching or pendent stems. The slender sepals and petals and wedge-shaped lip are green at the base and orange on the tips. Requires constant moisture. (Australia; spring and summer.)

Liparis delicatula is epiphytic and has ovoid pseudobulbs 1 cm tall, bearing one or two leaves tapering on both ends, 1.3 cm long. The erect, 4 cm, flowering stem holds a dozen yellowish buglike flowers 5 mm long. The sepals and petals are pointed and spreading, the fleshy lip is broad, curving upward and then sharply down, with a hairy tip. The huge, winged column looms over the lip. (Sikkim, Khasia Hills, and Assam; early summer.)

83. Lepanthes trilobata *is an exception in that the lip is large and stands under the column instead of surrounding it. Note the fishtail-shaped petals. The blossoms are all of 3 mm across.*

84. *Orchid flowers often show surprising features. It takes a close look at* Leptotes bicolor, *a lovely 4 to 5 cm flower, white with a magenta lip, to notice the threatening aspect of the column.*

85. Leptotes unicolor, *half the size of* L. bicolor, *is colored in shades of pink and magenta.*

86. Liparis keitaoensis *is the "silver cricket orchid" of Taiwan. The beautiful leaf, green, flecked with gray, is almost as attractive as the little silvery green blossoms.*

Liparis duthei, an epiphyte, has closely packed, egg-shaped pseudobulbs 1 cm tall, topped by single, linear leaves 2.5 to 8 cm tall. The flower stalk equals the leaf height and carries numerous, minute, pale green flowers 2 mm across. Their dominant feature is a broad, shield-shaped folded lip. (Sikkim.)

Liparis gambelei, another with buglike flowers, has a single, beautiful, deeply veined, oval leaf, ruffled on the edge, 8 to 10 cm long, whose basal sheath covers the young developing pseudobulb. The flower spike arises from within this sheath also reaching a height of 8 cm. The 5 mm flowers have inconspicuous dark green sepals and petals and a velvety, oval lip veined with brown-purple. Terrestrial in cool damp forests. (Sikkim; early summer.)

Liparis keitaoensis [Plate 86] is a terrestrial called the "silver cricket orchid" in its native land. It has a stunning, broad, heart-shaped leaf flecked with gray, at whose base there forms a rounded pseudobulb. An erect spike 15 to 20 cm long produces 20 to 30 flowers arranged spirally around the stem. They are pale green, translucent, 1.5 cm long, with filamentous sepals and petals and a rounded lip. The leaf is deciduous. (Taiwan; fall.)

Liparis perpusilla is epiphytic with egg-shaped pseudobulbs, to whose flattened apex are attached three narrow leaves 2.2 cm long. The inflorescence is 6 to 8 cm tall and bears a scattering of flowers much like those of *L. duthei*. Cool growing. (Sikkim.)

Liparis pygmaea is a tiny terrestrial, only 2.5 cm tall, including the ovoid pseudobulb and pair of oval leaves. The pseudobulbs are swathed in large, loose sheaths. The flower stem with its three blossoms is 3.5 cm tall. The tan flowers are 7 mm long, with narrow, backward curving sepals and petals and a tongue-shaped, spreading lip. From 13,000 ft (about 4120 m) elevation. Cold growing. (Sikkim; fall.)

Liparis rizalensis [Plate 87] is a chunky epiphyte with fat, pear-shaped pseudobulbs, each bearing a pair of broad leaves for a total height of 10 to 12 cm. The flower spike comes from the top of the maturing pseudobulb and bears 40 or 50 densely packed, 5 mm, red-orange blossoms, from which its nickname the "red cricket orchid" is derived. The yellow column pokes up from the folded lip and down-curving sepals and petals. Needs good light. (Taiwan; fall.)

Lockhartia

The "braided" leaves of *Lockhartia* give it a special charm, although the bright little flowers are attractive, too. The braided effect comes from the flat, triangular leaves that follow each other alternately up the dainty, graceful stem with their bases overlapping, a characteristic of several other genera as well. Leaves of this type are said to be "equitant." Flowers come from the axils of the upper leaves and are of two types, round or elongated. Plants may make stems somewhat longer than our limit, but are always dainty. Those that tend to remain upright can be grown in pots; those with trailing stems should be grown on a mount. New stems form almost constantly as older ones turn brown and lose their leaves. The latter can be cut off without repotting the plant. Some begin to flower when short, and all flower several times from the same stem. They like to be constantly damp but never sopping.

Lockhartia acuta averages more than 20 cm in height, but is unusually generous with flowers and is remarkable for having long, branched inflorescences, several at a time, which reach 8 to 9 cm. The blossoms are rounded, wide open, about 1 cm across, yellow or white with a yellow lip. The sepals and petals are broadly oval. The lip is rather flat, with low side lobes and a mid-lobe that has two points at the end and one on each side. The callus is a raised mound divided into two flat projections, all covered with glandular hairs. (Panama, Trinidad, Colombia, and Venezuela; Flowers over a long period, usually summer.)

Lockhartia longifolia has unusually long, slim leaves, hence its name. Its bright yellow, 1 cm flowers are completely round, with broadly oval, wide-spreading sepals and petals, and a rounded lip whose tip has two lobules. The crest is a depression encircled by an orange-colored ridge that is finely hairy, with a fleshy tooth at its apex. (Colombia, Venezuela, and Peru.)

Lockhartia oerstedii [Plate 88] has short leaves, making the leafy stem very narrow. The complicated yellow, 2 cm flowers come singly or in pairs. They have oval sepals pressed back against the ovary. The large petals arch sideways beside the dorsal sepal. The lip is the striking part of the flower. It is long and narrow, with its mid-lobe divided at the apex, flaring out from a ridgelike central section that is covered with fingerlike protuberances and speckled with brown. The side lobes are broad at the base, narrower and tongue-shaped as they curve up and over the crest to touch at their tips in front of the column. They are also striped with brown. The column is elegantly decorated with fan-shaped spotted wings. (Mexico to Panama; flowers all year.)

Ludisia

The single species in this genus is one of the jewel orchids, and is borderline in size after it has branched out a bit.

Ludisia discolor, long known as *Haemaria*, has velvety leaves in various color patterns. One is plain dark green on top, red-purple underneath; another is dark wine color with gold veins on the upper surface, pale rose underneath. The jointed stems are brittle and fleshy and branch easily, so that a plant soon becomes a mass of growths. Individual stems grow to about 15 cm, but, as branches come along their stems, they become trailing. The plant is lovely in a hanging pot. Although a terrestrial

87. Liparis rizalensis *earns the name "red cricket orchid" from its red-orange blossoms.*

88. *It is interesting to see how plant characteristics are repeated among various genera. A number of unrelated kinds have the general habit of the lovely* Lockhartia. *Shown here is* L. oerstedii.

101

that will grow in a soil mix, it can also be grown in fine bark. The flower spike arises from the tip of a new growth and is about 15 to 20 cm tall, producing many lovely little, white flowers 2.5 cm across. A unique characteristic is that the anchor-shaped lip and the huge yellow anther are twisted in opposite directions. The petals and the dorsal sepal form a hood, while the lateral sepals spread sideways. Requires shade and constant but moderate moisture. (South China, Burma, and Indonesia; fall and winter.)

Macodes

This genus is related to *Ludisia* and also has the lip twisted as in that genus. The small brown flowers are not as pretty; the plants are grown for their extraordinarily beautiful foliage. They are warm growing and require high humidity and good shade.

Macodes petola has broad, oval leaves 6.5 cm long in a flat rosette. They are velvety, dark green, with five strong longitudinal, golden veins and groups of smaller cross veins. The under surface is tinged with purple. (Sumatra to the Philippines; spring.)

Macodes rollinsoni has broad, dark brownish-green, velvety leaves 10 cm long, whose margin is wavy and bordered with white. (New Guinea; fall.)

Macodes sanderana has nearly round, velvety leaves 8 cm long, whose upper surface is deep green with a network of gold veins. The lower surface is purple. (New Guinea; fall.)

Masdevallia

The genus *Masdevallia*, queen of the *Pleurothallis* group, inhabits the high mountain country from Mexico to Peru, with the greatest concentration in Colombia and Ecuador. Over 300 species are known, among them some of the most beautiful, most colorful, and strangest flowers of the orchid family. In contrast to most other orchids, the showy parts of the flower are the sepals, which are broad at the base, joined for part or nearly all of their length to form a cup or tube, and often extended into tails. The petals and lip are tiny and contained within the cup or tube, sometimes hidden, sometimes exposed. They have two pollinia. The plants are epiphytic and have no pseudobulbs. Leaves grow close together from a creeping, branching rhizome, and most species spread rapidly into bouquets of leaves and flowers. The leaves are oar-shaped or paddle-shaped, with the blade or outer portion widening gradually or abruptly from a short or long petiole. The base of the stem is surrounded by one or more tubular bracts or sheaths, some small, some very large and loose, and the plants can often be recognized as masdevallias in the field by this characteristic. Flower stems come from the rhizome beside the leaves, either within or outside of these bracts. Most species are one-flowered, but a few have several blossoms at once or in succession.

Various authorities have divided the species into sections according to characteristics of the plants or flowers, but some of the divisions seem artificial, are difficult to use, and sometimes are not descriptive of their appearance. Therefore, since there are so many, samples of some types will be given in detail along with a list of a few similar ones. With few exceptions, they need shade, cool temperatures, and constant moisture.

Masdevallia amanda, a plant of 8 to 9 cm height, has dainty, pink and white flowers, several on a stem 12 to 16 cm tall. The blossoms resemble the open jaw of some reptilian creature, with a toothed upper jaw and a pair of fangs from the lower. The flower is 1.5 to 2 cm overall, with the sepal tails one-third of that. The sepaline tube is indented to form a little chin. (Colombia; flowers continually.) Similar species are *M. oligantha*, *M. caloptera*, *M. melanops*, and the somewhat larger *M. pachyura*.

Masdevallia aspera is 6.5 cm tall with a flower stem the same height. The sepaline cup is 1 cm long, filled with short white hairs and striped with yellow. The tails are 1.5 cm long on the dorsal sepal, 3.5 cm long on the laterals. (Peru.)

Masdevallia astuta: See *Dracula astuta*.

Masdevallia barleana, whose leaves range from 7 to 14 cm in height, is a squared-off version of the famous *M. coccinea*, which is too large for this category. The flowers are brilliant rosy-crimson. The sepaline tube is narrow, and the flattened portion of the sepals is 2 cm long. The flared part of the smaller dorsal sepal is pale pink striped with the dark tone, and has a 2.5 cm tail; that of the laterals is a solid color, and the tails, which come from their outer "corners," are 1 cm long. (Colombia; fall.)

Masdevallia caudata [Color Plate C-50] is intriguing and one of the most serenely beautiful of the genus. The plant is 7 to 9 cm tall with rather broad leaves. The flower, huge in proportion to the plant, has a total length of 12 to 15 cm, with the basal part 4 cm long and the tails individually 6 cm. The flower is basically yellow, the rounded dorsal sepal striped and lightly speckled with rose, and the somewhat narrower and longer laterals densely spotted and mottled. The tails are yellow. (Colombia; fall to spring.) A similar species is *M. triangularis*.

Masdevallia caudivolvula, named for its curly tails, is one of the strangest of the genus. The rather slender leaves are 10 to 13 cm tall, and the flower stems are the same length. The yellow, 3 cm blossoms have a globose cup and fleshy, wax-hard tails that curl like corkscrews [Plate 89]. The twist becomes tighter and tighter as the flowers age. (Colombia; summer to fall.)

Masdevallia chestertonii: See *Dracula chestertonii*.

Masdevallia ecaudata, whose name means "tailless," actually has little stubby prolongations of the sepals [Plate 90]. The plant is 5 to 8 cm

89. Masdevallia caudivolvula *is aptly named "curly tails."*

90. *Almost tailless,* Masdevallia ecaudata *is more open than many and allows its petals, lip, and column to be seen.*

103

91. *This little spiny flower was named the "hedgehog," the translation of the specific name of* Masdevallia erinacea.

92. *Masdevallia floribunda gives a wealth of tiny butter-yellow blossoms from the base of the 8 to 10 cm tall plant. Note the tube formed by the union of the sepals.*

tall and the flower stems slightly more. The sepal bases form a broad, open tube in which the petals, column, and lip are conspicuously centered. The flower is waxy, 1.5 cm long, cream or greenish white striped with purple even to the petals and column. The lip is yellow. (Costa Rica, Panama, Colombia, and Venezuela; mid-winter.) Similar species are *M. campyloglossa*, *M. livingstoniana*, *M. peristeria* (a huge flower), *M. peruviana*, and *M. weberbaueri*.

Masdevallia edwallii: See *Dryadella edwallii*.

Masdevallia erinacea [Color Plate C-51] was briefly called *M. horrida* before it was realized that it had been named *M. erinacea* decades ago. The name means "like a hedgehog," referring to its spiny bristles. The plant is a cushion of leaves 4 cm long by 2 mm wide, fleshy but not rigid. The delightful globular flowers [Plate 91] come singly on stems just taller than the leaves. They are 1.5 cm long and dangle short yellow, end-thickened tails from the tip of each sepal. (Costa Rica; summer.)

Masdevallia erythrochaete: See *Dracula erythrochaete*.

Masdevallia floribunda [Plate 92] forms a dense cluster of leaves 8 to 10 cm tall and gives a profusion of single flowers on horizontal stems 10 to 12 cm long. They are butter yellow lightly stippled with brown. The sepaline cup is 1.5 cm across. The dorsal sepal consists of a small triangle with a 2 cm tail; the laterals are almost round and have short tails tucked underneath. (Mexico to Costa Rica; spring and summer.) A similar species is *M. chontalensis*.

Masdevallia gemmata is tiny, only 4 cm tall, but with flowers as long as the leaves. The rose-colored blossoms are slightly translucent and come singly on threadlike stems 4 to 8 cm tall. From the short tube the dorsal sepal extends directly into a tail 2.5 cm long. The laterals are joined clear to their ends, forming a rectangular platform at whose outer corners straight tails 2 cm long project. (Colombia; midwinter.) Related species are *M. huebneri* and *M. triaristela*.

Masdevallia grandiflora was evidently so named because its blossoms are large for the plant, not because they are among the largest in the genus. The plant is 8 to 10 cm tall. The single, 4 cm flowers are pure white save for a touch of orange in the lip. The long sepal tails taper gradually from the narrow, triangular united bases that form a short tube. A plant with many blossoms appears to have a frill of white fringe around its middle. (Ecuador and Peru; winter or spring.) Comparable species are *M. strumifera* and *M. tubulosa*.

Masdevallia heteroptera is an uncommon species with flowers that look like big red insects [Plate 93] and leaves 9 to 10 cm tall. The total spread of a blossom is 5 to 6 cm from tip to tip of the thin tails. There is practically no tube. The dorsal sepal is cream color spotted with red and cupped over the column and the large, up-turned lip. The dark red lateral sepals are narrower, consisting of a flat, wide portion at the base with its edges rolled back, and a terminal filamentous tail. (Colombia; flowers almost all year.) A less bold looking species is *M. picturata*.

Masdevallia minuta is a real lilliputian. The plants are only 3 to 4 cm tall and the flowers, which occur down among the leaves, only 1 cm long. The white or greenish-white blossoms have their sepals united for almost their entire length, and only their triangular tips flare open at the end of the tube. The hidden lip is bright orange. (Venezuela, Surinam, British Guiana, Ecuador, and Peru; fall and spring.) A related species is *M. diantha*.

Masdevallia nidifica is about 7.5 cm tall and has little red and yellow flowers on threadlike stems of about the same height. The sepaline cup is 5 mm deep and hairy inside. The wide part of the dorsal sepal is heavily spotted with red, while the base of the lateral sepals is less so. The red or yellow filamentous tails are up to 4 cm long. (Costa Rica, Colombia, and Ecuador; winter and spring.)

Masdevallia rosea is dainty even though it reaches a height of 13 cm. The almost fluorescent rose-colored flowers [Color Plate C-52] come on slender stems a bit longer than the leaves. They are 5 to 8 cm long, with a narrow, brilliant orange tube. The small dorsal sepal and large flat laterals all point straight forward, lying almost flat on each other. The former has a short tail, the latter longer ones. (Ecuador; fall and winter.)

Masdevallia saltatrix [Color Plate C-53], 7 to 11 cm tall, has flowers with a protruding "tummy." The shiny dark red flowers are waxy, with a long curved tube swollen in the middle. The tips of the sepals flare outward at the open end, terminating in short tails. Total length of the blossoms is about 4 cm. (Colombia; flowers throughout the year.) A near relative is *M. angulifera*.

Masdevallia sprucei has rather rough leaves 7 cm tall and flower stems of about the same height. The yellow flowers are about 2 cm long, with broadly triangular sepals that end in fleshy white tails 1 cm long. The basal part of the dorsal sepal is velvety, and the surfaces of the larger laterals are papillose and marked with a large purple patch. (Venezuela, Colombia, and Ecuador.)

Masdevallia strobelii [Color Plate C-54] is completely charming, with leaves 4 cm tall and single orange and yellow flowers on stems of the same height. The orange sepaline tube is 1 cm long, the out-turned part of the sepals is yellow and furry inside, 1.5 cm across their open "mouth." Actually, the fur consists of stiffly upright, slender, fleshy "fingers." The 3.5 cm filamentous tails curve gracefully sideways or backwards. (Ecuador; early winter.)

Masdevallia susanae may be the smallest of the genus, with minuscule, round, fleshy leaves 3 to 5 mm long, held flat to the tree bark. The nearly tailless reddish flowers are 4 mm long, with the sepals joined for 0.5 mm. (Brazil; summer.)

Masdevallia tovarensis [Plate 94], serenely beautiful, is 10 to 13 cm tall and holds its pure white flowers on graceful stems that arch outward in all directions. The flowers come in twos, threes, fours, or fives, shoulder to shoulder in a circular arrangement. The sepaline cup is small,

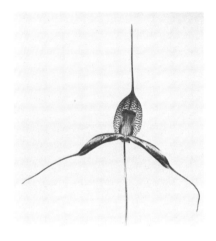

93. Masdevallia heteroptera, an odd one, has almost no sepaline cup and an unusually large lip up-turned against the column.

94. One of the loveliest of all is Masdevallia tovarensis, 10 to 15 cm tall, with flowers almost 6 cm long, including the tails. They are pure white, even the column.

and the dorsal sepal extends from it with a small triangular base and an erect 3 cm tail. The lateral sepals form a broad platform 2 cm long, squared off at the end, and their 1 cm tails often meet or cross. It flowers repeatedly from the same stems in succeeding seasons as well as from new ones. (Venezuela; usually fall to winter.)

Masdevallia wageneriana is a squat plant with thick, stiff, rounded leaves. The greenish-yellow or cream-colored flowers have an intriguing lip. It is a narrow, jiggling, red-speckled tongue, tipped with a most provoking red "blob" that must act as a lure for the insect pollinator. The flower, including the tails, is much longer than the leaves, with a broad, shallow sepaline cup. The broad base of the dorsal sepal forms a hood, the equally broad laterals spread flat, and all have tails 4 cm long. (Venezuela; fall to winter.)

Maxillaria

In some species of *Maxillaria* the derivation of the name is obvious, for they show a definite "jaw" or "maxilla" formed by the lip attached to the base of the column foot, hinged to it and mobile. In other species the jaw is not as apparent. The genus has some 300 or more species and spreads from Florida through Mexico and Central and South America as far as Argentina. Many are large, some awkwardly rambling, and some have flowers that are anything but graceful. But other large ones are beautiful, and some small ones completely charming.

Maxillaria arbuscula [Plate 95; also see Plate 9] is a decorative plant with slender branching stems clothed with short, straight leaves 2 cm long in ladderlike formation. One form makes small pseudobulbs at intervals along the stem. As years go by, some stems can become quite long, but there are always young ones coming along and branches on the older ones, so that the size of the plant can be controlled. The flowers are globose, 1 cm across, with rounded white sepals and petals sometimes lightly sprinkled with red dots, and a deep red lip. (Peru and Ecuador; almost continually in bloom.)

Maxillaria cobanensis has the distinction of being the smallest member of its genus in Mexico and Guatemala. The plant ranges from 4 to 10 cm tall, including the slender pseudobulb and its single leaf. The flowers, 1.5 cm across, come in succession on short pedicels among the pseudobulbs. They are a dull pinkish-tan veined with red-brown. The sepals are slender and spreading, the petals oval and held forward, the lip scoop-shaped and rather prominent. (Mexico to Costa Rica; summer.)

Maxillaria heterophylla has many varieties, among them the miniature variety *pygmaea*. Its neat, ridged pseudobulbs are 0.7 to 1.4 cm high, topped with a pair of pointed, divergent, slender oval leaves 1 to 3 cm long, and clustered along a rambling rhizome. The short-stemmed flower, 1.2 cm across, is a yellow globe from which a shiny, dark purple,

95. Maxillaria arbuscula *is a decorative plant with pink and white flowers.*

wet-looking lip protrudes. This flower type is seen in many of the small Brazilian species. (Brazil; midwinter.) Similar species are *M. spannagelii* and *M. pumila*.

Maxillaria horichii (syn. *Sepalosaccus horichii*) has rather graceful rambling stems from which pseudobulbs with single, sword-shaped leaves arise at intervals. From the base of the new growth, clusters of bright red to red-orange flowers appear. The 1 cm blossoms are tubular, with a prominent chin, and pointed parts that turn outward to give the front of the flower a star shape. (Costa Rica; winter.)

Maxillaria juergensis [Plate 96] is a perfect pincushion of needlelike leaves on tiny pseudobulbs. It grows rounder and fatter through the years. The ridged pseudobulbs are 1 cm tall, the leaves 3 to 4 cm long. The rhizome forms short, erect branches on which new growths come slightly higher each season, a process that gives the plant its widening, moundlike shape. A plant with hundreds of pseudobulbs may have a diameter of only 15 cm and height of only 7 to 8 cm. When in bloom, it is covered with blackish-red, globose blossoms just at leaf tip. They are 1.2 cm across, with bluntly oval sepals and petals and a protruding rounded, tonguelike lip with a shiny, juicy-looking surface. (Brazil; fall to winter.) Related species are *M. echinophyta*, *M. minuta*, *M. neowiedii*, *M. vernicosa*, and *M. vitelliniflora*.

96. *One of a group of Brazilian species,* Maxillaria juergensis *has nearly black flowers with wet-looking lips.*

Maxillaria perparva is the new name for *Bifrenaria minuta*. The plant has oval pseudobulbs 1.5 to 2 cm tall and slender, stalked leaves 10 to 12 cm long with several parallel veins. The rather open flowers are 1.5 cm across, similar to those just described but with a longer mentum (chin). They have brownish-purple sepals and petals and a maroon lip with a white border. (Venezuela; anytime of year.)

Maxillaria reichenheimiana [Color Plate C-55] is striking enough to be grown for its foliage alone. The broad blue-green leaves, beautifully mottled with gray, are 6 to 12 cm long, one at the top of the 1.5 cm pseudobulb and the other growing from the side. Single, large, showy, spidery flowers come in succession on 5 to 6 cm stems. The sepals and petals are very slender and pointed, cream color merging into gold. The lip is yellow. The sepals are 5 to 6 cm long, the petals 4 cm and crossed at their tips. (Costa Rica, Honduras, Trinidad, and Venezuela; late spring to summer.)

Maxillaria rufescens is popular because of its vanilla fragrance, and because it flowers freely and almost continually. It is variable in plant size and flower color, and some individuals may be too large for a miniature collection. Typical blossoms are 3 to 4 cm across, yellow with red spots, but some are plain yellow, and one form is white with a yellow lip. The sepals and petals are spatula-shaped and wide-spreading, the petals directed upward at an angle. The lip is tonguelike with small side lobes, and in heavily marked forms resembles the dorsal side of a bee. (Trinidad and Honduras south to Peru and Venezuela; flowers any time, mostly spring and summer.)

Maxillaria sophronitis (syn. *Ornithidium sophronitis*) has tiny pseudobulbs 1.2 cm tall and 2 cm leaves, one from the tip and one from the side. The spreading, creeping rhizome soon covers a mount. From among the leaves peek brilliant scarlet flowers 1.5 cm long with broad, triangular sepals that spread wide, shorter petals that touch at their tips, and a yellow lip that presents its papillose surface to the front. Best grown on a mount with good light and constant moisture. (Venezuela; winter.)

Maxillaria uncata [Plate 97] is a small plant with graceful stems covered with fleshy leaves. It makes a pretty pot plant; its stems, curling in different directions, lengthen slowly so that it takes many years for them to reach a length of 10 cm. The flowers, which grow close to the leaves, are rather inconspicuous, somewhat translucent, creamy pink or yellow striped with red, 1.2 cm long and somewhat tubular, with a long mentum. (Guatemala south to Brazil; fall and winter.)

Maxillaria variabilis is another popular and variable species. Because of their narrow, curving leaves the plants seem shorter than the actual leaf length of 15 cm. The leaves arise from flattened, cylindrical pseudobulbs 3 to 4 cm tall. The plants flower profusely, giving little yellow or red blossoms on short stems. They are 1 to 1.5 cm wide, with spreading sepals, forward-held petals, and a tongue-shaped lip. (Mexico to Panama; flowers any time of year.)

Maxillaria vittariaefolia has gently arching, ribbonlike leaves 9 cm long on crowded, globular pseudobulbs 5 to 6 mm wide. The delicate milky white flowers, 1 cm across, with slender sepals and petals are borne on stems 5 to 6 cm tall. The bright lip, with yellow side lobes and a red front lobe, adds to the charm of the flowers. (Costa Rica; spring and fall.)

Maxillaria wercklei is a diminutive, branching species. Some tiny individuals have pseudobulbs only 4 mm long, while others, somewhat larger, can be as tall as 2 cm. The leaves are single from the top of the pseudobulb and a few from the side, 1 to 3 cm long. The lovely little flowers also vary in size from 1 to 2 cm in diameter and are produced on short peduncles. They are round, wide open, with broad sepals and petals that are tan with rich red stripes, and a rounded lip of solid rose. (Costa Rica, Panama, and Colombia; summer and fall.)

Mediocalcar

The genus *Mediocalcar* ranges from Papua New Guinea to Samoa. The beautiful, succulent plants ramble and branch, forming mats of tiny fleshy stems and terete leaves, punctuated by bright little balloon-shaped or jug-shaped blossoms. The latter are so much alike among the various species that it is difficult to tell them apart.

Mediocalcar species, unidentified and perhaps new [Plate 98], sends its stems creeping over the mount, attached by a few wiry roots. The little pseudobulbs are mere swellings from the rhizome, with the ends

97. Maxillaria uncata *has pale, undistinguished flowers but makes a lovely little pot plant. Here it is growing in a 5 cm ceramic pot.*

98. Mediocalcar *is a New Guinea genus that has tiny red or orange jug-shaped blossoms. This plant, possibly a new species, is creeping and has tiny fleshy leaves.*

tipped up to give rise to four leaves each. Flowers come on very short pedicels from the base of older pseudobulbs. They are shiny yellow and orange jugs, 7 mm long, with the pointed tips of the sepals and petals turned outward at the tip. Must be kept moderately cool and be watered daily. (New Guinea; fall and winter.)

Megalotus————————————————————

The name *Megalotus* means "big ear." The new genus was created by L. A. Garay to separate what was *Sarcanthus bifidus* from that genus.

    Megalotus bifidus is a monopodial orchid with a short stem and two or three narrow oval leaves 10 to 12 cm long. The straight, slim, pendulous flower spike is some 15 cm long, bearing 70 or 80 flowers which open in succession so that 20 or so are in bloom at one time. The flowers are 1.2 cm across, cream color, the sepals and petals oval, the dorsal one forming a hood. The lip, often tinged with purple, is split at the outer end, lending the name *bifidus* to the species. The "ears" are on the column, flat, fleshy lobes that stand beside the stigma. (common in the Philippines; fall and winter.)

Meiracyllium————————————————————

The two charming species of this genus are well known and are often collected by lovers of miniature orchids. They have a creeping rhizome along which arise oval or rounded, thick, rigid leaves on short bract-covered stems that can hardly pass for pseudobulbs. Clusters of four to six perky, bright rose-colored flowers come from the base of the leaves.

    Meiracyllium trinasutum [Color Plate C-56] has nearly round leaves, 2.5 to 3.5 cm long, tipped with a short point. The blossoms are 1.5 cm across, with broad pointed sepals and petals and a pouch-shaped or cup-shaped lip with a pointed tip. (Southern Mexico and Guatemala; early summer.)

    Meiracyllium wendlandi (old name *gemma*) [Color Plate C-57] may have leaves either oval or nearly round, moderately or extremely thick, depending on the individual. The flowers are about 1.5 cm across, with more slender parts than the preceding, and a narrower, shallower lip. (Mexico, Guatemala, and El Salvador; fall to winter, sometimes spring.)

Mexicoa————————————————————

A beautiful little species was recently determined by L. A. Garay not to belong to *Oncidium*, where it had long been included, nor to any other established genus. He created a new one for it, *Mexicoa*, after its native

99. *Among nature's mysteries are the leafless orchids. A plant of* Microcoelia guyoniana *is a mass of gray roots with tiny spikes of white blossoms.*

100. *The flowers of* Microcoelia guyoniana *in detail.*

country. The old specific name was retained.

Mexicoa ghiesbreghtiana [Color Plate C-58] is a trim, dainty plant, with slightly fluted conical pseudobulbs 4 cm tall and slender, paired leaves 10 cm long. The inflorescence, about 14 cm tall, holds three to five striking blossoms 3 to 4 cm long. The oval sepals and petals are pinkish-yellow, broadly striped with brick red, the former wide-spreading, the latter held forward at an upward angle. The large, pale to rich yellow lip is four-lobed, the flat lateral lobes extending sideways, the mid-lobe divided at its tip. There is a shiny, fleshy, upside-down Y-shaped crest. (South central Mexico; spring, sometimes fall.)

Microcoelia

A genus of leafless orchids, *Microcoelia* furnishes conversation pieces for lovers of the unusual. The little plants are masses of roots which, except for the few that hold them to a small twig, seem not to have to cling to anything. New roots and sprays of minute white flowers come from the stubby little, bract-covered stem a few millimeters tall. They should be gathered from the wild on their own twigs, which in cultivation may be tied to a larger stick for support. The plants should be hung in a bright, cool, airy place, given a mist each day, and included in the regular fertilizer program.

Microcoelia exilis has rather fine, branched roots and arching 6 to 12 cm stems of 80 or more minuscule flowers that open in succession. They are completely round, fairly wide open, with broad sepals, petals, and lip. The spur is a tiny balloon tucked under the lip. (Malawi, Tanzania, eastern South Africa, and Malagasy; fall.)

Microcoelia guyoniana [Plate 99] has long, rather thick, unbranched roots. The numerous pendulous flower spikes [Plate 100] bear many utterly charming flowers 3 mm across, white, with transparent green spurs 3 mm long, in which the level of nectar can be seen. The blossoms open all at once, whether there are 20 on the stem or 80. (Kenya, Tanzania, Zambia, Malawi, and West Africa; summer.)

Microcoelia koehleri is a sturdier plant than the foregoing, with thicker roots and larger, but fewer flowers. The blossoms are 5 to 6 mm across, white sometimes suffused with pale pink, and with a brown or orange-brown stripe on the petals and lip. The column is unusually large. The S-shaped spur is 5 mm long. (Kenya, Uganda, Tanzania, and Zambia; late summer and fall.)

Miltoniopsis

Species of the type of *Miltonia vexillaria* have now been removed from that genus and placed in *Miltoniopsis*, a genus created for them long ago

110

and ignored until recently. Of this group, only one comes close to our limits and might even be a bit over, but it is too lovely to leave out:

Miltoniopsis roezlii [Color Plate C-59], an exquisite species, has slender, compressed pseudobulbs 5 to 6 cm tall, almost hidden by the basal leaves and bearing a single leaf from the top. The flower stem, 12 to 15 cm tall, bears two to five large, flat, marvelously fragrant blossoms 7 to 8 cm long, pure white except for a flare of purple at the base of the petals and yellow on the lip crest. The sepals and petals are broadly oval, pointed at the tips, and overlapping at the base. The huge spreading, slightly undulating lip has two sharp ears that project upward at the base of the column and three short keels. (Panama and Colombia; late summer and fall.)

101. Mormolyca gracilipes
*has a flower large for the
tiny plant.*

Mormolyca

This genus contains two insect imitators whose lips resemble the female of certain species of bee. In his efforts to mate with the flower, a process called pseudocopulation, the male removes the pollinia and later places them on another flower. Species transferred to this genus from *Cyrto-glottis* may also be insect imitators but information on this is not available at present.

Mormolyca gracilipes [Plate 101], transferred from *Cyrto-glottis*, has small pseudobulbs and single leaves, totaling a height of 5 to 10 cm. The large flower [Plate 102], 5.5 cm long, yellow-brown with some purple tinge, is held on a wiry stem 12 to 13 cm tall and lasts for three weeks. The sepals are broad at the base and taper to pointed tips, while the much smaller, thinner petals stand upright against the inner surface of the dorsal sepal. The small lip is dark purple-brown, with down-turned edges and a fleshy little tail tucked under the tip. It is hinged to the column foot and is mobile. (Venezuela, Colombia, Ecuador, and Peru; fall.)

Mormolyca peruviana, 10 to 15 cm tall with small pseudobulbs and a slender leaf, has a lip that looks exactly like a bee [Plate 103]. In fact, the male bee is obviously fooled into thinking that his female counterpart is partaking of nectar from the flower. The blossom is yellow-green with a few red stripes at the base of the spatula-shaped sepals and petals. The furry lip, 1.5 cm long, has a yellow background marked with red-brown. Cool growing with constant moisture. (Peru; fall to winter.)

Mormolyca ringens goes a bit over 15 cm, with fat, round, compressed pseudobulbs and single, slender leaves. It is never out of flower. On stems 24 cm tall arise single blossoms 2 cm long, yellow-green striped with red. The blunt sepals and petals have a little keel under the tip that ends in a sharp point. The petals stand up in front of the dorsal sepal. The tiny bee-like lip is also striped but is not furry. It has two raised, shiny, dark red "lumps," one in the center and the other at the base, and

102. *Front view of the*
Mormolyca gracilipes
flower.

103. *Mormolyca peruviana is pollinated by a male bee that is lured into thinking the lip of the flower is its female counterpart.*

104. Mystacidium aliceae *has the diameter of a fifty-cent piece and tiny, waxy green, long-spurred flowers.*

its tail (tip of the lip) is tucked under. (Mexico to Costa Rica; flowers all year.)

Mormolyca schweinfurthiana (formerly *Cyrtoglottis peruviana*) is similar to *M. gracilipes*, with taller pseudobulbs and leaves about the same size. The single flowers are also similar, but they have a much smaller lip, and the tips of the sepals curve backward. (Peru; summer.)

Mystacidium

Some of the most delightful and also some of the tiniest of Africa's monopodials are in the genus *Mystacidium*. The short-stemmed plants have few leaves. Flowers are mostly white, but a few are greenish or yellowish. They do well mounted on small slabs or branches with constant moisture.

Mystacidium aliceae [Plate 104], even in bloom, often covers no more than the area of a 50-cent piece. The leaves are 1 to 2.5 cm long with almost parallel sides and an unevenly bi-lobed tip with rounded ends. Several tiny flower spikes come at the same time, each with two to five waxy greenish blossoms. The flower is 5 to 6 mm across, with a short mid-lobe to the lip. The spur is 7 to 8 mm long, wide mouthed and narrowing to a blunt tip. (Natal and eastern Cape Province; summer.)

Mystacidium braybonae has leaves 3 to 6 cm long, with the longer of the end lobes sharply pointed. Pendulous stems hold five to ten pure white flowers 1.7 to 2 cm across, with petals that stand almost straight up, and a longer lip than in *M. aliceae*. The wide-mouthed spur is 2 to 2.2 cm long. (Transvaal; spring.)

Mystacidium caffrum [Color Plate C-60] is a tiny plant with narrow leaves which on a mature plant can be 4 to 6 cm long. The plant illustrated was collected as a seedling and is flowering for the first time. The flower is distinctive for its broadly rounded parts and green column. The blossom is 1 cm across, the spur 2.5 cm long, wide at the mouth and inflated at the end. Several inflorescences may come at once, bearing from ten to 12, closely set flowers. (Cape Province, Natal, and Transvaal; winter or spring.)

Mystacidium capense [see Plate 5] is a highly decorative plant, with leaves 6 to 8 cm long and sprays of six to ten, good-sized, pure white flowers 1.8 to 2.3 cm across, with spurs 4 to 5 cm long. The flower parts are slender, the lip long and narrow; the spur, whose mouth is fairly narrow, is straight and gradually tapers to a point. (Cape Province, Natal, and Swaziland; early summer or fall.)

Mystacidium flanaganii is another tiny one, with three to five leaves 1.5 to 3 cm long. Sprays 5 to 6 cm long carry eight to ten, yellowish-white flowers. The blossoms are 0.8 to 1 cm across, with a short, pointed lip, and a 2 to 2.5 cm, wide-mouthed, tapering and slightly curved spur. It is cool growing. (Cape Province, Natal, Swaziland, and Transvaal; winter.)

Mystacidium gracile is leafless, but it can make an occasional tiny leaf that soon falls. The roots are bluish-green, thin and unbranched. Pendulous spikes carry four to seven flowers 1 cm across, white or greenish-white, with a long, pointed lip, and a tapering spur 2.5 cm long. (Cape Province and Natal; spring.)

Mystacidium pusillum covers about the area of a 25-cent piece. Its two or three leaves are 1.7 to 2.7 cm long, and the flower sprays, only 1.5 to 1.7 cm, bear three to five greenish-white flowers 6 to 7 mm across which become yellow with age. They have a pointed lip with undulating sides and a spur with a proportionately large mouth that curves as it tapers to a fine point. (Cape Province; winter.)

Mystacidium tanganyikense has short leaves and green or yellowish flowers, slightly fragrant. The blossoms are 1 to 1.2 cm across, with a three-lobed lip and a thin spur 1.7 to 2.1 cm long. (Tanzania, Zambia, and Malawi; spring and summer.)

Mystacidium venosum [Plate 105] is next to *M. capense* in size, with leaves 3 to 5 cm long. The inflorescence holds four to seven or more white flowers 1.5 to 2 cm across. The flower parts are narrow and pointed, the lip similar in shape to the petals. The spur is narrow mouthed, about 4 cm long. (Cape Province, Natal, Swaziland, and Transvaal; fall.)

Nageliella

Two charming little species make up this genus, still known by some as *Hartwegia*. They have gray-green, fleshy, narrow leaves mottled with purple, and small, rich violet flowers. Plants are usually small, but rare individuals can attain greater height.

Nageliella angustifolia, the less common of the two, is usually around 8 to 10 cm tall. The stem is only slightly thickened where the leaf arises. The leaves are slender, tapering evenly to the pointed tip, and slightly rough, mottled with gray or purple. The slender flower stems are 9 cm tall arising from the juncture of leaf and stem and bear clusters of blossoms that open in succession [Color Plate C-61]. Additional flowers come from the same growth in succeeding years. The satiny, bright rose-purple blossoms are 1.3 cm across, wide open with broadly oval sepals and petals. The lip is remarkable. Its base clasps the lower part of the column and forms a shallow horizontal sac. The outer part then bends sharply downward, with its fluted edges turned in to form a shallow bowl. (Guatemala; summer to fall.)

Nageliella purpurea has broader, somewhat thinner leaves than the foregoing. Average plants are 11 to 12 cm tall, with flower stems twice that height. The wide-open, red-purple flowers are 1.5 cm across, with a broad dorsal sepal, rounded laterals, and much narrower petals. The lip forms a vertical sac at the base of the column, its small outer lobe spreading flat from a curved, three-keeled crest. (Mexico, Guatemala, Honduras; summer.)

105. *Not much larger vegetatively than* Mystacidium aliceae *is* Mystacidium venosum, *but its blossoms are huge for the plant, being 1.5 to 2 cm across, with spurs 4 cm long. Shown here are two plants.*

Nanodes

This old generic name has been revived for the species for which it was created, *Nanodes discolor*, which was for many years incorporated into *Epidendrum* as *E. schlechterianum*. The much beloved species spreads through many countries. (Some other species once called *Nanodes* are now in the genus *Neolehmannia*.)

Nanodes discolor has short branching stems, completely clothed with the clasping bases of short, fleshy, rigid leaves whose upper section is triangular, turned sharply outward, and deeply channeled. The stems reach some 6.5 cm in length and form dense mats. The flowers just barely protrude from the last leaf axil, occurring in pairs or triplets. There are at least two flower forms. One is longer than wide, 2 cm high, with the dorsal sepal standing straight up and the petals held down beside the column. Its color is green flushed with pink and brown, and the lip is brown with maroon on each side. Another has rounder flowers 1.5 cm across, with wider parts, and the petals are held at a less pronounced angle. The color is pinkish-green and the lip pale green. In both, the sepals and petals are finely toothed on the edges. (Mexico through Central America, Trinidad, and South America to Brazil, Venezuela, and Peru; spring and summer.)

Neodryas

The small genus *Neodryas* is related to *Cochlioda*. The species have eye-catching, little brightly colored flowers whose chief distinction is a peculiar double-auricled column.

Neodryas rhodoneura has oval compressed pseudobulbs 1.5 to 4 cm tall, bearing a single, narrow leaf from the top and several from the sides. The pseudobulbs and leaf bases are attractively tinged with reddish-brown. Leaves are 8 to 14 cm long. Branched inflorescences bear 30 or more 7 mm flowers that open over a long period. The sepals and petals appear to be solid rose color, although they are really heavily veined with rose on a pink background. The dorsal sepal is oval and hooded, the laterals united except for the tips, and the petals are round and concave. Lip and column are bright orange and fill the center of the globose blossom. The fat column has a pair of down-hanging auricles that meet in front under the anther and has ear flaps on each side. The fleshy lip turns down sharply in front, while its four-keeled crest bends in the middle to nestle under the column tip. (Peru and Bolivia; fall and winter.)

Neodryas weberbauerana is similar, with bell-shaped, nodding flowers, orange to dark red. The lip has a simple spatulate callus. (Peru.)

*Neofinetia*_____

A single lovely monopodial species comprises the genus *Neofinetia*.

    Neofinetia falcata [see Plate 11], the Japanese "wind orchid," is a miniature version of a strap-leaf vanda, with a short stem and several pairs of nearly flat, keeled leaves 5 to 9 cm long. The plant branches freely from lower leaf axils. Flowering stems, about 7 cm long and several at a time, bear half a dozen pure white flowers, deliciously fragrant in the evening. They are about 3 cm long, not including the gracefully curved 6 cm spur. The dorsal sepal and petals flare upward, the lateral sepals curve down and outward, and the short, three-lobed lip turns down from beneath the column. Grow on the cool side of intermediate temperatures. (Japan, Korea, and Ryukyu Islands; summer to fall.)

*Neolehmannia*_____

This genus is closely related to *Nanodes*. Among the species relocated here are two that were familiar as epidendrums and two others less well known.

    Neolehmannia medusae (was *Nanodes medusae*), named for Medusa of the snaky locks, is a famous and spectacular plant. At its largest size it would have to be considered borderline, but its stems can be within the 12 to 15 cm limit. The stems are fleshy, soft and limber, clothed with pale green, fleshy leaves 5 to 8 cm long, triangular, deeply veined, and all facing upward. They clasp the stem with their bases. The huge flowers, 6 to 7 cm across, come in triplets at the end of the stems, two on top and one underneath. The slender sepals and petals are greenish, densely stippled with brown. The ruby-red lip is round, 4 to 5 cm wide, edged with long, thick fringe. Its center is almost black and covered with shiny papillae that give it a wet look. It is cool growing and does best in a hanging basket or pot or on a mount, with medium light and constant moisture. (Ecuador; summer.)

    Neolehmannia peperomia is vegetatively similar to *N. porpax* although a bit smaller. The flowers are much like it in shape and size, but they are all-over brownish-red tinged very slightly with green. The lip is not quite as broad. (Brazil; spring.)

    Neolehmannia porpax [Plate 106], formerly known as *Epidendrum porpax*, is a famous little species that smothers a slab with branching, 4 to 6 cm stems covered with shiny green, 1.5 cm leaves. Single flowers come at the tip of each stem, and a plant in bloom appears to be covered with a host of shiny beetles. The flowers are 2 cm long, with the green dorsal sepal and petals standing above the lip, the laterals united at their base and hidden behind it. The shiny, smooth, red-brown lip is rounded and has a greenish border. (Mexico to Panama and south to Venezuela and Peru; summer to fall.)

    Neolehmannia viridibrunnea is similar to *N. porpax* vegetatively.

106. Neolehmannia porpax, with its beetle-like flowers, was long known as Epidendrum porpax.

115

The flowers are about the same size but differ in color and shape. The sepals and petals, all of which spread starlike above the lip, are greenish-cream, and the lip, which is longer than wide, is pinkish-green. (Venezuela and Colombia; winter.)

Nidema

Nidema is another one-species genus removed from *Epidendrum*.

Nidema boothii has slightly curved, flattened oval pseudobulbs that grow crowded together, and a single slender leaf that brings its height to 15 to 17 cm. The fragrant flowers, borne four or five to a 10 cm stem, are cream color with a streak of orange on the lip. They are about 4 cm across, with slender sepals 2 cm long, shorter petals, and a tongue-shaped lip hinged to the short column foot. The column is raised above the lip for its entire length. (Mexico to Cuba and Dutch Guiana; fall to spring.)

Notylia

Two types of plants were formerly represented in *Notylia*. Those with pseudobulbs are retained in *Notylia*, and those having a fan of equitant leaves surrounding a barely perceptible pseudobulb are now called *Macroclinium*. A characteristic of both is the position of the pollinia on the back side of the column tip, covered by a long, slim anther cap under which lies the long stipe (stalk) connecting them to the viscid disc protruding from just under the tip of the cap. All have a spade-shaped lip, with a narrow "claw" representing the handle of the spade. The mosquito-like flowers are from a few millimeters to 1 cm long. There are many species in each group.

Notylia barkeri, a widespread species, is one of the better known and also one of the larger kinds. It has pseudobulbs 1 to 3.5 cm tall, oval and compressed, with a single leaf, usually around 10 to 15 cm long, sometimes longer. The pendent flower spike can be 30 cm long with many 7 mm flowers that are white, sometimes spotted with yellow. (Mexico to Panama; summer.)

Macroclinium bicolor is a glorious little species about 10 cm tall, with a fan of flat leaves, the central one of which arises from a minuscule psuedobulb hidden in the depths of the fan. Usually more than one spray of flowers develops, each with a dense tuft of feathery blossoms whose sepals are white or green and petals and lip are lavender with purple spots. (Mexico, Guatemala, Costa Rica, and El Salvador; summer.)

Notylia longispicata is characterized by a tremendously long flower spike with over 100 blossoms. It is the pseudobulb type, with a leaf from the top and one from the side. (Brazil; spring and summer.)

Macroclinium mirabilis, called *Notylia norae* for a while, is probably the smallest of the genus, the fan of few leaves being only 1.2 cm wide and the flower spike with its pair of blossoms 2 cm tall. The flower is 6 mm long, lilac color, sometimes with a dark spot or two. (Venezuela and Peru; anytime of year.)

Notylia nana may be the smallest of the pseudobulb type, averaging only 5 cm in height. It has one oval leaf from the top and another from the base of the entirely hidden pseudobulb. The pendent flower spray, 3.5 to 10 cm long, holds 25 or more greenish-white flowers. (Trinidad and Venezuela; spring.)

Notylia tridachne has an oval, ridged pseudobulb 3 cm tall, and three broad leaves, one from the top and two from the sides. The 20 cm spike holds many greenish-yellow 1 cm flowers spotted with orange. (Mexico, Guatemala, and El Salvador; spring.)

Macroclinium wullschlaegeliana is a tiny plant with a fan of few leaves, 3 cm tall. An arching spray bears four or five 1 cm flowers. The sepals are translucent yellow-green and curved backward. The petals are white with large purple blotches. The filamentous column sticks straight out of the flower, holding its big, fat orange anther far in front of the lip. (Venezuela, Guyana, Surinam, Brazil, Colombia, and Peru; winter and summer.)

Notylia xiphophorus [Color Plate C-62] is an exquisite species with a fan of flat, dark red, rough leaves 3 cm tall, mottled with gray-green. They give many wiry inflorescences 3 to 5 cm long, at whose tips the 1 cm flowers come in "dandelion puffs." They are translucent rosy-violet with a darker lip. New branches come from the old flower stems in succeeding years, adding to the number of flowers each season. (Ecuador and Peru; spring and summer.)

Oakes-Amesia (syn. *Sphyrastylis*)

This genus was named for the late Oakes Ames, Harvard's distinguished taxonomist and orchidologist. It consists apparently of one species, a relative of *Ornithocephalus*, found so far only in Panama, but it may possibly dwell elsewhere:

Oakes-Amesia cryptanthus has a fan of flat, equitant leaves 5 cm high. The 7 cm flowering stem holds many diminutive blossoms 6 mm long, of complicated structure. The sepals are pointed oval, the petals triangular, all white, with their edges finely toothed. The lip has erect side lobes and a three-part mid-lobe that resembles a small cap with ear flaps. Down the center of the lip runs a narrow tube that opens at the apex of the lip under a band of short hairs. The column is short, with the anther bent over like a nodding head. The rostellum projects way beyond the anther and is three-lobed. (Panama.)

107. The beauty of an Oberonia *is the combination of a dainty plant and the fairy-like sprays of minuscule blossoms. This one is* Oberonia japonica, *whose plants are 1.3 cm tall and flowers 0.5 to 1 mm long.*

Oberonia

At first glance, plants of *Oberonia* could be mistaken for species of either *Lockhartia* or *Ornithocephalus*, for they have equitant leaves either in a fan or on a tall stem. The flowers and flowering habits are entirely different, however. In *Oberonia* the flower stem comes from the apex of the growth and is a "rat tail" of minuscule blossoms packed solidly around the stalk. The genus spreads through India, Malaysia, Australia, New Guinea, Fiji Islands, and East Africa. It requires a strong hand lens, not just the ordinary magnifying glass, to see the flower details. The plants are attractive in themselves, and when there are several fans in flower, the delicate, trailing inflorescences add to their beauty. Buds open first in the center of the spike, then at the tip, and finally at the base. They can be grown on slabs or in pots, and require constant moisture.

Oberonia iridifolia is one of the larger species, with tapering leaves in a low fan. Side leaves are short, the central ones up to 15 cm in height. The flower spike is 15 to 20 cm long, covered with 2 mm, golden blossoms. The sepals and petals are triangular, the latter toothed on the edges, and the lip has squarish, fringed side lobes and two small, fringed lobes on the center section. (India through Malaysia and the Pacific Islands; fall to winter.)

Oberonia japonica [Plate 107] is surely from Oberon's own garden, an exquisite little plant with a slightly elongated fan 1.3 cm tall bearing five leaves 0.5 to 1 cm long. The filamentous flower spike is 3 cm tall, with some 50 blossoms 1 to 2 mm long. They have translucent green sepals and petals and red-gold side lobes on the fringed, four-lobed lip. (Japan, Korea, and Okinawa; fall.)

Oberonia palmicola is a magnificent spectacle when covered with flower spikes. It forms a mass of fans 1 to 6 cm tall whose green leaves are often suffused with pink. The abundant, curving, pendent flower spikes are 5 to 15 cm long and bear hundreds of translucent coppery-red blossoms. They are simple, not fringed, 1.5 mm in diameter. (Australia; spring and fall.)

Octomeria

The genus *Octomeria* is one of the many relatives of *Pleurothallis*. The species are neat plants with straight stems and single, fleshy leaves. Some are quite tall, and some smaller ones can become so with optimal conditions. The true miniatures are unpretentious but pretty. Flowers come singly or in clusters from the juncture of stem and leaf, which is often midway between the base and top of the plant. They have eight pollinia. The genus ranges from Honduras through Trinidad and Tobago, to Venezuela and Brazil.

Octomeria complanata has flattened stems 8.5 cm tall, 2 cm wide, and only 2 mm thick, with a leaf of the same width and thickness, 4 cm long. The flowers come one at a time from the base of the leaf and are 0.9 to 1.7 cm long. They are brownish-red, sometimes markedly veined with purple. The sepals and petals are narrowly oval, the lateral sepals united for part of their length. The lip is three-lobed, with pointed, up-curving side lobes and a pair of keels on the crest. Warm to warm-intermediate. (Venezuela, Brazil, and Peru; winter or summer.)

Octomeria gracilis is a dainty plant 8 cm tall, with needlelike leaves on thin stems. The pale yellow flowers, 6 to 7 mm across, come in clusters and are slightly nodding, with slender sepals and petals, and a rectangular lip with armlike, in-turned side lobes. (Brazil; all year.)

Octomeria integrilabia has slender stems 3 cm tall, with wider leaves 3.5 cm long. Flowers come in succession. They are large for the plant, 1.2 cm across, with oval, straw-colored sepals and petals, and a rounded, quite plain, darker yellow lip without side lobes. (Venezuela and British Guiana; any time of year.)

Octomeria minor is similar to the foregoing in shape and size. The 1 cm, pale yellow flowers, which come in succession, have more pointed sepals and petals and a very small lip that is yellow tipped with maroon and whose basal edges turn up. (Venezuela and British Guiana; winter to spring.)

Octomeria nana [see Plate 4] can have stem-and-leaf 6 to 14 cm tall on the same plant. The stems are 2 mm wide, the rigid leaves 5 mm thick, channeled on the upper surface. Sparkling, translucent flowers come one to three at a time. They have the usual oval sepals and petals, perhaps a bit broader than in some species, brownish-yellow, with a rectangular lip that is pale yellow. The sides of the lip bend upward in the middle where diagonal ridges slant inward. (Venezuela; winter to fall.)

Octomeria steyermarkii is one of several new species found in Venezuela. This one is unusual for its spidery flowers. The plants range from tall with short flowers, to short with tall ones—from those 12 cm tall with flowers of 2.2 cm, all the way to those 5 cm tall with flowers of 8 cm,—in other words, the shorter the plant, the longer the flowers. The small blossoms have sepals and petals that taper to short tails, while in the large ones the tails are long and filamentous. Color ranges from cream tinged with pink, to pink, to brownish-purple. (Venezuela; any time of year.)

Odontoglossum ————————————————————————

The genus *Odontoglossum* has been divided into several new genera, only two of which are applicable to miniatures. These are given here along with the old genus name to assist in making the transition.

Odontoglossum (Lemboglossum) cervantesii [Color Plate C-63] is one of the loveliest of the genus, indeed of the orchid family. Its slightly four-angled, conical pseudobulbs are 3 to 4 cm tall, and the single leaf is usually 10 to 13 cm long, occasionally more. The 15 to 20 cm arching flower spray holds four to six fragrant, satiny, white, sometimes pink, blossoms. The decorative flower, 6 to 7 cm across, has oval, slightly crinkled sepals and petals with concentric circles of brown bars on the front and back of their lower third. The lip is heart-shaped from a narrow basal claw, and has a slightly scalloped edge and a few brown bars at its base. It may be grown either cool or intermediate, with a bit less water when resting. (Mexico and Guatemala; fall or spring.)

Odontoglossum (Lemboglossum) ehrenbergii is similar to the better known *O. rossii*, and their equally colorful flowers can easily be confused. *O. ehrenbergii* is smaller, the pseudobulbs up to 3 cm high, and the single leaf 5 to 13 cm tall. The flowers [Plate 108] come at the same time as the new growth. The blossoms are 3 to 4 cm across, three or so to the spray. The sepals are strongly barred with brown on a white background. The petals and lip are white when the flower opens but soon become tinged with red. The sepals are slim and pointed, the petals broader, and the lip heart-shaped with a ruffled edge. The crest is yellow, with raised sides under the column, and two small points descending onto the claw of the lip. Cool growing. (Mexico; summer.)

Odontoglossum (Lemboglossum) galleottianum is a charming little cousin of *O. cervantesii*. The pseudobulbs are 4 to 6 cm tall, slightly four-angled, covered with purple spots and clothed with large bracts that soon become papery. The single, curving, 10 to 18 cm leaf is slender and pointed. An arching, 7 to 10 cm inflorescence holds four or five sparkling snow white, slightly translucent, 6 to 7 cm flowers marked with a few pinkish-brown spots at the base of the pointed sepals and petals. The dorsal sepal backs the tall, erect column which has a pair of long, finger-like "wings" curving down beside the stigma. The lateral sepals spread horizontally, while the broader petals swing upward, their tips curved back. The long arrowhead-shaped lip has a scalloped edge and is without side lobes. The prominent callus is boat-shaped, yellow veined with brown on its upturned basal edges, and spotted lightly on its out-thrust, bilobed outer end. From cool cloud forests up to 3000 m. (Mexico, states of Oaxaca and Guerrero; summer.)

Odontoglossum (Ticoglossum) krameri [Color Plate C-64] is serenely beautiful. Its round, 4 cm pseudobulbs are compressed to sharp edges and bear single leaves 10 to 15 cm long. The 10 to 20 cm flower spray holds three to five round, soft pink to rose blossoms 3 cm across. The sepals and petals are broadly oval, the lip skirtlike from a narrow claw. The claw is fleshy, spotted with brown, and has two raised keels that diverge onto the broad outer lobe and are delineated from it by brown lines. (Costa Rica; late summer.) There is a lovely white form that retains the yellow crest and flowers a bit earlier. It is from Costa Rica and possibly Panama.

108. Odontoglossum (Lemboglossum) ehrenbergii *has blossoms that open white but soon become tinged with red. The bars on the sepals are brown.*

Odontoglossum (Ticoglossum) oerstedii [Plate 109] has tiny pseudobulbs 2 cm tall, rather conical, and pinched and curved at the top. The single, stalked leaf is 7 to 13 cm tall. The flowers [Plate 110] come singly on erect stems almost as long as the leaves. They are little shallow saucers, 3.5 cm across, with overlapping sepals and petals, and a heart-shaped lip that has small side lobes. The saddle-shaped, yellow crest is spotted with orange. Cool growing. (Costa Rica and Panama; spring.)

Odontoglossum (Lemboglossum) rossii, mentioned before with *O. ehrenbergii*, differs from it in its larger size, in the fact that the flowers come from the mature growth, and in floral details. It is supposedly the better known of the two, but they have possibly long been confused. The longer flower spray bears blossoms almost twice as large, 5 to 7.5 cm, with spotted rather than barred sepals. The petals also have spots toward their base. The petals and lip are white, but there is a pink form. Cool growing. (Mexico; winter.)

Odontoglossum (Lemboglossum) stellatum is a coppery-brown star. The plant has oval, compressed pseudobulbs 3 cm tall and single leaves 5 to 8 cm long. The flower stem comes from the base of the mature pseudobulb and is about the same length as the leaves. The blossom is single, 4 cm long, with very slender sepals and petals. The roundish lip has deeply lacerated edges and a white border and is veined and tinged with pinkish-lavender in the center. The basal section turns up tightly beside the column, and it and the column are covered with fine, short hairs. (Mexico, Guatemala, and Venezuela; fall, winter, or spring.)

109. Odontoglossum (Ticoglossum) oerstedii.

110. The single white blossoms of Odontoglossum (Ticoglossum) oerstedii *are almost completely round, 3.5 cm across.*

Oeonia

The half dozen monopodial species of *Oeonia* have little climbing stems clothed with small alternate leaves. They root at every leaf axil. The flower stems are erect, tall for the plants, and on their outer half bear numerous white flowers shaped like some of the variegata oncidiums.

Oeonia elliotii has leaves 2.5 to 4 cm long and an inflorescence that reaches 23 cm. The three to five flowers are about 1.8 cm long, with narrow sepals and petals and a three-lobed lip whose mid-lobe is two-thirds the length of the flower. Its side lobes are deeply divided from the mid-lobe, which is itself notched at the end. The 4 mm spur has a wide mouth. (Malagasy; summer.)

Oeonia oncidiiflora has branching stems that soon cover a mount. The flower stems bear three to seven greenish-yellow blossoms 2.5 cm across, whose tiny sepals and petals are held entirely above the lip. The side lobes of the lip are small, the large mid-lobe divided into two diverging round lobes at the end. (Malagasy; fall.)

121

111. Oeoniella polystachys
*is a most unusual little
monopodial. The 3.5 cm
blossoms are deliciously
fragrant. The trumpet-
shaped lip is formed entirely
by the side lobes, the mid-lobe
being a tiny spike.*

112. Oncidium abortivum
*suffered a mutation eons
ago that caused it to abort
all flowers except those
at the tips of the branchlets
on the flower spray. The
little bursts of bracts
represent flowers that failed
to form.*

Oeonia rosea has smaller flowers on shorter stems. They are 1.5 cm in diameter, with green sepals and petals and a rose-colored lip. (Malagasy; winter.)

Oeonia volucris has the tallest inflorescence of the group, reaching 35 cm. The ten or more white blossoms, 2.5 cm wide, have longer sepals and petals in proportion to the lip than other species, and the lip is narrower and less divided at the tip. (Mascarene Islands; spring and summer.)

Oeoniella

There are perhaps three species in this genus, one said to be doubtful, one little known, and the third a well-known beauty:

Oeoniella polystachys is a dainty plant of branching stems clothed with narrow, spatula-shaped leaves 5 to 7 cm long. The arching flower spike [Plate 111], 15 to 18 cm long, bears a double row of exquisite and unusual, fragrant, white flowers, 3.5 cm across, with narrow, wide-spreading sepals, smaller petals, and a trumpet-shaped lip. The side lobes form the bell of the trumpet, then become narrow at their base to enfold the column, and end in a 3 mm, green spur. The mid-lobe of the lip is merely a short little point. (Malagasy and the Comoro and Seychelle Islands; fall to spring.)

Oncidium

The genus *Oncidium* is a fantastic assortment of over 750 species that spread from Florida and Mexico through Central America and the West Indies deep into South America to Uruguay and Argentina. As mentioned above, it is related to *Odontoglossum*, *Brassia*, and *Miltonia*, and many intergeneric hybrids have been made between them. The lip swings out at a right angle to the column and usually has many tubercles or little spikes on the crest, whose size and arrangement are often the important means of distinguishing one from another.

Oncidium abortivum is an interesting member of a group with both perfect and aborted (defective) flowers. Borderline in size, it ranges from 12 to 20 cm tall, counting the oval pseudobulbs and single leaves. The 30 cm branched flower spray holds perfect flowers only at the tips of the branchlets [Plate 112]. Elsewhere, where there should be blossoms, there are merely bursts of tiny yellow bracts. The yellow flowers are 1.5 cm across, curiously shaped, with an S-shaped column, a lip with huge side lobes and a tiny triangular mid-lobe, and inconspicuous sepals and petals striped with brown. (Venezuela; spring.)

Oncidium barbatum has pseudobulbs 3 to 4.5 cm tall and leaves 6 to 10 cm long. Its ungainly 2 to 2.5 cm flowers are borne on a branched stem 30 cm long. If you disregard the dark green, brown-mottled sepals and petals, you are faced with what appears to be a yellow duckling trying to take flight on undeveloped wings. The column is its head; the large, paddle-shaped side lobes of the lip its wings, and the broad and finely fringed isthmus and tiny hatchet-shaped mid-lobe its body. (Brazil; spring.) Similar species are *O. suscephalum* and *O. reisei*.

Oncidium (Tolumnia) calochilum [Plate 113] is a unique little plant. It has no pseudobulb and only three or four rounded, toothpick-like leaves 5 cm long. The spectacular flowers [Plate 114] come on a short stem often one at a time, sometimes two or three and are huge for the plant, 3 to 4 cm long. They have sharply pointed, green sepals and petals and a bright yellow, arrow-shaped lip, surrounded by fringe. The crest holds five slender, sharp spikes directed forward, and the side lobes look like another pair of spikes. (Hispaniola and Cayman Islands; spring.)

Oncidium cheirophoroides (syns. *luteum* and *pittieri*) was named after *O. cheirophorum*, because its flowers are remarkably similar although the former look less birdlike. *O. cheirophoroides* has an almost indistinguishable pseudobulb, well hidden in the basal folds of the leaves; one arises from its top and several from the sides. The leaves are 9 to 13 cm long, broadly oval. The 24 cm flower spray holds many waxy yellow blossoms 1.5 cm long, shaped like a cross. The lip has horizontally spreading side lobes, a narrow fan-shaped mid-lobe, five protuberances on the crest, and a horn curved toward the base of the column. The column is winged and is hooded by the dorsal sepal. (Costa Rica; fall.)

Oncidium cheirophorum is a long-time favorite for its densely covered spray of yellow flowers that look like a flight of birds. It has rounded pseudobulbs compressed to sharp edges, 3 cm tall, and stippled with purple. The single leaves average 20 cm in height. The waxy blossoms are 1.5 cm across, and it is the lip that looks like a bird, the sepals and petals being reflexed and not seen in front view. The broad side lobes are the wings, the mid-lobe the tail, and the curved horn at the base of the lip the neck and head. The fleshy crest is divided into four lobes. (Nicaragua to Colombia; fall.)

Oncidium concolor comes just within the 15 cm limit, with pseudobulbs 1.5 cm tall and leaves less than 15 cm. The pendent inflorescence bears six to 12 lovely flowers 4.5 cm long. The greenish-yellow or pure yellow sepals and petals are narrow, the petals held upright beside the dorsal sepal, and the lateral sepals hidden behind the large lip. The bright yellow lip flares like a long skirt from a narrow base and is somewhat ruffled. The crest bears two parallel keels. (Brazil; summer.)

Oncidium cornigerum is another that just meets our limit, with slender ridged pseudobulbs and narrow leaf. The flowers [Color Plate C-65] are somewhat nodding on a branched, pendent stem. The crest of the lip bears horns, as the name indicates, and the long, narrow central portion has various protuberances marked with red that altogether give the appearance of a large ant. The dorsal sepal and petals are bright red-

113. *The plant of* Oncidium (Tolumnia) calochilum *has one to three flowers on a plant that consists of a few little toothpick-sized leaves.*

114. *The flower of* Oncidium (Tolumnia) calochilum *is decorative, with a bright yellow lip and green sepals and petals.*

brown barred and trimmed with yellow and, with the lip, give a four-part effect. The lateral sepals, hidden behind the lip, are united almost to their tips. The column has a pair of tiny ciliated arms just beneath the anther. (Brazil; late summer.)

Oncidium crista-galli is a petite beauty but not easy to grow. It has a small pseudobulb enveloped by several 7 cm leaves and a huge flower on a short stem. The blossom is 3.5 cm long, canary yellow, with lightly spotted sepals and petals and a few spots on the base of the lip. The lip has ruffled side lobes wider than the mid-lobe, and the latter is itself divided into two rounded side sections and is bi-lobed at the tip. The plant should be grown on a mount or in a small pot in bright light and should have constant moisture. (Panama; flowers variably.)

Oncidium dayanum is an example of a lovely group of Ecuadorian species that look very much alike. Space prevents describing them all; in fact, only detailed specifications, drawings, and photographs of the 22 members and several varieties can fully separate them. The plants of *O. dayanum* have conical, slightly fluted, compressed pseudobulbs 4 cm tall and paired, slender leaves 12 cm long. The arching flower spike holds five to seven exquisite blossoms 3 cm long, white, daintily spotted with violet [Color Plate C-66]. The sepals and petals are broadly oval, coming to a sudden point The lip has rounded side lobes separated by a gentle semicircular indentation from the wide-spreading, kidney-shaped outer lobe. (Ecuador; spring and summer.) This species is often mistaken for *O. phalaenopsis*. Two other species in this group are shown in [Plate 115], *O. spathulatum* and *O. tripterygium*. Others with which you may be familiar are *O. nubigenum*, *O. cucullatum*, and *O. olivaceum*.

Oncidium desertorum: See *O. guianense*.

Oncidium edwallii [Plate 116] is a modest little species, nicely proportioned, with single, thick, fleshy, rigid leaves 2 to 4 cm tall on rounded, compressed pseudobulbs 1 cm high. The flower spike is 10 cm tall and carries seven or eight yellow-tan blossoms 1.5 cm long. The sepals and petals are broadly oval, pointed, and wide-spreading. The lip is longer than the other parts, gold color, with a narrow isthmus and an indented fan-shaped mid-lobe. The crest bears four rather large, blunt projections, in whose center is a smaller one. The column has white oval wings. (Brazil; spring.)

Oncidium endocharis was overlooked for many years in Mexico but has now been collected by a number of people. Shiny, plump pseudobulbs 2.3 to 3.5 cm tall, compressed to a sharp edge and stippled with purple, bear paired leaves 8.5 cm long that are deciduous in winter. The 28 cm flower spike holds several distinctive 3 cm flowers. The slender sepals and petals are entirely brown except for yellow tips, and the large, blunt-tipped, pure yellow, oval lip has a heavy crest consisting of seven protuberances. Cool growing, dry rest in the winter. (Mexico; spring or summer.)

115. Two of a closely related and very lovely group of species are (left) Oncidium spathulatum *and (right)* O. tripterygium, *which are white decorated with rose and violet.*

116. A neat little plant in every way, Oncidium edwallii *has little yellow and tan blossoms.*

Oncidium globuliferum: See *O. scansor*.

Oncidium (Tolumnia) guianense belongs to a charming group called the "variegata oncidiums," named for one of the members, *O. variegatum*. Their leaves are equitant, in fan formation, and appear to be folded and grown together from the mid-vein, so that the upper edges are actually two sharp, sometimes toothed, ridges. Central leaves are taller than the side ones. There are some 30 species in this group, only a few of which can be described here. *O. guianense* has a fan of wide, bronze-green leaves 4 to 7 cm tall, and a spike 16 cm long holding a dozen or more perky, bright yellow flowers 2 to 2.5 cm across [Plate 117]. The petals are almost duplicates of the broad kidney-shaped lip, lacking only the side lobes and crest. The winged column is a decorative part of the flower. The insignificant sepals are held in back. (Haiti and Hispaniola in general; spring or fall.)

117. Oncidium (Tolumnia) guianense *has petals that almost repeat the lip.*

Oncidium harrisonianum is similar to *O. edwallii* in some ways, but the flowers are rounder and broader, 2 cm long. The pseudobulbs are rounded and compressed, 2.5 cm tall, and the single leaf is stiff, broad, deeply veined, and 7 to 11 cm long. The many-branched inflorescence is 30 to 40 cm long, and holds a large number of flowers. The sepals and petals are dull gold with blotches of red-purple running down the center. The lip is pale yellow marked with purple on the narrow isthmus. The crest bears five, fingerlike protuberances. (Brazil; spring and summer.)

Oncidium (Tolumnia) henekenii is one of the most delightful of insect imitators. Affectionately called the "bee" orchid, it is one of the variegata group, although it looks nothing like them florally, forming a fan of few, stiff, broad, sharply curved, reddish-green leaves. The inflorescence gradually increases in length as one 2 cm flower after another is formed, up to 15 or so through many months. (Don't cut it off until you are sure no more blossoms will come.) At one time thought to be pollinated by a spider, it has recently been observed being pollinated by a bee. As far as its appearance is concerned [Plate 118], it could look like either. The dorsal sepal and petals stand up behind the column; the laterals lie behind the lip. The furry lip is purple-black with a velvety pink crest and a narrow border of pink. Spiky protuberances stick out on either side of the lip, giving a semblance of legs. Must be grown on a bare stick in bright light and given only a light daily mist, as it does not tolerate much moisture. (Hispaniola; late winter through summer.)

118. An insect imitator, Oncidium (Tolumnia) henekenii *looks more like a spider than a bee, but is pollinated by a male bee fooled into thinking that this is the female of its species.*

Oncidium heteranthum is another that forms perfect flowers only at the tips of the branchlets of the inflorescence, giving groups of bracts—aborted flowers—elsewhere [Plate 119]. It is more beautiful than *O. abortivum*, with a long willowy flower stem that can reach 2 m. Its old Costa Rican name, *O. asparagoides*, is more descriptive of its habit, for the inflorescence does look something like an asparagus plant. Plants can be both over and under 15 cm. The blossoms are 2 cm long, bright yellow, with tiny sepals and petals held back to allow the lip to be the con-

119. Oncidium heteranthum *dramatically shows its aborted flowers, the clusters of bracts along the stem.*

120. Oncidium limminghei *is a tiny, creeping relative of the well known* O. papilio.

121. *Almost a caricature,* Oncidium macropetalum *illustrates the extreme variations exhibited by the orchid family.*

122. Oncidium meirax *produces a few small flowers on a zigzag stem. The triangular, bumped-up lip is its attractive feature.*

spicuous part of the flower. The crest has numerous protuberances, and the column is quaintly hooded by a pair of large, folded wings. (Costa Rica, Panama, and the northern half of South America; fall through winter.)

Oncidium hians makes a delightful appearance. It is a compact plant 10 cm tall that makes many leads close together. The pseudobulbs are round and flat, and the leaves are oval, stiff, and thick. Its greatest charm is its numerous zigzag, bouncy flower stems that hold about ten blossoms of the edwallii type spaced rather far apart along their 30 cm length. A plant in bloom has an airy, lacy aspect. The 1.5 cm blossoms have broad, oval, pointed, concave sepals and petals, brownish-green tinged slightly with red, all held up away from the lip. The white lip is fiddle-shaped with erect side lobes and a kidney-shaped mid-lobe that is finely toothed and ruffled on the edge. The crest bears four fat, out-turned, white fingers dotted with red. The broad column wings dip down almost to touch the side lobes of the lip. (Brazil; summer and fall.)

Oncidium hookeri, *O. raniferum*, and *O. loefgrenii* are so much alike that they may eventually be combined into a single species. The plants are small and dainty, one of the species only half the size of the others, with ridged pseudobulbs that vary from flat-conical to slim-conical; all have a pair of short leaves. Height ranges from 8 to 15 cm. The flower spike is 15 to 20 cm long, with short side branches, and bears up to 60 bright yellow, doll-like blossoms, 0.7 to 1 cm long [Color Plate C-67]. Sepals and petals are tiny, and the lip is the conspicuous part of the flower. In all three species, the lip has a long mid-lobe, stubby side lobes, and a large, waxy crest shaped like a sitting frog. (Brazil; fall and winter.)

·*Oncidium limminghei* [Plate 120] is a relative of the famous *O. papilio* and *O. krameranum* but is the wee one of the lot. The tiny pseudobulbs and mottled leaves, 2 and 3.5 cm long respectively, creep along a branch or trunk, bearing at intervals a single flower on a stem 15 cm long. The blossom is 3 to 3.5 cm across, with oval, dull brown sepals and brighter petals often faintly barred with yellow. The lip is 3 to 3.5 cm across, creamy yellow spotted with brownish-orange, and has large, horizontal side lobes and a triangular mid-lobe. The column has large, flaplike auricles which are bilobed and edged with whiskers. Must be grown on a mount. (Brazil and Venezuela; summer to fall.)

Oncidium loefgrenii: See *O. hookeri*.

Oncidium longipes: See *O. uniflorum*.

Oncidium macropetalum has huge petals that give it a humorous look [Plate 121]. The plant has conical, fluted pseudobulbs 2.5 to 3 cm tall and paired leaves that arch horizontally and are 10 to 11 cm long, occasionally longer. The astonishing flowers are 3.2 cm long, bright yellow with a few brown spots on the lip crest, and tall, stalked, bannerlike petals. The lip is small, with armlike side lobes and a kidney-shaped mid-lobe. (Bolivia and Brazil; winter.)

Oncidium meirax is a petite plant with bright green, oval pseudo-

126

bulbs 1.5 to 2 cm tall and leaves 3 to 5 cm long, one from the top and several from the sides. The zigzag, three-angled flower stem holds half a dozen long-lasting, little 1.5 cm flowers whose striking feature is their fat lip [Plate 122]. The slender sepals and petals are yellow with broad brown bands. The triangular yellow lip is humped up in the center and bears on the top a fleshy, three-parted crest of brighter yellow. A few pale brown patches cover its surface. The column is a decorative feature, as it stands above the lip like some small creature. (Greater Antilles, Colombia, Ecuador, Peru, and Venezuela; spring.)

Oncidium morenoi is one of the gems of the genus [Plate 123]. The pseudobulbless fleshy leaves are small versions of the large "mule ear" orchids. They are 7 to 10 cm tall, speckled or mottled with red. The stiff little branched flower spray stands erect, 5 to 9 cm tall [Plate 124] and is densely covered with minute but voluptuous blossoms 6 mm wide, sparkling white except for the two large fleshy, papillose yellow cushions on the wide-spreading "fleur-de-lis" lip [Color Plate C-68]. The oval sepals and petals complete the circular shape of the blossom. (Bolivia; fall or winter.)

Oncidium nanum is another with small "mule ear" leaves 12 cm long, dull green, lightly spotted with purple. The shiny, waxy, golden, saucer-shaped flowers are borne close together on a pendent spray and open over a long period [Plate 125]. They are 1.2 cm in diameter, with concave sepals and petals spotted with red. The modest, spreading lip is not spotted, but its lumpy, darker callus is slightly so. (British Guiana, Venezuela, Peru, and upper Amazon area; summer to fall.)

Oncidium onustum has handsome, conical pseudobulbs ribbed with light green and spotted between the ribs with purple. The single stiff, channeled leaves are 10 to 14 cm long. The branched flower spray [Plate 126] holds many lovely, flat flowers that are pure yellow except for sometimes a few lines on the saucer-shaped crest. They are 2 cm long, with tiny sepals, broad petals, and a spreading lip whose narrow side lobes lie along the margin of the mid-lobe. (Ecuador; summer and fall.)

Oncidium (Tolumnia) pulchellum is a lovely member of the variegata group [Color Plate C-69]. The plants have fans of ten or so leaves up to 12 cm tall and produce erect flower stems 30 to 35 cm long, bearing 20 or more 3 cm blossoms. The full, flat flowers are light pink with some brown markings on the toothed crest. The sepals are minuscule, the petals broad and spreading, and the lip is rounded, with the side lobes overlapping the skirtlike mid-lobe. (Jamaica; spring and summer.)

Oncidium pumilum has tiny pseudobulbs and very thick "mule ear" leaves 4 to 8 cm tall, dark green, sometimes sparsely stippled with purple. The branched inflorescence can reach 15 cm in height, although it is often shorter. The densely packed, 5 mm flowers are straw-colored and bear a resemblance to those of *O. morenoi*, with slender sepals and petals and a large three-lobed lip. The fleshy divided crest is the same color as the lip and has raised, bumpy ridges. The side lobes of the lip are concave

123. Oncidium morenoi *is a perfect gem, with fleshy "mule ear" leaves and a short spray of most unusual little blossoms.*

124. *The spray of* Oncidium morenoi *is crowded with the tiny round flowers, which have a big, three-lobed lip decorated with cushions of yellow bumps.*

125. Oncidium nanum *has saucer-shaped, waxy flowers of rich gold. The plant is a little "mule ear" type.*

126. Oncidium onustum *gives lovely flat flowers whose only deviation from pure yellow is the tiny red spotting of the unusual shield-shaped crest.*

and curl down beside the mid-lobe, which has a rectangular tip. A distinctive feature of the column is its armlike wings, which form a perfect anchor spreading to either side of the anther. (Brazil and Paraguay; summer to fall.)

Oncidium raniferum: See *O. hookeri.*

Oncidium reisei is similar to *O. barbatum* but smaller, daintier, and prettier. Its conical, flattened, four-keeled pseudobulbs are 3 cm tall, bearing a single leaf from the top and three from the sides. The inflorescence is a many-flowered branched spray. The blossom has oar-shaped sepals and petals, yellow heavily banded with light brown. The bright yellow lip has a broad fringed isthmus, rounded side lobes, and a kidney-shaped mid-lobe. (Brazil; fall.)

Oncidium scansor (known to many as *O. globuliferum*) is a remarkable climbing plant, difficult to grow and more difficult to flower. Little flat, rounded pseudobulbs 2 cm tall, with oval leaves 5 cm tall, are spaced far apart on a vining stem, each taking root. The question has arisen as to whether the stem is actually an inflorescence rather than a rhizome and the plantlets "keikis" formed at the same nodes as the flowers (or without the flowers, if the plant fails to bloom), much as plantlets form on flowering stems in other genera. As soon as the plantlets mature, they send out other vining stems, along which other little plantlets soon develop. When flowers reluctantly appear, they come singly on short stems beside each pseudobulb, and are 3 cm in diameter. The sepals and petals are small and brownish-yellow, and the wide, kidney-shaped lip is bright yellow. The side lobes are small and blunt, and the crest is a spotted triangular plate under or in front of which appear several pointed protuberances. The plant should be mounted on a good-sized log or "round" of cork bark and given plenty of moisture. The runners (stems) may have to be trained around the log, but they will vine on anything they find. (Costa Rica to Venezuela; summer.)

Oncidium (Tolumnia) triquetrum is a delightful member of the variegata group but different from the typical ones. Its leaves are more open at the top, appearing almost three-keeled. They are in fans of three or four, 8 to 12 cm tall. The red and white flowers are 1.2 cm across, several to a spray 10 to 18 cm long [Color Plate C-70]. The narrow sepals are dull red bordered with white and the broad, diamond-shaped petals white, streaked or mottled with red. The beautiful lip has fan-shaped side lobes. The heart-shaped mid-lobe has a patch of solid red in the middle with red veins running out toward the edge. The crest is a mere shiny yellow knob. (Jamaica; winter or summer.)

Oncidium uniflorum and the very similar *O. longipes* may be but one variable species [Color Plate C-71]. It is certainly difficult to see any differences between them. They have oval pseudobulbs 2 cm long and one or two leaves averaging 10 cm in length. Both belong to the barbatum group with their circular, spiky, fringed lip isthmus and oar-shaped petals and sepals. However, these species produce only one, two, or three flowers, 2.5 to 4 cm long, on short inflorescences. A plant soon covers a little log or other mount and is a bouquet of blossoms when in bloom. (Brazil; summer to fall.)

Oncidium (Tolumnia) variegata, for which the variegata group is named, is a variable and pretty species [see Plate 7]. The fan stands about 7 cm tall and has four to six rigid, curved leaves with saw-toothed edges. The 30 cm flower stem bears many delightfully colored blossoms 2.5 cm long. They range from white to pink to lavender, with touches of all three colors in each flower, and they have bars of brown on the small sepals and petals and dots of brown around the yellow, spiky crest. The sepals and petals are small, the lip full-skirted with rounded side lobes. (Cuba, Hispaniola, Puerto Rico, and Virgin Islands; summer and fall.)

Oncidium viperinum, a relative of the well-known and much larger *O. varicosum,* is a diminutive plant whose conical pseudobulbs are 1.5 to 2.5 cm tall, fluted and somewhat four-angled and lightly speckled with purple. The paired leaves are slender, 5 to 6 cm long. The arching flower stem reaches 30 cm in length and holds a number of blossoms 2.5 cm across. The sepals and petals are 8 mm long, oblong, red-brown barred with yellow, and the 1 cm long, sulphur yellow lip is squarish and heart-shaped. (Uruguay, Paraguay, Brazil, and Argentina; flowers at various times.)

Oncidium waluweva, a close relative of *O. cornigerum,* also appears to have a large ant on the lip. The plant has conical, slightly compressed, rough-surfaced pseudobulbs 2 to 3.5 cm tall bearing a single leaf 8 to 9 cm long. The pendent flower stem holds up to 15 nodding blossoms 1 cm long [Plate 127]. They are creamy white, with concave sepals, broader concave petals barred with deep cerise, and an elongated lip with a triangular apex [Plate 128]. On the midline of the lip, a series of cerise tubercles form the image of an insect, which is further carried out by two red streaks at the "head" end that resemble antennae. The column has long, narrow, fuzzy arms that arch down toward the lip. (Brazil; fall to winter.)

127. *A curious species that may be an insect imitator is* Oncidium waluweva, *for the humps and markings on the lip do simulate an insect. The spray of the nodding blossoms are white and red.*

128. *A flower of* Oncidium waluweva *seen from below.*

Ornithocephalus

This is the best known of the several related genera, yet many of the species are difficult to separate. The flowers are tiny and complicated, and differences in their parts are sometimes only slight. They are fascinating when viewed with a magnifying glass, and their fairylike sprays of blossoms are beautiful under any circumstances. H. F. Loomis wrote, in the April 1954 *American Orchid Society Bulletin:*

"Would you not be thrilled to pick up a curious little orchid plant and . . . discover that the tiny blooms, closely packed on their ascending spikes, looked not so much like flowers as a rookery of water birds, with wings outstretched, on the instant of taking flight together?"

129

129. *Tiniest of the genus,* Ornithocephalus bonplandi *has blossoms as large as those of other species.*

130. Ornithocephalus cochleariformis *has extra thick, sharply pointed leaves and fuzzy flowers.*

131. Ornithocephalus gladiatus *makes a lovely arrangement on a tree fern ball.*

Their name refers to the "bird-head" column, a little head (the anther) with a long beak (the rostellar process), at the end of which is the viscid disc. The plants have fans of flat leaves whose basal sheaths overlap. Flower spikes come from leaf axils, often a great many at a time. In nature the plants grow on small twigs and in cultivation do well on mounts or small branches or in small pots, with care to keep them damp but not overwet. The original plant may continue to grow for many years, with the old leaves falling as new central ones form. In the meantime, basal plantlets may grow to form nice clumps, or they may be removed and planted separately.

Ornithocephalus bicornis is one of the most familiar of the genus. The leaf fans are 3 to 5.5 cm tall, the numerous leaves rather short and rigid. The 6 to 7 cm spike and its bracts, the ovary, and backs of the sepals are covered with fine hairs. The blossoms are greenish- or yellowish-white, 4 mm across, with rounded sepals and petals. The lip, 4 mm long, has a fleshy globose base with two diverging blunt horns and a long tonguelike mid-lobe that curves up and out. (Guatemala to Panama; winter and spring.)

Ornithocephalus bonplandi [Plate 129] is a lilliputian among miniatures [Plate 129]. The plant is 3 cm wide and 2 cm tall, dark green, with fuzzy roots. The tiny flower spike reaches a height of 4 cm and bears three or four translucent, pale green flowers, large for the plant at a diameter of 6 mm. The oval sepals have dorsal keels ending in sharp points. The petals are broader at the outer end than at the base. The tongue-shaped lip is straight-sided, with a pair of gold-colored, shiny, wet-looking winglike calluses at its base. Requires a damp and shady spot. (Colombia and Venezuela; winter and spring.)

Ornithocephalus cochleariformis [Plate 130] has wide leaves that taper rather suddenly to sharp points. The fan can be 12 cm tall, with fuzzy flower spikes of the same height. The white blossoms are about 6 mm across, with the round sepals and somewhat squared petals also fuzzy on the back, the hairs at the tips a bit longer, creating short tails. The shell-shaped, green lip is broad, concave, with a pointed, up-turned tip and a round, saucer-shaped callus. (Panama; spring.)

Ornithocephalus gladiatus [Plate 131] has been made to encompass a great many other species, that is, many others have been reduced to synonymy with it, among them *O. inflexus*, *O. iridifolius*, and *O. tripterus*. When you view plants of these various types, they do look different, but they evidently grade together in order to have been considered variations of the same type. The plants average 8 cm tall, wider than high. The extremes in flower form range from one with slender petals smooth on the edges, to one whose petals are broad fans on narrow stalks with their edges finely toothed. The various components of the species range from Mexico through Central America, to Trinidad and Tobago, and through almost all of South America. Flowering time for the group varies throughout the year.

Ornithocephalus inflexus: See *O. gladiatus.*
Ornithocephalus iridifolius: See *O. gladiatus.*
Ornithocephalus tripterus: See *O. gladiatus.*

Ornithochilus

If a bird could carry a pair of pinwheels as it flies, then *Ornithochilus fuscus* is the image of that bird. It is monopodial, apparently one of two species in this genus, the other one extremely rare.

Ornithochilus fuscus is only 4 cm high, with three or four horizontal, narrow, oval, light green leaves 10 to 11 cm long. The branched flower spray, up to 10 cm in length [Plate 132], holds a flock of whimsical little, gold and rust blossoms, each 8 mm long. The broad, striped sepals and narrow petals arch over the rest of the flower like open wings. The long, conspicuous column has a head and beak like a bird. The lip is the remarkable part of the blossom: The front section [Color Plate C-72] is carved into two red wheels edged with fingers of gold and red. Its basal section forms a wide funnel constricted suddenly to a blunt, curved tip, the body and tail of the "bird" [Plate 133]. (Thailand, Burma, Himalayas, Laos, Vietnam, and Hong Kong; summer and again in winter.)

132. The branched flower spray of Ornithochilus fuscus.

133. Ornithochilus fuscus. *A single flower, in which the bird-head column and the rest of the lip, including the spur, can be seen.*

Ornithophora

The succession of orchid names coined to indicate some likeness to a bird makes a fascinating study. This one means "bird bearing," which a glance at the column and folded-back sepals and petals explains.

Ornithophora radicans is possibly the only species in the genus. It has thin, narrow pseudobulbs 4 cm tall and grasslike leaves 17 cm long. On each slender stem among the leaves sit up to ten tiny flowers [Plate 134]. They are 5 mm long, with greenish sepals and petals, and a wine-colored column. The lip has a narrow basal section or "claw" on which there are a rounded yellow knob and a spoon-shaped protuberance. The front lobe of the lip is white, with a down-turned outer part and earlike projections toward the rear that give it something the shape of an anchor, and it has four raised keels on the curved part. The column sits erect and completely exposed over the lip. (Brazil; summer and fall.)

134. Ornithophora radicans, *a 5 mm flower, easily earns its name, "bird bearing."*

Pabstiella

This is a new genus created in honor of Guido F. J. Pabst to receive a delightful species removed from *Pleurothallis*.

Pabstiella mirabilis is about 5 cm tall and has 1 cm, waxy white flowers with almost a spur formed by the attachment of the lip to the

very long column foot and covered by the united portion of the lateral sepals. The "spur" in fact looks like a handle to the flower. The tips of the lateral sepals curve out above the "spur," while the petals and dorsal sepal form the upper half of the flower. Half a dozen or so blossoms are borne on the branched inflorescence just about at leaf level. (Brazil, spring.)

Pachyphyllum

The members of *Pachyphyllum* are delicate, dichaea-like monopodials. A plant can flower when only 2 cm long and continues as it grows taller and branches out. The alternate fleshy leaves are attached to sheaths that clasp the stem and remain on the older part after the leaves fall. Roots arise along the stem. Tiny flowers come singly or in clusters from the leaf axils. The sepals and petals are more or less connected to each other at the base to form a tube. In some species the squarish or triangular lip is attached to the lateral sepals as part of the tube; in others, the lip has a long claw and is free. Broad wings form a full-length cloak on the column. The plants are best grown on a mount and kept shaded and moist.

Pachyphyllum gracilimum has flat, pointed leaves 6 to 8 mm long, ciliated on the edges and flower stems shorter than the leaves bearing three or four minuscule blossoms. The yellow-green flowers are 3 mm long, with the lip forming part of the tube. The ovary is much larger than the flowers. Cool growing. (Peru; winter.)

Pachyphyllum hispidulum has leaves 3 to 5 mm long, and they and the floral bracts are hairy on the edges. The pale green, fleshy flowers are slender bells 2.5 mm long occurring singly or in pairs. (Costa Rica to Peru and Venezuela; spring and fall.)

Pachyphyllum pectinatum has 5 to 8 mm leaves that curve in an arc and are finely toothed near the end. The tip bears a needlelike point. The white flowers are bell-shaped, with keeled and pointed parts, and the ovary is three-winged. Cool growing. (Peru and Bolivia.)

Pachyphyllum schultesii has leaves whose sides fold upward strongly and are toothed near the tips. The rounded single flowers are white and green, 2 mm long, with wide column wings that clasp the callus of the lip. (Colombia and Venezuela; summer.)

Panisea

Apparently only about four species are known in the genus *Panisea*. They are somewhat related to *Coelogyne* and are all from the Himalayas.

Panisea tricallosa is about 7 cm tall, including the oval 2 cm pseudobulb and slender leaf. The flowers are borne one or two to a short stem and are tan color, about 1 cm long, not opening fully. The lip has

135. Panisea uniflora is a translucent, yellow-green flower with orange swellings on the lip.

three calli, as the name indicates and is attached to an S-shaped claw. Cool-intermediate. (Assam and Thailand; spring.)

Panisea uniflora is a much prettier species. The pear-shaped pseudobulbs are 2 cm tall and have paired, 8 cm leaves. The lovely, translucent yellow-green flower [Plate 135] is 3 cm long, with slender, gently tapering, wide-spreading sepals, and smaller petals constricted at their base. The lip is oval, with small, upright, orange side lobes, four keels down the center, and an orange swelling at the end of each keel. (Himalayas, Burma, Thailand and Laos; summer and fall.)

Paphiopedilum

The Asiatic slipper orchids, so much loved everywhere, belong to the genus *Paphiopedilum*. These wonderful terrestrial orchids, with their fans of plain or mottled leaves, have been subjects for hybridization for generations, yet the species are as charming as the hybrids. When the hybrids reached their maximum size, amateurs began wishing for new and daintier types. Hybridizers, beginning by remaking the old primary hybrids, have now come forth with many novelty types, including "pygmy paphs," small plants with average size flowers. Among the many species are a few that come within, or just over, our limits for miniatures. For convenience, we'll divide them into groups with broad and narrow petals.

Broad petal group

Paphiopedilum bellatulum, with beautifully rounded flowers, is the most famous of this group and also the one most often used in hybridization. The narrow leaves are some 15 cm long, deep green mottled with light green on the upper surface and purplish underneath. The bowl-shaped flower, which is pubescent on the back, is 6 cm across and stands just at leaf level on a very short stem. Its round dorsal sepal and round petals are white with large rose-purple spots, entirely overlapping to form a background for the small, lightly spotted, egg-shaped lip. The united lateral sepals stand behind the lip. Grow warm or at the warm end of the intermediate range, with bright light part of the day and shade the rest. Pot in fir bark with some shell or limestone chips added, and do not keep so wet as most other paphiopedilums. (Burma and Thailand; spring to fall.)

Paphiopedilum concolor has dark green leaves mottled with gray-green, about 15 cm long. The yellow flower is 7 cm across, variably spotted with purple and pubescent on the back. Its parts do not overlap. The dorsal sepal is almost round, while the petals are oblong and directed downward. The lip resembles an elongated egg. Culture as for *P. bellatulum*. (Burma, Cambodia, Laos, and Thailand; spring.)

Paphiopedilum delenatii is unique in that the flowers are similar

to those of *Phragmipedium*, which is native to tropical America. The plant is of the ordinary paphiopedilum type, however, with as many as seven pairs of rather short leaves, dark green, mottled with light green above, finely spotted with purple underneath. Two or three lovely pink, lemon-scented flowers, about 6 cm across, are held on red stems about 20 cm tall. The small, pointed dorsal sepal and the rounded, horizontal petals are light pink and covered with fine hairs. The globe-shaped lip is darker pink, and the large staminode is mottled with purple. Culture is difficult, and each grower who succeeds with it seems to have a different system. As a starter, it is suggested that it be grown like *P. bellatulum* and given a drop in temperature, to 50°F (10°C) at night for a few weeks, to encourage flowering. (Indo-China; late winter, spring.)

Paphiopedilum godefroyae is not unlike *P. concolor.* The leaves are mottled dark and light green above, and are crimson underneath. The 6.5 to 7 cm flowers are white or pale yellow with purple spots that coalesce into lines. The rounded dorsal sepal is of modest size. The flattish petals are large, oval, and directed downward, with their upper edges folded back. The lip is slender, egg-shaped, and lightly spotted. Warm growing. (Birdsnest Islands in the Gulf of Siam; summer.)

Paphiopedilum leucochilum has recently been distinguished from *P. godefroyae* by its pure white, unspotted lip. Background color of the flowers can be white or pale yellow, and parts other than the lip are spotted with red-purple. The petals are concave or more or less flat. (Islands in the Indian Ocean off the west side of the Malay Peninsula; early summer to fall.)

Paphiopedilum niveum tends to be smaller than all the preceding species, with dull, dark green leaves motttled with gray-green, rich violet on the back. The dainty flowers, sometimes paired, are white, 5 to 7 cm across, on stems 8 to 10 cm tall. The rounded, somewhat fan-shaped dorsal sepal is concave, pubescent, ruffled on the edge, and lightly stippled with purple on back and front. The pubescent petals are broadly oval, curved in a bit at the tips, and spotted on the basal half. The rather slender, egg-shaped lip is white with a few spots on the incurved edges. Culture is difficult. If a regular paph mix is not suitable, and the bark-shell or bark-lime chips do not work either, try growing in scoria (porous volcanic rock). Be sure to flush pots thoroughly every other watering before applying fertilizer. (Loncavi and Tambilan Islands; early summer.)

Narrow petal group (of easier culture than the preceding)

Paphiopedilum charlesworthii [Color Plate C-73] is a stunning species with narrow leaves that range from 8 to 12 cm in length and are green on top, lightly speckled with purple underneath. The single flower stands on a 15 cm stem, its 8 cm spread almost overshadowing the plant. The huge dorsal sepal is wider than tall, 7 cm across, white densely veined with red-violet. The horizontal petals are yellow, net-veined with brown, and the disproportionately small lip is brown tinged with yellow. (India, Bengal, and Burma; late summer to fall.)

Paphiopedilum fairrieanum has narrow, plain green leaves that can reach 20 cm but often remain shorter. The flowers are 9 to 10 cm long, fuzzy on the back, single or in pairs and have an oriental look [Plate 136]. The dorsal sepal is tall, narrowed to a peak at the top, ruffled on the edge, and rounded through the middle. The petals curve down from their base and then turn out and up and are very finely ruffled on the upper edge where there are also groups of brown hairs. Both sepals and petals are beautifully veined with red and green on a white background. The lip is brownish-green, dimly net-veined in a darker tone. There are several color variations, ranging from wine red to green and white. Does well in either cool or intermediate temperatures. (India and southern Sikkim; fall and winter.)

Paphiopedilum spiceranum is a bit larger vegetatively than the preceding species, with broader leaves, plain green except for a tinge of purple at the base, and occasionally a white or light green border. The flowers are 6 cm across, held singly or in pairs on stems 20 cm or more tall. The beautiful dorsal sepal is broad with a turret shape created by folding and bending at the sides and top. It is pure white except for a dark crimson-purple stripe down the center. The petals are narrow, ruffled on the edges, yellow-green spotted with purple and have a median stripe of purple. The rather large lip is brown flushed with crimson. Cool growing. (Assam; fall to winter.)

Paphiopedilum venustum has beautifully mottled, rather sharply pointed leaves that are purple on the underside, 10 to 15 cm long [Plate 137]. The flowers, usually single on stems 12 cm tall, are 7 cm long, 9 cm from tip to tip of the petals. The onion-shaped dorsal sepal is beautifully marked with long and short green veins on a white background. The basal half of the petals is yellow with green veins, the outer half merges into red. The edges are hairy, and there are a few black warts sprinkled over the surface. The lip is yellow net-veined with green. This was the first *Paphiopedilum* to be introduced to science, in 1820, although it was discovered in 1816. Warm or intermediate. (Sikkim and India; winter.)

136. Paphiopedilum
fairrieanum *has delightfully
oriental-looking flowers.
The plant is just at the
limit of miniature size.*

137. Paphiopedilum
venustum *is easy to grow
and becomes a many-flowered
plant.*

Papillilabium

The only species of *Papillilabium* is a petite monopodial with, it is said, the strongest fragrance of any Australian orchid.

Papillilabium beckleri bears a few 2 to 5 cm leaves and a shorter inflorescence with three to eight flowers 5 to 7 mm across and 1 cm long. The sepals and petals curve inward at the tips so that the laterals embrace the rather long spur that descends between them. The blossoms are pale green lightly speckled with brown or purple, and the lip is green and purple, its outer lobe divided in three and lined with white hairs. (Australia; early spring.) A similar species is *Schistotylus purpuratus*.

Papperitzia

There is only one species in the genus *Papperitzia*, a diminutive plant with charming but strange green flowers.

    Papperitzia lieboldii has a 5 mm pseudobulb hidden at the base of its fan of four leaves, which are 2.5 to 3.5 cm long, slender and curving. Six to 12 long and narrow flowers 1.5 cm long are borne on a drooping stem [Plate 138]. The dorsal sepal and the joined laterals are concave and open up like the halves of a shellfish. The pointed petals flare up beside the column, which has huge wings that curve around in front of it to form a cape-like circle. The lip has a funnel-like base that stands up beneath the column in contact with the wings. Below this, the lip swings out at a right angle and becomes a fleshy tongue. Just at the curve there is an erect fleshy pad. The sac or lower part of the lip-funnel is filled with hairs, although these cannot be seen unless the flower is cut in half. The little plants should be kept on their original twigs if possible, fastened against sphagnum moss on a piece of cork bark. They should be kept damp and fairly well shaded. (Mexico; early summer.)

138. Papperitzia lieboldii *has strange, little pale green and cream flowers, 1.5 cm long. (From a Kodachrome by Eric Hagsater.)*

Phalaenopsis

The famous large hybrids of *Phalaenopsis* no longer overshadow the completely charming small species and hybrids being made with them, for the latter are colorful and available. *Phalaenopsis* is a genus of monopodials with fleshy leaves that may be succulent or tough and hard, according to the species and conditions of culture. The sepals and petals are the showy parts of the flower, but the lip is decorative and usually attractively and curiously shaped.

    Phalaenopsis equestris is quite variable, with a number of named color forms. Plants can be small and dainty, with drooping leaves up to 12 cm long or larger and sturdier, with leaves up to 20 cm long and 6.5 cm wide. The plants often make side growths that flower along with the original one. Spikes come several times a year; they increase in length over many months and open their flowers two or three at a time while more buds form. The blossoms [Color Plate C-74] are about 2.5 cm wide and are rosy-lavender, white tinged with lavender, or all white. Some have a yellow crest, others a white one, both types usually dotted with brown or purple. The sepals are oval, a little shorter than the rounder petals. The lip has a gently pointed oval mid-lobe and small, upright, narrow side lobes, broader at the tip than at the base. The crest bears an erect two-keeled callus. (Philippines; flowers all year.)

Phalaenopsis lueddemanniana has light green oval leaves which, like those of the above species, vary greatly in size, ranging from 12 to 20 cm in length. It has a peculiar flowering habit: The stems are thick, succulent and round, often branching, and are covered with green bracts. They can continue to grow for a year or more without producing any flowers and then, for no apparent reason, suddenly given forth blossoms their en-entire length and remain in flower for months. The inflorescences normally range from 10 to 30 cm in length. The fragrant, extremely waxy flower [Color Plate C-75] is 5 to 6 cm across, pale pink on the back and rich rose-violet with light crossbars on the front. The sepals and petals are oval, the lateral sepals the larger. The lip has tall, squared side lobes that curve forward to touch in the center, half violet and half orange, and a long mid-lobe whose almost parallel sides turn slightly down. A raised cushionlike keel bearing numerous bristles lies along the outer half of the lip and projects somewhat beyond its tip. Many of the so-called color forms, such as one-time var. *hieroglyphica* (a larger plant), are actually distinct species. Accepted varieties are: var. *delicata*, white with the end portions of the sepals and petals barred with cinnamon or ochre while the basal halves are barred with amethyst; and var. *ochracea*, light yellow with bars of ochre and only a tinge of purple at the base of the parts. (Philippines; flowers variably.)

Phalaenopsis pallens tends to be smaller in size than *P. lued-demanniana*, with shorter, fewer-flowered inflorescences. The blossoms are 3.5 to 4 cm across, white or cream color with a few broken bars of cin-namon brown on the sepals and petals, and a white lip. The outer lobe of the lip may flare on each side of the tip into lacerated or toothed extensions, or it may have only a few teeth on both sides of the tip. The cush-ioned part of the keel is set back from the tip. The erect side lobes are squared at the ends, with sharply pointed corners. (Philippines; fall.)

Phalaenopis lobbii was long considered a variety of *P. parishii*. Its leaves are broadly oval, rarely longer than 8 to 9 cm. In its native habitat it endures a severe dry season during which its leaves fall, but, in damper niches and in cultivation, it usually retains them. Several inflorescences about as long as the leaves appear simultaneously, each bearing four to six rather delicate flowers about 2 cm across. The sepals and petals flare backward a bit, while the semicircular lip juts forward. The lip in the type species is all purple, whereas that of the variety is white with a broad brown vertical stripe on each side. The lip callus in the variety consists of a raised crescent, lightly toothed around its edge, in contrast to that of the type, which is edged with long fringe and has in addition four long fila-ments. (Eastern Himalayas; spring.)

Phalaenopsis pulchra, once considered a variety of *P. luedde-*

manniana, is similar to it in plant characteristics and general flower shape [Color Plate C-76]. It is silvery white on the back, brilliant deep rose-violet on the front, with only the faintest hint of crossbars. The distinctive lip has erect yellow side lobes. The front lobe makes a right-angle turn forward from its narrow base and spreads into a slender fan which is toothed on the front edge and covered with scattered papillae. The cushion keel bears a few hairs toward the middle only. (Philippines; summer to fall.)

139. Phymatidium tillandsioides *looks like a small tillandsia plant.*

140. Phymatidium tillandsioides. *Its flowers are only 5 mm across, lovely and intricately formed.*

Phymatidium

A relative of *Ornithocephalus*, the genus *Phymatidium* has about 13 tiny, delicate species. They have no pseudobulbs and consist of a more or less dense fan or tuft of leaves. They require shady, damp locations but must be grown on a mount with good aeration and not be overwatered.

Phymatidium antioquiense vegetatively resembles an ornithocephalus plant, with a sparse fan of narrow, flattened, sword-shaped leaves 2 cm long. The 3 cm spikes hold four or so minute, light green flowers 6 mm long. The tiny sepals and petals are 3 mm long, directed backward. The narrow lip is bent back at its tip and bears a fleshy, yellow callus at its base and tiny papillae on its surface. The white column is straight and thick, large for the flower, covered on its front surface with papillae. (Colombia.)

Phymatidium cundinamarcae has a fan of flattened leaves, wider than those of the preceding species, and 2 cm tall. The 4.5 cm inflorescence is warty and holds a few flowers 7 mm long that are light green with a dark green lip and a broad oval callus covered with papillae. The column is straight. (Colombia.)

Phymatidium delicatulum has tufts of leaves like the finest blades of grass; the whole plant is 3 to 4 cm high. A profusion of spikes bearing three to five flowers each creates a bouquet of tiny blossoms. The flowers measure about 5 mm across, with oval sepals and petals and a fan-shaped lip all light green speckled with green. The lip callus is a fleshy, shiny green saucer, behind which, at the base of the column, are three green knobs. (Brazil; summer.)

Phymatidium histeranthum has fewer and smaller grassy leaves and is only 2 cm tall. The flower spikes are few but covered for their whole length with tiny snow-white blossoms. The sepals and petals are pointed oval, the lip rather heart-shaped. (Brazil; summer, fall and winter.)

Phymatidium tillandsioides is aptly named [Plate 139], for it resembles a tiny tillandsia plant, as does to a slightly less degree *P. delicatulum*. The innumerable, delicate light green leaves form a thick tuft 3 cm tall, from which arise a few short flowering stems each bearing three or four white blossoms 5 mm across [Plate 140]. The sepals and petals are narrow and pointed. The fringed lip is a narrow triangle that curves up at the tip; it bears a fleshy, green, concave callus of the same shape and three green knobs at its base. (Brazil; summer.)

Physosiphon

One of the *Pleurothallis* group, *Physosiphon* has only a few species, all with small tubular flowers. The plants have single leaves with several tubular sheaths at their base. Each leaf axil produces a flowering stem that may have one or 100 blooms, depending on the species.

Physosiphon lansbergii [Plate 141] is 3 to 6 cm tall, with tiny, paddle-shaped leaves and a single slender flower. Some plants produce very short flowering stems, often shorter than the leaves; others have stems that exceed the leaves in length. The blossom is 1 to 1.2 cm long, tubular, with the narrow sepals united for half their length and turned out slightly at their tips. They are white or greenish-white at the base; the tips may be white or yellow. Inside the tube are hidden the tiny white petals, yellow lip, and yellowish column, all about 2 mm long. Cool. (Bolivia, Venezuela, and Ecuador; fall and winter.) (May now be *Musclevallia* [1996].)

141. Still on its original twig, Physosiphon lansbergii *is a minute plant with long-lasting tubular flowers. (May now be* Musclevallia *[1996].)*

Physosiphon pubescens is a tiny creeping plant that spreads mat-like on its native trees and on a mount in cultivation. The very fleshy leaves are 1.2 cm long, close together. The little paired flowers, 1 cm long, are hidden among the leaves. They face each other like the heads of tiny cobras in conversation. The fat tubes are curved so that the only slightly open ends bend down, giving them the cobralike appearance. The edges of the minuscule lip and column hood are fringed. (Brazil; spring.)

Physosiphon tubatus spreads rapidly into a dense cluster of leaves 15 to 17 cm tall. It flowers prolifically, and each 20 cm spike bears 20 to 100 blossoms 1 to 2 cm long. The tubular section is green, the outer portion orange. A flowering plant is a charming sight. (Mexico and Guatemala; summer.)

Pinelia

The tiny species of *Pinelia* are structurally related to *Laelia*, *Epidendrum*, etc., and, along with the genus *Pygmaeorchis*, are the true lilliputians of the group. The pseudobulbs are egg-shaped or globose and the leaves pointed oval, thick and rigid, with the mid-vein showing only on one surface.

Pinelia alticola is scarcely 1 cm tall, including leaf and pseudobulb. The 5 mm flower is single, bell-shaped, white tinged with maroon-pink. The pointed sepals are a little longer than the spatula-shaped petals. The projecting lip is boat-shaped, with its sides turned up and the tip closed over. The callus is a transverse ridge. Grow damp with good light. (Venezuela; fall.)

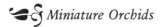

Pinelia paulensis is similar in plant characteristics, 1.5 to 2 cm tall. Its blossoms are light green, 7 mm long, the lip oval, with its sides rolled up to create the impression of a sharply pointed horn. (Brazil; summer and fall.)

Pityphyllum

The pseudobulbs in this genus look like minuscule cacti. They alternate along a pendent rhizome. The genus has four or so species, whose tiny pine-needle-like leaves stand in a tuft on the top of the pseudobulb. Single, minute flowers arise on short stems from axils of the sheaths along the rhizome. They do not open fully but hold themselves half closed. All probably do best kept damp in cool temperatures.

Pityphyllum amesianum is perhaps the prettiest vegetatively. The tiny, fluted, barrel-like pseudobulbs, 9 mm long, are topped by a flat-spreading tuft of twenty to forty 5 mm leaves. The cream and white flowers, with slender parts, are less than 5 mm long. (Colombia and Venezuela; fall.)

Pityphyllum antioquense has only three or four leaves 6 cm long and pseudobulbs 1 to 1.5 cm tall. The little, half-closed flowers are 5 mm long, white and cream, with slender parts that taper to a rather long point. (Colombia; winter).

Pityphyllum laricinum has pseudobulbs 8 mm long, with three or four 1.5 cm leaves. Its flowers are pale yellow and only 3 mm long. (Peru; summer to fall.)

Pityphyllum pinoides has pseudobulbs 1.2 cm long and three or four leaves 2.5 cm long. The flower is 3.5 to 4 mm long. (Ecuador; winter).

Platyrrhiza

This genus has only one species, a tiny plant with roots that are large for its size and probably contain chlorophyll to help make up for the small size of the leaves; it is related to *Ornithocephalus*.

Platyrrhiza quadricolor has a fan composed of a few leaves 2 to 2.5 cm tall and a spike about 5 cm high bearing several, brightly colored blossoms 7 mm across. The tiny, narrow, greenish-white sepals and petals are held back from the forward-curved, green and yellow column and jutting lip. The lip is white with a yellow tip and has a broad front lobe and rather long and narrow side lobes. (Brazil; winter.)

142. Platystele compacta is an attractive little plant with many stems holding clusters of 3 mm blossoms that keep coming for over a year.

Platystele

The genus *Platystele* is related to *Pleurothallis* and contains several charming species with minuscule flowers. Leaves are of the more or less typical paddle shape. The flowers have wide-spreading parts, sepals alike, petals smaller but similar to the sepals, and a fleshy, velvety lip. The short column has broad wings that form a hood and two pollinia. Grow either in pots or on mounts, damp, and with medium shade.

Platystele compacta [Plate 142] forms a veritable cushion of narrow leaves 3 cm long and innumerable spikes of tiny yellow flowers. The name *compacta* was chosen apparently because the flowers are densely packed together, although they never fill the whole spike, but are clustered at its end. Spikes keep lengthening as time goes on, forming flowers for a year or more. New spikes start in early spring. The blossoms are 3 mm across, with rounded parts and a heart-shaped lip. (Costa Rica, Guatemala, and Honduras; flowers all year.)

Platystele johnstonii is a remarkable species. The very small leaves, only 4 mm long, are rounded and arise alternately on a creeping rhizome, forming dense mats. The amazing creamy white, pubescent flower is 2 cm tall overall, with petals and lateral sepals forming a little star over which towers the tall dorsal sepal, four times the length of the rest of the flower. The orange lip is a mere 1 mm long, with a papillose surface. (Colombia, Ecuador, and Venezuela; fall.)

Platystele misera has leaves 6 to 7 cm long, and it, too, forms a cushion with almost ever-flowering spikes. The flowering stems are filamentous, twice the length of the leaves when young, growing longer with time. The blossoms [Plate 143] are 7 mm across, translucent, tan or green suffused with purple, and have tapering sepals and petals. The velvety, tongue-shaped lip is thickened at the tip, and its edges are rolled under. The white anther makes a conspicuous eye spot. (Colombia; flowers continually).

143. Platystele misera
continues to form its 7 mm purplish blossoms for a year or more.

Platystele ornata is 2 to 2.5 cm tall, with flower stems shorter than the leaves. The exquisite blossoms are just over 1 mm across, bright purple, with an unusual surface texture described as "bubbly," and glandular projections on the edges. The sepals are rounded, the petals slender, and the lip a pointed velvety heart. (Venezuela; flowers any time of year.)

Platystele ovalifolia has oval leaves 5 mm long that overlap each other as the rhizome branches and wanders. Three or four flowers 1.5 mm across, pale cream color, appear one at a time on short stems. Cool growing. (West Indies, Trinidad, Surinam, British Guiana, and Venezuela; flowers any time of year.)

Platystele stenostachya has at least two forms. Any plant will have leaves of different lengths, but those from more northern regions, Mexico and Central America, seem to be larger, up to 5 cm tall, while those from farther south, Venezuela and Colombia, only occasionally reach 4 cm. Also, the northern ones are more compact and spread more rapidly, filling pot after pot as they are divided. The flowers of the northern areas [Plate 144] are 3 to 4 mm across, yellow, with a relatively large velvety orange lip and yellow anther. The blossoms come on short stems down

144. Platystele stenostachya
has short stems of flowers down among the leaves. In the northern form, shown here, they come at intervals rather than continuously.

141

among the leaves. The stems produce up to a dozen flowers in succession, and additional stems come one after another from the same leaf. The southern form is not so compact, and the flowers are less hidden. They are 2 to 3 mm across, green, with a heavily papillose purple lip with a white margin, and a purple anther. Up to 25 are borne in succession on a neat herringbone inflorescence. (Mexico through Central America to Venezuela and Colombia; chiefly summer.)

Plectrophora

About four species of *Plectrophora* are known to date. They have fans of sturdy, flattened leaves similar to those of *Ornithocephalus*, spreading out from very small pseudobulbs, yet structurally the flowers are related to *Comparettia*. The handsome flowers are bell-shaped with a fairly long spur and a lip that rolls around the column.

 Plectrophora calcarhamata has a fan of up to eight rather broad, flat leaves, 8 to 10 cm long. The single cream-colored flower has highly ruffled petals and lip that overlap to form a bell about 3 cm long. Its spur is 3 to 4 cm long and makes a definite hook or almost a complete circle on the tip. (Brazil; summer.)

 Plectrophora cultrifolia has only two or three leaves in its fan, and they are 7 cm long. The single flower comes on a short stem from beside the very short pseudobulb [Plate 145]. It is a waxy, ruffled bell, 2 cm long not including the 2 cm spur, creamy white except for the yellow center in the lip. The broad oval sepals, the rounded, ruffled petals that overlap above the column, and the rounded, ruffled lip create a very compact flower whose rather thick, pointed spur extends straight back, sometimes slightly curved at the tip. (Brazil; summer.)

Pleurothallis

In a genus of 1000 species, such as *Pleurothallis*, there are a great many of similar appearance whose separation into individual species depends on minor differences. We can select only a few, trying to pick some that are attractive or intriguing, but having to neglect many.

 Pleurothallis has two pollinia. Some of its relatives also have two, others four, six, or eight. Two types of column are present: one that is dilated at the base with a pedestal-like foot and a stigma that looks "squeezed" so that it protrudes on either side of the rostellum (true of species with heart-shaped and near-heart-shaped leaves); and one that is slender, with a longer foot and a stigma centered underneath the anther as in cattleyas. The sepals may be entirely free or somewhat joined, and the lip is moveably attached to the column foot. Leaves can be paddle-shaped or heart-shaped, broad or slender, on long stems or short. Most are native

145. Plectrophora cultrifolia *is a rare and beautiful little orchid. All of its parts are broad and contribute to the formation of a round cup with a sturdy spur.*

142

to the cool cloud forests and therefore do best with cool, damp conditions in cultivation. A few prefer intermediate conditions. If a plant refuses to flower under one set of conditions, move it to another.

Pleurothallis amparoana is one of the loveliest. Its leaves are oval, 5 to 9 cm long. The inflorescence holds six to eight, almost transparent, delicate white blossoms tinged with green on the back, 1 cm long [Plate 146]. The lateral sepals form an oval bowl whose margins are densely covered with long, white, in-turned hairs in which it is easy to imagine an insect becoming entangled. The dorsal sepal, whose undersurface is also hairy, slants over the bowl. The column would be part of the insect trap with its several, long points. The inconspicuous petals are 2 to 3 mm long. (Costa Rica; winter).

Pleurothallis barbulata is 0.5 to 2 cm tall, with 5 mm flowers that appear large for the plant. They come on stems twice the height of the leaves and are yellow suffused with purple. The broad, pointed dorsal sepal and united lateral sepals are concave. The slender petals are edged with short hairs. Main feature of the flower is the slender, beardlike lip edged with long hairs. (Mexico through Central America, across northern South America and south to Ecuador; flowers continuously.)

Pleurothallis calyptrostele forms a mosslike mat of tiny leaves 1 to 1.6 cm tall [see Plate 2]. The white or greenish-white flowers are 5 mm long, three or four to a filamentous stem. They have pointed sepals, of which the laterals form a sharp chin. (Costa Rica and Panama; fall.)

Pleurothallis ciliaris is an example of species that resemble *Lepanthes* vegetatively, having ciliated, funnel-shaped bracts along the stem and rounded leaves. In this species, which is some 8 cm tall, the leaves are dark green on top, purple underneath. Up to 12 successive short spikes of tiny, hard, ciliated flowers appear at the back of the leaf. The blossoms are deep wine-red, often suffused with green, and have white petals. (Mexico to Peru and Venezuela; flowers repeatedly with a slight pause between times.)

Pleurothallis cobraeformis has slender leaves on long stems for a total height of 9 to 15 cm. The round, nodding, 1 cm flowers look like little cobra heads and come one at a time at the juncture of leaf and stem. The concave dorsal sepal and united laterals are broadly rounded, yellow-green spotted with purple, and from between them appear mustachio-like petals that are red with toothed edges. The little lip curves around the column. (Panama; flowers continuously.)

Pleurothallis comayaguensis is a creeping plant with rounded, overlapping leaves 6 cm long and 6 cm spikes of three or four minute, red flowers. The blossoms are about 4 mm long, with an upright dorsal sepal and united laterals, and fringed petals, lip, and column. (Guatemala and Honduras.)

Pleurothallis cypripedioides has flowers almost identical to those of *P. amparoana* except that they are red and open in succession on a zigzag stem. (Ecuador; spring to fall.)

146. Pleurothallis amparoana *has little bowls filled with in-turned hairs. These tiny, furry flowers may be insect traps.*

Pleurothallis flexuosa is 6 to 9 cm tall with slender, pointed leaves on short stems. The flowers come on bouncy, wiry, zigzag stems, opening one at a time as more buds form, until 18 to 20 have bloomed. They are yellow-green spotted with purple, 7 mm long, shaped like a gaping snake mouth, and covered inside with white wooly hairs. Petals, lip, and column are maroon. (Colombia, Ecuador, Peru, and Venezuela; flowers all year.)

Pleurothallis grobyi is common and well known, typical of a great many with sprays of little yellowish or greenish flowers marked with brown or purple. The plant is usually 4 to 7 cm tall, and the inflorescence is just taller than the leaves. The 5 mm blossoms open only part way, barely showing the small petals and lip within the concave dorsal sepal and longer, united laterals. Some 30 different names have been found to be synonymous for this species. Intermediate. (From Mexico to northern South America and the West Indies; spring and summer.)

Pleurothallis hirsuta can be small or may reach 15 cm in height. The flower stems are filamentous, taller than the leaf, and bear a few, greenish-yellow flowers spotted with purple, 6 to 7 mm long. The inner surface of the dorsal sepal and dish-shaped, united laterals is covered with unruly purple hairs. Intermediate. (Mexico, Guatemala, and Honduras; flowers variably.)

Pleurothallis intricata is a minute plant, 1.5 cm tall, with a zigzag stem of relatively large white flowers with a gold lip. The sepals extend into wide-spreading tails, giving the flower a diameter of about 1.5 cm. (Colombia, Ecuador, and Venezuela; March.)

Pleurothallis minutallis is a colorful and popular species. The leaves are 1 to 2 cm long on very short stems and form a rather dense mat. Flower stalks are about the same height as the leaves and bear two or three, nicely open, 5 mm blossoms, with pointed oval parts. The dorsal sepal is yellow-green with a few purple spots, the laterals yellow with orange tips, the petals yellow with red tips, and the jutting, tongue-shaped lip red-purple. (Mexico and Guatemala; winter.)

Pleurothallis mirabilis, see *Pabstiella mirabilis*.

Pleurothallis niveo-globula, or "little snowball," is a charming plant, 2 to 6 cm tall, with leaves 1.5 to 2.5 cm long, shaped like elongated hearts. Each of the successive blossoms arises from the base of the heart on a hairlike stem 1.5 cm tall [Plate 147]. The almost-closed bell is nodding, 2 mm long, crystal white, hiding within its overlapping parts the minuscule lip and column. (Ecuador; flowers continually.)

Pleurothallis pergrata is an astonishing species 3 to 6 cm tall, vegetatively like *Lepanthes*, with ciliated, tubular bracts along the stem, and a small rounded leaf. Long-tailed flowers, huge for the plant, appear one at a time from the top bract. The base of the flower is not wide open, but the sepals extend into wide-spreading tails 2 cm long, the dorsal one becoming a mere thread. The flowers are commonly maroon, but a yellow

147. Pleurothallis niveo-globula is a dainty plant with elongated heart-shaped leaves and tiny, white globe-shaped blossoms on hairlike stems.

form is known. (Panama and Colombia; flowers repeatedly throughout the year.)

Pleurothallis pterophora is a lepanthiform plant, 8 to 11 cm tall, with leaves spotted with brown on the back when young and stems of little white dancing bells. The 6 to 7 mm flowers have a sparkling texture and open all at once on thin, upright, zigzag stems 12 cm long. So delicately are they attached that they jiggle with the slightest air movement. The sepals of the nodding flowers spread half open, the laterals united and double-keeled on the back. (Brazil; flowers several times a year.)

Pleurothallis racemifera (syns. *quadrifida* and *giesbreghtiana*) is typical of those with stems of many alternate, nodding, white or yellow flowers [Plate 148]. This species is 15 cm tall, the flower stems two or three times that, with stems of 20 or more sparkling, faintly fragrant, yellow-green flowers 7 to 9 mm long [Plate 149]. They are quite open, the lateral sepals united, and the petals and lip large for the genus. The plant is easy to grow in either cool or intermediate temperatures. (Mexico; winter.)

Pleurothallis rubroinversa is a pretty little heart-leaved species 10 to 15 cm tall, with red flowers 1.5 cm long resting on the base of the leaf. The pubescent sepals are broadly oval; the horizontal, relatively large petals and the small rounded lip are toothed on the edges and warty on the surface. (Ecuador; flowers repeatedly from the same leaf.)

Pleurothallis samacensis is almost impossible to tell from its near twin *P. setigera*, which comes only from South America. The plant is 2 to 3 cm tall and has a few-flowered spike 4 cm high. The spiky flowers are 1 cm long, yellow-green marked with purple. The slender, pointed sepals are free-spreading and covered with bristles on the back side. The prominent 4 to 5 mm long petals have long teeth on the basal third, and their tips are extended into tails. (Guatemala and Venezuela.)

Pleurothallis schiedii is curious and charming. The dense cushion of leaves is 3 to 5 cm tall. The 1 cm flowers are reddish or grayish spotted with dull red and open perfectly flat [Color Plate C-77]. Their sepals are fringed with motile, wax-covered hairs that not only jiggle in the gentlest breeze but twist and turn at the slightest change in humidity, flapping back and forth across the face of the flower. Surely their action provokes the attention of the flies that pollinate them. The flower spikes continue to lengthen and form more flowers from the time they open the first bud until they reach some 12 to 14 cm over a year later. (Mexico; all year.)

Pleurothallis sonderana, about 3 cm tall, is pretty because of the little bouquet of golden orange flowers it bears [Color Plate C-78]. They come on slim stems just above the level of the fleshy, straight leaves and are 5 mm long, three or four to a stem. The blossoms are quite plain, with slender sepals and tiny, undecorated petals and lip. (Brazil; fall to winter.)

Pleurothallis spiritu-sanctensis, one of the smallest of orchids, presses its tiny leaves to the bark of its native trees, wandering over trunk

148. *Typical of dozens of its genus,* Pleurothallis racemifera *has sprays of nodding blossoms.*

149. *From the underside of* Pleurothallis racemifera, *the flowers show their sparkling, translucent texture.*

145

and branch. The leaves are rounded, 3 to 3.5 mm long, and overlapping. The red flower stem rises to a height of 2 cm and bears brightly colored flowers 6 mm long, twice the size of the leaves. They have long slender, pointed, wavy sepals, yellow, striped with red-orange, smaller but similar petals, and an orange, tongue-shaped lip. (Brazil; winter.)

Pleurothallis talpinaria is unusual in that the lip is the showy part of the flower. The plant is about 10 cm tall. The 2 cm flower is long and narrow, green spotted with purple [Color Plate C-79]. Several blossoms follow each other, coming from the bract at the junction of leaf and stem. The slender dorsal sepal and united laterals open wide to show the long, thin column and spectacular lip. The latter has a slender claw, from which it spreads into a three-lobed section. It is white, with a red collar at the neck and side lobes that curl into complete circles edged with red and decorated with "eyelashes." The mid-lobe is carved into lengthwise lobes and flushed with red. (Colombia, Ecuador, Peru, and Venezuela; summer and fall.)

Pleurothallis tridentata is a beautiful little pot plant whether in bloom or not [Plate 150]. Its heart-shaped leaves are red-bronze when young, light green when mature, and stand on stiff, thin, 8 to 12 cm stems. The yellow-green flowers, 7 mm across, nestle one after another at the base of the leaf. They have rounded dorsal and united lateral sepals, narrow horizontal petals, and a tongue-shaped lip. (Colombia, Ecuador, Peru, and Venezuela; flowers continually.)

150. Pleurothallis tridentata *makes a pretty pot plant. Tiny yellow flowers nestle at the base of the leaves.*

Podangis

A single exquisite monopodial species makes up this genus.

Podangis dactyloceras has an erect fan of dark green, rather tough, flattened, pointed equitant leaves 4 to 8 cm tall. The odd, translucent, crystal-white flowers arise from a short stem at the base of the fan, opening in quick succession so that all six to 15 are open at once. In spite of their delicate appearance, they are long-lasting. The rounded sepals, petals, and mouth of the lip form a completely round vertical bowl, 0.7 to 1 cm wide, that leads into the descending spur. The funnel-shaped spur, 1.5 to 2 cm long, expands suddenly at the end into a fishtail-shaped tip, so transparent that the level of nectar within it can be seen. The green anther cap decorates the center of the flower. (Tanzania, Uganda, and West Africa; spring through fall.)

Podochilus

The plants of this genus are beautiful vegetatively, some resembling *Lockhartia*, others more like *Dichaea*. Their stems grow in clumps.

Podochilus cultratus has very closely overlapping flat, triangular leaves on a stem 15 cm tall. The 2 to 3 mm, globe-shaped flowers, which come in small groups from the stem tips, are white flushed with pink, with a short fat chin. (Sikkim, Assam, Burma, and Nepal; late fall.)

Podochilus khasianus has willowy stems 10 to 15 cm tall with linear leaves 1 cm long, spaced 6 to 7 mm apart. Three or four minute, tubular flowers, 2 cm long, come at the stem tips. They are white, flushed with yellow. (Sikkim, Khasia Hills, and Assam; early fall.)

Polyradicion

The famous "ghost orchid" or "white frog orchid" of Florida belongs to this genus of few species. It is a leafless monopodial.

Polyradicion lindenii sends its long gray-green roots over the branches of trees in deeply shaded forests. The large white flowers come one at a time on a stem that holds them suspended in the air so that the "ghost" appears disconnected from its plant. The sepals and petals form a star 3 to 4 cm across. The 7 to 9 cm long lip is shaped like a frog, even to the curving, dangling legs (extensions of the mid-lobe). The flower also has a long spur that curves down beyond the lip to a length of 12 to 13 cm. Warm temperatures, shady, and damp. (South Florida and Cuba; winter into summer.)

Polystachya

The genus *Polystachya* contains numerous pretty species in the Old World and some less showy ones in the New World. Most have pseudobulbs and hold their flowers in a nodding position so that they open downward, the lateral sepals spreading apart to reveal the underside of the lip.

Polystachya aconitiflora is grasslike, 10 to 12 cm tall, with thin stems and single leaves. Short flower stems hold two or three bell-shaped blossoms, 1.2 to 1.4 cm across, in shades of pink to lavender, with a purple lip. (Uganda and Congo; spring.)

Polystachya bella has oval, much flattened pseudobulbs on a creeping, climbing rhizome, and paired, oval leaves. It is one of the larger species and very handsome, reaching 15 cm in height. The flower spike is 16 cm tall and holds a dozen or more yellow or orange flowers with slender, pointed parts. Cool growing. (Kenya and Uganda; summer or winter.)

Polystachya brassii is deciduous and flowers while leafless. The nearly round pseudobulbs are very tiny, olive green or dark purple, wrinkled, 8 mm high, often buried in lichens on the host trees. The three or four very narrow leaves are 8 cm tall. Before the new leaves start, the lovely pink flowers appear on a 1 cm stem from the tip of the old pseudobulbs. They are 5 mm long, white on the outside, tinged with pale lavender or pink within. (Malawi; spring.)

151. Polystachya pubescens
has a flower spike that
continues to form buds
for many months.

152. *The flower of*
Polystachya pubescens *is*
yellow striped with brown
and bears tufts of hair on
the lip.

Polystachya latilabris is a slender plant 12 to 13 cm tall, with thin stems and tough, narrow leaves. Three or four lovely, waxy flowers are borne on a stem shorter than the leaves. They are round and open [Color Plate C-80], about 1 cm across, white or cream color with a rose-colored lip and anther. (Kenya; spring.)

Polystachya ottoniana is a showy species with asymmetrical pseudobulbs shaped like flat-lying, elongated pears, bearing three or four slender leaves 6 to 10 cm long. The flowers, 1 to 1.4 cm across, are white, set off with a bright yellow stripe on the lip. Does best on a mount. (South Africa; spring to fall.)

Polystachya pubescens [Plate 151] is a delightful species with upright 6 cm pseudobulbs and two or three 6 to 8 cm leaves. The fuzzy inflorescence grows to 24 cm and forms buds for a long time. Ten or more flowers are open at once, with the final number some 25. The bright yellow blossoms are wide open, 2 to 2.4 cm across [Plate 152]. The lateral sepals are striped with brown on their lower half and covered with a few sparse, short hairs. The lateral lobes of the lip bear tufts of tall, yellow hairs, and the mid-lobe also has a few. (South Africa; fall through winter.)

Porpax

This is a genus of curious plants whose tiny flattened, disc-like pseudobulbs are pressed to the branch on which they grow. They are 1 cm in diameter, covered with net-veined sheaths, and bear small deciduous leaves. A pair of tiny tubular flowers sits right on top of the pseudobulb, before or after the leaves fall.

Propax elwesii, mistakenly called *P. meirax*, has small, very crowded pseudobulbs 1 cm across and small leaves that fall before flowering. The dull brown flower is a narrow tube 1.2 cm long, almost completely closed. A single bract stands behind the flower. The chin is rounded and fairly long. (Sikkim; fall).

Porpax fibuliformis has leaves about 2 cm long on 1 cm pseudobulbs. It flowers before they fall. The fat, 2 to 3 mm blossoms are tubular, shaped by the joined sepals to look like a slightly open, rather hooked beak. The tips of the petals can just be seen within the opening. The dull red flower is covered with short hairs. The column foot forms a blunt chin with the lateral sepals. (Sikkim; fall.)

Porroglossum

The curious insect-trapping genus *Porroglossum* is close to *Masdevallia*. Many species have been discovered in the past few years, and new ones will undoubtedly turn up. The leaves, shaped like those of *Masdevallia*, are finely pitted or reticulated. The flowers have a sensitive lip that closes when the callus on its narrowed crest is touched—by an insect, a drop of water, or an instrument held by a human hand; sometimes the lip closes at night (in response to darkness or to a drop in temperature?). The sepals are united to form a shallow cup whose base is a translucent window. The tips of the sepals end in a knob or tail. The stiff narrow petals come together in a circle around the anther. The S-shaped lip is hinged to the column foot by a long slender claw. Its outer lobe is triangular and edged with hairs. It hangs down when open, and when the callus on its center hump is touched it rises up against the barrier formed by the petals, forming a chamber that holds the insect until the lip relaxes and opens again [see Plates 153 and 154]. Some species snap the lip shut so fast that if you were to touch it with a pencil it would catch the tip before you could jerk it back. Others raise the lip slowly until it is almost in contact with the petals and then snap it shut. All are cool growing and require damp conditions and medium shade. They flower throughout the year, usually many times from the same stem.

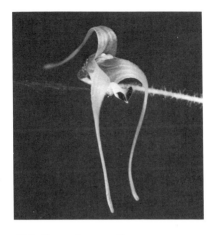

153. Porroglossum flowers have a sensitive lip that snaps shut when its crest is touched by a visiting insect. Porroglossum echidnum is shown here with its lip open.

Porroglossum amethystinum is 8 to 9 cm tall with flower stems 20 cm long that bear a succession of 2 cm, amethyst-colored blossoms. The sepaline tube is carved into ridges and hollows. The dorsal sepal curves backward and has only a rudimentary tail. The lateral sepals have sparsely pubescent, fleshy, 1 cm tails. (Ecuador; flowers off and on all year.)

Porroglossum chondylosepalum is 5 to 7 cm tall with 14 cm flowering stems. The sepals form a deep cup, and their tips end in knobs instead of tails. The flowers are 7 mm long, heavily stippled with rose on a white background. (Ecuador; flowers variably.)

Porroglossum echidnum is 6 to 7 cm tall with hairy flower stems 14 to 16 cm tall. The yellow blossoms are striped with orange, and the edges of the front lobe are red [Plates 153 and 154]. The tails of the sepals are up to 2 cm long, and either the dorsal or all of them are folded back. (Colombia, Ecuador, and Venezuela; flowers at intervals throughout the year.)

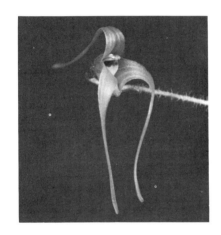

154. P. echidnum with the lip closed. Note the tiny armlike petals that form a barrier around the tip of the column into which the lip fits.

Porroglossum eduardi is an odd one, both because of its rambling nature and its more or less closed, tailless flowers. The lateral sepals are united for most of their length, creating an elongated saucer from the top of which the short-tailed dorsal sepal turns sharply upward. The blossoms are bright red, and several are open at once. (Colombia; flowers variably.)

Porroglossum mordax, 8 cm tall, is peculiar in that the creamy yellow sepals are toothed on the edges and have stubby, blunt, purple- or brown-spotted tails. The sepaline tube is longer than wide and quite open. The elongated section of the lip is dark purple, while the outer edges are cream color. (Colombia; flowers variably.)

Porroglossum peruvianum is 4 to 5 cm tall with rough leaves stippled with purple on the back. The symmetrical flower is greenish-yellow suffused with wine color. The fleshy tails are dull orange. The flower has a spread of 2 cm from the tip of the top tail to the bottom ones. (Peru; flowers continually.)

Porroglossum rodrigoi, 2.5 to 5 cm tall, has tiny beautiful leaves, net-veined with dark green and stippled with purple on the back. The threadlike flower stems are 9 to 10 cm tall. The 1 cm flowers are rather like those of *P. amethystinum* in that the cup is ridged and grooved, and the dorsal sepal ends in a rudimentary tail. The flower is rosy-violet, the short tails of the lateral sepals are orange, and the lip is tipped with dark purple. (Colombia; flowers throughout the year.)

Porroglossum sergii is of the *P. amethystinum* type, with yellow flowers 2 cm long, veined with violet, and with a red band across the mid-lobe of the lip. (Colombia; flowers variably).

Porroglossum xipheres is of the *P. echidnum* type. It has a hairy flowering stem and yellow-green brown-bordered flowers with short, fleshy tails. (Colombia; flowers variably.)

Promenaea

Related to *Zygopetalum*, the genus *Promenaea* consists of about 15 species. They are small plants with rounded, compressed, slightly four-angled pseudobulbs, and paired, rather soft leaves. The charming flowers come on relatively short stems, sometimes reaching above the middle of the leaves, sometimes close to the base of the plant.

Promenaea ovatilabium is about 5 to 8 cm tall and grows more rapidly, forming a lovely bouquet of flowers on stems a bit longer than those of the following species [Color Plate C-81]. The blossoms sometimes come in pairs and are pure bright yellow, unspotted except for a few red dots on the side lobes of the lip and the front surface of the column. They are 5 cm across and slightly concave, with a long oval lip that has a three-part callus at its base and tall, rectangular side lobes. (Brazil; spring and summer.)

Promenaea paulensis is 10 to 11 cm tall, with rather slender pseudobulbs 2.2 cm tall, and narrow, pointed leaves. The flowers [Plate 155] come singly and are 4 to 5 cm across. The dorsal sepal which arches over the column and the wide-spreading laterals are pointed oval, white spotted with red, and have a line of larger red dots down the center. The petals are shaped like the sepals but are a bit smaller and more densely spotted and point forward. The lip has large, erect side lobes and a spreading, somewhat triangular mid-lobe whose edges roll down, and it is more densely spotted than the other parts. The crest bears a dark red, raised callus. (Brazil; summer.)

Promenaea stapelioides is not unlike the foregoing. The plant is shorter, the leaves and pseudobulbs broader, and it is 5 to 8 cm tall. The 5 cm flowers are similarly shaped but the parts are broader [Plate 156]. The color ranges from cream to deep yellow, and the purple spots merge into dense bands over the whole flower, except for a clear border

155. Promenaea paulensis, *like others of its genus, is a delightful modest-sized plant with spotted blossoms. Its flowers are red on white.*

156. Promenaea stapelioides *is even more densely spotted, purple on a creamy yellow background.*

150

around the edges. The lip is solid dark purple inside and bears a ridgelike rounded callus. (Brazil; summer.)

Psygmorchis

Long included in *Oncidium*, and familiar by that name, the species of this genus have fans of flattened leaves without the channel along the tops typical of the variegata group. The flowers are large in proportion to the size of the plants. They are difficult to keep in cultivation and may have a short life in nature.

 Psygmorchis glossomystax is a tiny jewel. Its fan is 1.5 to 3 cm across, with eight to ten leaves, and its flowers 1 to 1.5 cm long. The blossoms, bright yellow except for a few brown markings, come singly on short stems. The sepals and petals are minute, making the beautiful lip the showy part of the flower. It has side lobes extending horizontally and a divided mid-lobe separated from them by a narrow isthmus. The crest bears four armlike protuberances trimmed with little erect fingers or hairs. The column has large wings. The plant must be mounted and have perfect drainage, high humidity, and good light. (Mexico south to Brazil and Peru; flowers any time of year.)

 Psygmorchis gnomus is rarely seen and may be scarce in nature. It is 3 to 5 cm wide, with pale yellow flowers about 1 cm long, similar to those of *P. glossomystax* except for the crest, which is a flat, raised ridge with several tonguelike extensions. (Guatemala and Costa Rica; winter.)

 Psygmorchis pumilio is about the size of the above two species and has usually one, but occasionally two or three flowers to a stem. They are pale yellow, with a lip broader than long whose side lobes usually overlap the mid-lobe. The crest is bipartite, dilated in front, with toothed margins. (Southern Brazil.)

 Psygmorchis pusilla [Plate 157] is the species most often seen in cultivation, yet it seems to have a life span of but a few years. Its fan is 6 cm wide, and the inflorescence produces several flowers in succession, 2.5 cm across. The minute sepals and petals are yellow or greenish-yellow barred with brown or red-brown [Color Plate C-82]. The lip is yellow except for some brown spots on the basal section and the crest. The middle lobe of the lip is divided into four lobes. The crest is formed of several smooth raised plates whose edges curve up or down. The white column wings are beautifully fluted and frilled. (Mexico to Trinidad, Brazil and Bolivia; spring and summer.)

157. *The exquisite* Psygmorchis pusilla *is charming and decorative but may have a normally short life span, especially in cultivation.*

Pterostylis

This is the genus of "greenhoods" native to Australia and its neighboring islands. The species of *Pterostylis* have a sensitive lip that, when touched by an insect, flips back against the column wings. The pollinator-to-be is trapped in the resulting chamber and it can get free only by forcing its way out between the anther and lip or by waiting for the lip to reopen. The plants are terrestrial and grow from small tubers. The leaves appear first, in some species a flat rosette, in others a taller whorl, and the flower stem appears from the center. The dorsal sepal and the petals form a hood around the column; the lateral sepals may be joined and curve up beside the hood, or hang down. The lip is attached by a hinge and has a peculiar appendage at its base—a little tuft of hairs at the end of a strap, whose function is unknown.

The tubers should be planted in a pot of sandy loam; a cymbidium mix suits them well. The leaves dry up after flowering and the pots should be kept on the dry side until new growth appears. The tubers will increase in number and will grow and flower for two or three years without being disturbed. Eventually, they should be removed during a dormant period, when the leaves have died down, and put in new pots. All are cool or cool-intermediate growing.

Pterostylis banksii has a leafy stem 15 cm tall on which the leaves decrease in size from the bottom upward. The single flower is produced on this stem and is 5 to 7 cm long, with a sharply pointed hood [Plate 158]. The lateral sepals are joined for half their length, their tips spreading sideways beside the hood. The lip is slender. The flower is all green, with a bit of red on the tip of the lip. (New Zealand; midwinter.)

Pterostylis baptistii has a flower similar in shape to *P. banksii* but it is somewhat larger, pale creamy green suffused with pink, and translucent. The leaves form a basal rosette. (Australia; summer.)

Pterostylis barbata has a flower shaped like a peanut, pale green net-veined with dark green and brown. The hood is almost closed, allowing only a slit for the very slender lip to enter when it flips back. The lip has a few long hairs along its edge. It has pink-tipped leaves along the stem and some leaves also on the flowering stem. (Australia; spring).

Pterostylis biseta is pinkish-brown. The lateral sepals hang down from the hood and are joined at the base. Their edges have short hairs and their tips extend into long tails. The little oval lip is edged with long bristles. The leaves are in a basal rosette. (Australia; summer).

Pterostylis curta, another one like *P. banksii*, develops a 15 cm flower stem arising from the rosette of leaves. (Australia; fall.)

Pterostylis nutans has a rosette of leaves with ruffled edges. The flower is smaller than the preceding and nodding; otherwise, it is similar to *P. banksii*. (Australia; summer).

Pterostylis plumosa resembles a green peanut whose lip has a rich plume of golden hairs. (Australia; spring.)

158. A "greenhood" orchid, Pterostylis banksii *has a sensitive lip that snaps up against the column when touched by a visiting pollinator.*

Pygmaeorchis _____

A sort of third cousin to *Pinelia*, the single species of *Pygmaeorchis* is one of the smallest of the *Laelia* group.

Pygmaeorchis brasiliensis has a tiny, globular pseudobulb and paired slender leaves for a height of 1.4 cm. The single, 3 mm greenish-pink flower appears between the leaves on a short stem. It is round, not fully open, with a spiny ovary, broadly oval sepals, narrow petals, and an oval lip with two raised ridges that are hairy on the inner ends. (Brazil; winter.)

Quekettia _____

This genus of two species is related to *Capanemia*, with a fan of three to six slender leaves that spring from a swollen pseudobulbous base concealed by bracts.

Quekettia microscopica has three gray-green, 6 cm leaves heavily spotted with purple. The few-flowered, simple or branched inflorescence is about 1.5 cm long. The 5 mm flowers are narrow and tubular, bright yellow-green, and the tips of the sepals and petals turn outward just slightly. The tip of the golden yellow lip emerges a little way from the tube, showing the two maroon spots near its tip. The lip has a transverse hairy callus near the base. (Amazonas, Brazil, Argentina, and Venezuela; flowers any time of year.)

Quekettia pygmaea is 4 cm high with six leaves covered with large mottlings of red-brown. The many-branched, filamentous flowering stem, 2 to 6.5 cm long, holds 40 or more round, bell-shaped blossoms. The narrow sepals, the laterals partially united, and the rounded petals are white, the arrow-shaped lip yellow. (Trinidad and Venezuela.)

Rangaeris _____

The monopodial genus *Rangaeris*, with its lovely spurred, white flowers, is distinguished by having two separate viscid discs for the pollinia and a lip larger than the sepals and petals.

Rangaeris brachyceras has a short stem with narrow, flat, alternate leaves 6 to 12 cm long. The numerous little inflorescences are just about leaf length and hold six to 15 flowers in a spiral formation around the stem. Blossoms are 8 mm long, white or pale green, and faintly fragrant. The dorsal sepal stands erect, the laterals point down and forward, the triangular petals turn slightly forward, and the rounded lip curves up, sending its short spur straight down. (Western Kenya, Uganda, and west to Nigeria; summer and fall).

Rangaeris musicola resembles a small vanda vegetatively, with a few slender leaves 6 to 10 cm long on a short stem. The lovely waxy, white flowers are round, 1.2 to 2 cm in diameter, with an erect dorsal sepal, petals and lateral sepals that flare backward, and a pointed, heart-shaped lip with a gently ruffled edge. The long, graceful pendulous spur is 6 to 7 cm long. The sweet perfume is strongest in the daytime. (Kenya, Uganda, Tanzania, and West Africa; midwinter.)

Rangaeris rhipsalisocia has a fan of flattened, pointed leaves 8 to 12 cm long. The inflorescences, taller than the leaves, bear eight to 15 white, star-shaped flowers 1 cm across. The lip is slightly three-lobed, pinched-in in the middle, and the green spur, only 1.5 cm long, extends back along the ovary and then turns its tip down. (Uganda and West Africa; summer.)

Restrepia

Another of the *Pleurothallis* group, *Restrepia* is distinguished by the long platform made by the united lateral sepals, and by the upright dorsal sepal that tapers to a knob-tipped filament, petals similar to this on a smaller scale, and a small lip that lies nearly flat on the sepaline platform. The oval leaves are held on slender stems whose bases are covered with loose, papery bracts. The flowers arise one at a time from the juncture of leaf and stem. The plants thrive in cool or cool-intermediate temperatures with medium shade.

Restrepia antennifera has broad oval, pointed leaves on stems with brown-spotted bracts, the plants being 6 to 11 cm tall. The 4.6 cm flowers come on stems shorter than the leaves. The dorsal sepal is translucent white at the base, striped with purple, and it tapers to a green filament with a purple knob. The united laterals are yellowish-brown with purple stripes. The petals are similar in color to the dorsal sepal. The lip is slender, warty, undulating, tan with maroon spots. The base of the column is swollen and covered with short hairs. (Colombia, Ecuador, and Venezuela; flowers irregularly through the year.)

Restrepia elegans [Plate 159] is 13 to 16 cm tall with beautiful large flowers. The blossoms are 5 cm long, the dorsal sepal and petals are translucent white striped with dark red, and the united laterals are orange, densely spotted with dark red and velvety on the upper surface. The spotted lip has almost straight sides and a forked tip and is covered with tiny bumps. Its edges are finely toothed. (Venezuela; fall and winter.)

Restrepia filamentosa is 12 cm tall with slender oval leaves. The flowers are about 3 cm long, similar in color to *R. antennifera*, without the swollen base to the column. (Panama; fall.)

Restrepia muscifera is 7 to 12 cm tall, with leaves more slender than some, on tall stems covered with spotted bracts. The delightful flowers [Plate 160] are 2 to 2.5 cm long, with the rather stocky dorsal sepal nearly erect and the united laterals broader and rounder toward the

159. Restrepia embodies all the good qualities of orchids: It is a compact, attractive plant and flowers over and over from the same growths. The long, knob-tipped dorsal sepal, united lateral sepals, and filamentous petals are characteristic of the genus. Shown here is Restrepia elegans, *which is spotted with dark red.*

tip. The flower has a pale yellow-green background and red-violet spots that are largest at the base of the sepaline platform, smallest on the lip. Two raised yellow eye spots are situated at the base of the lateral sepals. (Mexico to Panama; flowers nearly all year.)

Robiquetia

The monopodial genus *Robiquetia* has a dozen or more species, some of them quite large. The plants have spikes of small waxy flowers.

Robiquetia paniculata has narrow leaves 6 to 9 cm long on a stem that grows long with age. The descending, rather open flower spike is 6 to 16 cm long and holds numerous greenish-white flowers 6 to 7 mm long. The dorsal sepal forms a hood with the small petals, while the lateral sepals spread wide like wings. The lip has large triangular side lobes that curve up beside the column, a slightly boat-shaped mid-lobe, and a short spur whose fluted tip is inflated like a minute balloon. (Thailand.)

Robiquetia rectifolia is a much smaller species with a stem 2 cm long and four or five leaves 1 to 4 cm long. The spike of numerous, minute, green flowers reaches a length of 7 cm. The blossoms are 2 mm across, with sepals and petals curving forward at their tips, and a triangular lip leading into a funnel-shaped spur. (Australia; winter.)

160. Restrepia muscifera *is yellow-green spotted with purple and has two yellow eyes at the base of the column.*

Rodriguezia

Related to *Oncidium*, the 30 or so species of *Rodriguezia* are characterized by a false spur formed by the reflexed lateral sepals that come together so that their edges touch or overlap. The lip has a small backward projection from its base that is not a true spur either.

Rodriguezia batemanii has oval compressed pseudobulbs 4 to 5 cm tall that bear a single 10 cm long leaf from the top and several from the sides. The short arching spike carries three to eight 6 cm, white flowers tinged with rose. They have broad dorsal sepal and petals and a wide, rather short lip with ruffled edges and two wavy, yellow keels down the center. (Amazon region of Peru to Colombia; spring and summer.)

Rodriguezia candida is a beautiful plant 10 to 15 cm tall, with dense spikes of very full, overlapping flowers. The blossoms are 5 to 6 cm long, waxy white, finely dotted with deep pink on petals and lip. The dorsal sepal is concave, the broad petals curve outward. The lip has a long midsection ruffled on the edges and bears two raised keels that spread apart and then come close together at the ends, at which point three short, pink keels extend a little farther. The end of the lip is broad and bi-lobed. (Brazil, Guyana, and Venezuela; winter.)

Rodriguezia granadensis is 12 cm tall, including the 2 cm pseudobulb. The lovely round flowers have broad ruffled petals and a

155

short, scoop-shaped lip. There are several colors—bright yellow, rose, pink, and white. Five to eight blossoms are borne on the 15 cm spike. (Colombia; spring.)

Rodriguezia lanceolata (syn. *secunda*) is the best known of the genus. Plants can be a bit large for our limits but can also run small. The species is loved for its bright rosy-red blossoms, borne all on the same side of the arching stem. They are 2 to 3 cm across and quite round. The dorsal sepal and petals project forward, the oblong lip curves down in front, and the "spur" formed by the lateral sepals curves forward under the lip. (Mexico to Colombia, Brazil, Venezuela, and Trinidad; fall.)

Rodrigueziella

A genus known previously as either *Hellerorchis* or *Theodorea*, *Rodrigueziella* is related to *Gomesa* and has perhaps half a dozen species. They are small plants with slender, oval pseudobulbs and soft, grassy leaves.

Rodrigueziella gomesioides has pseudobulbs 2 to 3 cm tall and paired leaves 8 to 10 cm long. The delicate inflorescences, shorter than the leaves, bear ten or more fragrant, 1 cm, brownish-green flowers with a yellow lip. The slender sepals and petals all curve forward and the pointed, fiddle-shaped lip hangs down between the lateral sepals. The crest has a pair of fuzzy orange keels. (Brazil; spring.)

Rodrigueziella handroi has wider pseudobulbs and leaves but is a shorter plant. The arching flower spikes hold about ten nodding, 1 cm flowers. The sepals and petals are nearly alike, oval, coming to a sudden, sharp point, pale yellow-green striped with dark green. The lip has a narrow, down-turned mid-lobe with rolled-in sides, and two curved, hairy keels. The column is also hairy. (Brazil; spring to summer.)

Saccolabiopsis

The genus *Saccolabiopsis* has about seven small monopodial species. The column has a long rostellum and equally long armlike wings projecting under it. They are best grown on mounts.

Saccolabiopsis armitii is a pendulous plant with a short stem and three to six leaves 1.5 to 6 cm long. More than one flowering stem can be produced at a time. They are 3 to 9 cm long and bear a wealth of tiny blossoms all facing forward. The flowers are 3.5 to 4 mm in diameter and twice that in length. The nearly round dorsal sepal and petals curve forward at the tips, the long lateral sepals hang down and curve around the long blunt spur like a cape. They have a thickened ridge down the center. The lip is white, its mid-lobe jutting forward to make a right-angle curve with the spur. The anther is red. (Australia: spring.)

Saccolabiopsis tenella is 4 cm tall with four or five leaves and inflorescences 4 to 8 cm long. The numerous 2 mm blossoms extend straight out from the stem on ovaries 3 mm long. They are green with a white lip, the oval sepals and petals spreading wide, and the fleshy lip opening into a very fat, short spur. (Borneo.)

Sarcochilus

Most of the dainty, vanda-like species of *Sarcochilus* are Australian. They are monopodials with sprays of little round flowers whose chief characteristics are a short spur on the front lobe of the sac-like lip and thick, platelike calli on its basal parts.

Sarcochilus australis is said to be difficult to grow but lovely and worth trying if plants can be obtained. It has three to seven leaves on a short stem and produces numerous pendulous sprays of blossoms 1.4 to 2.4 cm long. The brownish-green sepals and petals are free-spreading, the latter attached to the sides of the long column foot. The lip dominates the flower. It is white, with huge, erect side lobes striped with red, and a sac-like mid-lobe from whose bottom projects the solid, down-curving spur. (Australia; spring.)

Sarcochilus ceciliae has branching, tufted stems 2 to 12 cm long, with narrow, channeled, brownish-green leaves 4 to 8 cm long. The inflorescences are erect and bear a dozen cup-shaped, rosy-pink flowers 4 to 6 cm across. The sepals and petals spread wide. The lateral lobes of the lip are covered with hairs, and the mid-lobe is filled with them. The spur is only 1 mm long. (Australia; spring.)

Sarcochilus falcatus has several leaves 5 to 16 cm long, and short stems of delightful crystal white flowers 2 to 3.5 cm in diameter. The rounded sepals and petals spread flat. The lip is small, with up-curving side lobes striped with red, and a fat, protruding spur under the mid-lobe. The front of the column is also striped with red. (Australia; spring or fall.)

Sarcochilus hartmanii can grow quite large in nature but often remains small in cultivation. The plant might average 15 cm in height. It is easy to grow, makes side branches freely, and gives many sprays of round, white flowers 1 to 3 cm across [Plate 161]. The broad sepals and petals almost overlap and are sometimes spotted with red near their base. The lip is tiny, with semicircular side lobes striped with red and tinged with yellow, and has a little blunt spur. The species is semi-terrestrial, grows well in a cymbidium mix, and should be generously watered in the summer and left a little drier in the winter. Cool growing. (Australia; spring.)

Sarcochilus hillii has slender, quill-shaped leaves, 1.5 to 10 cm long, which curl at the tip, and sprays of dainty blossoms on zigzag, threadlike stems. The blossoms are 0.6 to 1.1 cm across, frosty white or pink, with roundish sepals and petals tipped with a point, and a lip whose side lobes are striped with purple and whose center is filled with hairs.

161. *A lovely little monopodial Australian species is* Sarcochilus hartmanii, *which gives many round white flowers, 1 to 3 cm across.*

Does best kept a bit dry in a humid atmosphere. (Australia; spring.)

Sarcochilus segawii is an exquisite, leafless orchid [Color Plate C-83]. The flower stems hold from four to 12 fat, round blossoms 1 cm across, of a sparkling texture [Color Plate C-84]. The broad, pale green sepals and petals are nearly round, and the lip is cup-shaped, cream color with touches of orange. (Taiwan; winter and spring.)

Scaphosepalum

A comical member of the *Pleurothallis* group, *Scaphosepalum* is characterized by a swollen mustache-like or cushion-like section of the lateral sepals from which short or long tails extend, and a long tail on the dorsal sepal. The over 40 species have two pollinia. The plants are generally 8 to 15 cm tall, with paddle-shaped leaves. The flower stems continue to make blossoms for a long time, even up to a year or more. They are cool growing and require constant dampness and medium shade.

Scaphosepalum lima [Color Plate C-85] is 14 cm tall, and its blossoms measure 3 cm across the lateral sepals. The flowers, with a white background spotted and veined with red, continue to form for a year on a slightly warty, zigzag stem. The long dorsal sepal, shaped like the head and beak of a stork, juts out over the cup formed by the basal union of the lateral sepals. These sepals separate and turn out at right angles, widen into sections covered with white fur, and then lengthen into tails. The minute petals and lip are within the cup. (Colombia; flowers all year.)

Scaphosepalum swertiifolium is 13 to 15 cm tall, with leaves a bit thinner than some and more pointed. The flowers come on fairly long pedicels on a straight, smooth inflorescence. They are almost solid rose-red and have a broad sepaline cup and tails that curve in a semicircle. (Colombia; fall and spring.)

Scaphosepalum verrucosum is 8 to 18 cm tall, usually in the smaller range. The flowering stem is zigzag and warty. The 1.5 cm blossoms [Plate 162] range in color from grayish-tan spotted and veined with red, with an orange sepaline thickening, to pink spotted with rose-violet and a cerise sepaline thickening. The thickenings of the lateral sepals are velvety, triangular cushions, flat where the sides of the two cushions meet, rounded over the ventral sides, and extending into pointed tails of a paler hue. (Colombia; flowers all year.)

162. Scaphosepalum verrucosum *has comical flowers whose dorsal sepal is extended in a long beak and whose lateral sepals thicken into velvety cushions at the base and then thin out into tails.*

Scaphyglottis

The genus is characterized by the plant's habit of making new pseudobulbs on top of older ones. The species have four pollinia. The flowers are small but charming.

Scaphyglottis amethystina has pseudobulbs about 8 to 10 cm tall with paired, slender leaves. The blossoms come in clusters from the apex of the psuedobulb, opening in quick succession. They are 1 to 1.5 cm across, white to lilac, veined with lavender. The sepals are broad, the laterals forming a short chin, and the lip is three-lobed, broader than long. (Costa Rica and Panama; spring.)

Scaphyglottis livida makes many branches. Its flowers are pale yellow-green, sometimes tinged with pink or lavender, about 8 mm across. They have a fairly long, down-turned, channeled lip. (Mexico, Guatemala, and Honduras; winter.)

163. Scaphyglottis prolifera *is a small plant with tiny flowers of translucent white tinged with green or lavender and a dark purple column.*

Scaphyglottis prolifera has pseudobulbs 2 to 5 cm tall that sometimes form more than one new pseudobulb from their tips. They root readily at the nodes, allowing the grower to reduce their height by removing the top pseudobulbs and potting them separately. The particularly pretty flowers are 1 to 1.2 cm across, white, yellowish or greenish, veined with deep pink or blue, and of crystalline texture [Plate 163]. They have a squarish fan-shaped, lavender lip and an eye-catching, red-purple column. (Guatemala, throughout Central America, the West Indies, and northern South America; winter and spring.)

Scaphyglottis pumila is a tiny plant 2 to 3 cm tall, with oval pseudobulbs, and a single, narrow, rather rigid leaf. The single translucent flower is tan or white tinged with green and has a rectangular lip with a V-shaped, purple stripe down the center. Cool growing. (Mexico; spring.)

Schlimia

Some four species compose the charming genus *Schlimia*, which is related to *Gongora* and *Stanhopea*. The plants have oval, tapering pseudobulbs and single, pleated leaves. The inflorescence is pendent, and the hooded flowers open downward.

Schlimia alpina, now includes as synonymous *S. trifida* and thus has a wide range of sizes. Small plants come just within our limits, with pseudobulbs 2.5 cm tall and broad leaves 10 to 15 cm high. The flowers are waxy, cream color, about 5 cm long. The lateral sepals form a tall, helmet-shaped sac, from under which the petals, dorsal sepal, and orange-tipped column protrude. Cool growing; should be planted in a basket. (Colombia; winter.)

Schoenorchis

Schoenorchis is a genus of monopodials, many of which have fairly long stems and extremely small flowers. The one given here is a short-growing little gem with relatively large blossoms.

Schoenorchis fragrans (briefly and erroneously called *Smitinandia ambikanum*) is 1 to 2 cm tall, with thick, rather rough, closely set,

1 to 1.5 cm leaves. From the leaf axils come dense clusters of exquisite waxy, 1 cm, blush-pink flowers of unusual form. The short sepals and petals spread wide to form a little saucer, under which hangs the proportionately long lip, with its fat spur directed backward and its sac-like front lobe forward, thrusting ahead of it a hooked projection. Warm growing. (India and Thailand; summer.)

Sedirea

This is a new genus created by Garay and Sweet to accommodate a single species once included in *Aerides* as *A. japonica* but distinctly different from members of that genus.

Sedirea japonica resembles a little phalaenopsis in plant habit, with two to three pairs of flat-lying oval leaves 7 to 10 cm long. The flower spike can reach 15 cm and bears 6 to 10 fragrant, waxy blossoms, 3 cm long. They are white or green to greenish yellow, with purple bars on the basal half of the lateral sepals; the lip is barred and spotted with the same color. The sepals are spatula-shaped; the petals are broader and held forward, abruptly squared off where they constrict to a basal claw. The lip is narrow at the base and flares into a ruffled lobe on each side. The short spur juts forward under the lip. (Japan; late spring.)

Sigmatostalix

A dozen or so intriguing species, relatives of *Oncidium*, make up the genus *Sigmatostalix*. The outstanding feature is the disproportionately long column with an enlarged tip, which gives some the appearance of a minuscule cycnoches (swan orchid).

Sigmatostalix amazonica [Plate 164] has rather translucent, flattened, oval pseudobulbs 4 cm high, and thin single leaves up to 8 cm tall. Two or three inflorescences can come from one pseudobulb, each bearing a double row of 20 or more tiny dancing figures [Plate 165]. The blossoms are 1.2 to 1.3 cm long, with narrow, yellow-green sepals and petals barred with brown. The rich yellow lip is shaped like a slim skirt. The callus is a thickened cushion hollowed on the front surface. (Colombia, Peru, Venezuela, Surinam, and Brazil; winter and summer.)

Sigmatostalix crescentilabia is 15 cm tall, including the 3 to 4 cm pseudobulbs and slender leaves, one from the top and one from each side. The 1.5 to 1.7 cm flowers are even more like dancing figures than the preceding species. They are lined up on the top side of the stem, lip uppermost [Color Plate C-86]. The downswept sepals and petals form the green, red-speckled skirt; the claw of the lip is the neck, surrounded by the shawl-like mid-lobe; and the large, round callus of the lip is the head. The very long column swings out horizontally. (Peru; fall.)

164. Sigmatostalix amazonica has flowering stems crowded with dancing blossoms.

165. The little flowers of Sigmatostalix amazonica are about 1.2 cm long, clothed in yellow and yellow-green.

Sigmatostalix graminea (syn. *peruviana*) [Plate 166] is only 4 to 5 cm tall. Tiny compressed pseudobulbs 1 cm high bear single leaves on top and six or more from the sides. The 5 mm flowers are bright and eye-catching despite their small size [Plate 167]. The column is not so long as in other species but nevertheless a prominent part of the flower. Sepals and petals are pale yellow with a wide red stripe, and the petals have a tooth at their base. The round, full lip is deep yellow, and its waxy callus consists of two wavy plates, one on top of the other. (Peru; flowers at any time of the year, mostly spring to fall.)

Sigmatostalix guatemalensis appears to have a fan of leaves, but actually there is a single top one and several others from the base of a tiny hidden pseudobulb. The whole plant is about 7 cm tall, usually tinged with red. The 1.5 cm flowers look like a row of birds sitting on a wire, with their tails hanging down. As buds develop from both sides of the stem, they all turn up to open in a double row, facing alternately left and right. The dorsal sepal and petals hang on one side, the lateral sepals on the other. They are green, barred and blotched with brown. The long-clawed, anchor-shaped lip is brown at the base, yellow around the edge. The tall column is barred with brown except for the all-yellow tip. (Mexico, Guatemala, Costa Rica, and Panama; summer.)

Sigmatostalix hymenantha, a most amazing little plant, is 12 cm tall and has a much-branched inflorescence 10 to 24 cm long, delicate as asparagus fern. At the tips of all the branches come an almost never-ending array of minuscule, translucent flowers. They are only 3 mm long, white, with a rather stocky column, reflexed sepals and petals, and a turned-down lip with a large, double, cushion callus that is orange in the center. (Costa Rica and Panama; flowers all year.)

Sigmatostalix pandurata is a near twin to *S. graminea*. The flowers are 8 mm across, with straight, wide-spreading sepals and petals, and a three-lobed lip. The column is taller, with a red "neck." (Colombia; spring to fall.)

Sigmatostalix racemifera ranges from 7 to 15 cm tall, with straight stems of tiny flowers. The blossoms are translucent, pinkish-white, with a ruffled, tooth-edged lip that supports a large, solid, cushion-like callus. The lip is spotted with orange, and the callus is orange with a band of red at its base. (Panama; fall.)

166. Sigmatostalix graminea, *only 4 to 5 cm tall, is eye-catching with its tiny bright yellow flowers.*

167. *A single flower of* Sigmatostalix graminea, *5 mm across, reveals fascinating detail.*

Smitinandia

This is a new genus created in honor of Tem Smitinand, co-author with Gunnar Seidenfaden of *The Orchids of Thailand*. (A genus honoring Seidenfaden has also been created, but the plants are above our size limit.) *Smitinandia* is closely related to *Ascocentrum*, and its type species was *Saccolabium micranthum*.

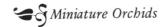

Smitinandia ambikanum: see *Schoenorchis fragrans.*

Smitinandia micrantha is a modest monopodial plant 8 cm or more tall, with narrow leaves 11 cm long. The fleshy inflorescence, 7 cm in length, bears numerous, small, waxy flowers, white with purple on the lip and anther; sepals and petals are sometimes spotted with purple. The blossoms are round, 7 mm across, with broadly oval sepals and narrower petals. The oblong outer lobe of the lip is held horizontally, its base forming a rounded sac or spur at whose entrance is a thickening that almost closes the opening. (spotted form: Himalayas; white form: Langkawi.)

Sophronitella _____

A genus of a single species, *Sophronitella,* is most closely related to *Sophronitis.*

Sophronitella violacea has slim pseudobulbs 1 to 2.5 cm tall and a single, erect, stiff, narrow, rough-textured leaf 3.8 cm long. The lovely rose-violet flower is an open bell, 2 cm long, its slender oval sepals and petals and slightly wider lip all spread open at the same angle. The tip of the column is much darker and lends a sharp accent to the center of the flower. Does best on a mount, with once-a-day misting, in a bright, humid atmosphere. (Brazil; summer.)

Sophronitis _____

The species of *Sophronitis* are glorious little orchids. The genus is an important member of the *Laelia* group, and one species, *S. coccinea,* has been much used in hybridization for its red color [Color Plate C-87]. Two general types of *Sophronitis* occur: the small-flowered but charming *S. cernua* and its varieties, whose flowers are short-lived; and *S. coccinea* and several similar species, whose blossoms last far longer. All have small pseudobulbs and thick, tough leaves and for the most part do well in cool-intermediate temperatures with generous humidity and medium light. The *coccinea* group can be grown either in pots or on mounts, but the *cernua* group does best on mounts, which they soon cover. The members of the *coccinea* group come from such varied habitats that one often has to move them around to find what suits each one. So subtle are their differences that it is often difficult to distinguish the species from each other, and while several will be given here, exact determination of any you may acquire may need the help of an expert.

Sophronitis cernua: two varieties.

Sophronitis cernua has peudobulbs that are fat cylinders when young, becoming flattened and wrinkled when old. They are 1.5 to 2 cm long and grow right and left of the creeping rhizome. The oval or rounded leaves are stiff and thick, 2 to 3 cm long. The 2 cm flowers come in clusters of two to four on a short stem. Typical plants have orange flowers and grow near sea level, which is why they are called var. *littoreana*. Farther inland and at higher elevations a dark red-orange variety occurs, called *mineira* [Color Plate C-88]. In both, sepals and petals are of equal size, broadly oval and pointed, and the lip is broad and scoop-shaped, shorter than the other parts. The column has fat, down-pointing auricles or wings tipped with purple, which create eye spots in the center of the flower. The var. *mineira* is a bit larger in all ways, and so is a rare, pale yellow form. (Brazil; fall.)

The *Sophronitis coccinea* group.

Sophronitis brevipedunculata has short, fat pseudobulbs 1 to 1.5 cm long, covered with bracts that shred to fibers and soon disappear. The leaves are 2.5 to 4.5 cm long. The rosy-red blossoms come on peduncles shorter than the leaves and are about 5 cm across. The sepals are narrow, the petals twice their width, and the lip is long and slender, orange within and veined with the basic flower color. (Brazil; late fall.)

Sophronitis coccinea [see Color Plate C-1] has slim, erect pseudobulbs 3 to 4 cm tall, and narrow oval leaves 6 to 7 cm high, whose mid-vein is dark purple. The perfectly flat flowers vary in size, 4.5 to 6 cm wide on the average, and are orange to red-orange in color, sometimes pure scarlet. The petals are much wider than the oval sepals. The small pointed lip enfolds the column, and is light orange within and symmetrically veined with scarlet. The peduncle lengthens, and the flower increases in size over a period of weeks, lasting for months. (Brazil; fall through winter.)

Sophronitis mantiqueirae is similar vegetatively to the preceding, with pseudobulbs 2 to 2.5 cm long and leaves 3 to 3.5 cm. Its rich red blossoms are wider than long, 6 to 7 cm across, and the petals are more rounded at the tips. The lip has fewer dark lines, and these are irregular. The var. *parviflora* is a smaller plant with flowers half the size. (Brazil; summer, fall and winter.)

Sophronitis wittigiana has almost the smallest plant of the group but the largest flower [Color Plate C-89]. The short, fat pseudobulbs range from oval to chunky, the leaves curving sharply back. The plant is squat, not erect, 4 to 6 cm tall, with blossoms 7 to 9 cm across. A young or newly collected plant may have smaller blossoms, but they will become larger in succeeding years. The flower increases in size, and its pedicel grows longer for several weeks after opening. The flowers are a distinctive shade of rosy-pink or pink-violet, which gave them one of their older names, "rosea." Their parts are rounder than in other species. (Brazil; fall through winter.)

Spathoglottis ───────────────────────────────────

Terrestrial orchids of great beauty, *Spathoglottis* consists mostly of species

168. Spathoglottis affinis
has a tall spike bearing large
butter-yellow flowers lightly
marked with purple.

169. Stelis argentata
shows exquisite detail
in a tiny, silvery flower
whose diameter is 1 cm.

too large for our purposes. Two, however, are dainty enough to be considered. They have small, irregularly shaped pseudobulbs that should be planted just at or below the surface of sandy-loam soil. Paired soft, narrow, pleated leaves arise in the spring, and soon the tall flower spike appears. In fall the leaves die down, and the pot of pseudobulbs should be kept somewhat dry until the following growing season.

Spathoglottis affinis probably grows taller in nature than in cultivation, except where it can be grown outdoors in a warm climate. The leaves reach 15 to 20 cm in length. The fuzzy flower spikes are 30 to 40 cm tall and bear six to 15 or more butter-yellow blossoms 3.5 to 4 cm across [Plate 168]. The oval sepals and petals are similar, the former veined with purple. The lip is three-lobed, the lateral lobes erect and striped inside with purple, and the mid-lobe spreading from a narrow isthmus to a heart-shaped outer section. (Malaya; late summer or fall.)

Spathoglottis altigena has three or four pleated leaves 25 cm long, from pseudobulbs that are round and a bit flattened. The 35 cm flower stem holds upwards of ten, rose-violet blossoms 3.5 cm across, with a darker lip and column. The sepals are oval, the petals a bit broader. The lip has a gold-colored isthmus decorated with a few hairs, while the end lobe is short and rounded, coming to a sudden point at the tip. (New Guinea; summer.)

Sphyrarhynchus

One small monopodial species makes up the genus *Sphyrarhynchus*.

Sphyrarhynchus schliebenii has flattened roots and two or three pairs of slender leaves 2 to 3 cm long. At the base of the stem come several little sprays of three to six wide-open flowers, 2 cm across, white except for a green patch at the base of the lip. They have slender, pointed sepals and petals and a pointed lip that leads into a bulbous spur. (Tanzania; spring.)

Stelis

The species of *Stelis* have among them many of delicate beauty and some that are quite fantastic. The genus is related to *Pleurothallis* and the plants are pretty much like those of that genus, ranging from 1 to 30 cm in height. More than 500 species are known, and new ones are being found all the time. Many look alike to the casual eye; in fact, even with a magnifying glass it is difficult to tell the difference between some, especially those that are symmetrical, three-pointed stars. Others diverge widely from the typical shape. Chief characteristics of *Stelis* are the tiny petals with swollen edges, a very small, fleshy lip, and a column with three lobes at the tip and a rather long membranous beak.

Stelis argentata is a well-known and much loved species. The plants are 10 to 15 cm tall and the flower spike twice that, bearing 30 or more beautiful translucent blossoms 1 cm across, sometimes plain, sometimes covered with hairs [Plate 169]. The color varies from silvery lavender to pink with a brown suffusion. The petals and lip surround the column with three fleshy crescents. (Mexico through Central America and all of northern South America; winter and spring.)

Stelis gemma, whose name means "web foot," is a fairly recent discovery. The shape is brought about by the union of the sepals in such a way that the dorsal is in the center, and the laterals curve up to join it [Plate 170]. The flowers are large and there are many on a 10 cm stem [Plate 171]. They are 1.3 cm from top to bottom, with exceedingly tiny petals, column, and lip. The color is greenish red on the furry front surface, shiny red on the back. (Ecuador; flowers several times a year.)

Stelis inaequalis is 5 cm tall with fewer blossoms to the stem. The flower gives the impression of having two parts, with the oval dorsal sepal forming the upper half and the united laterals the lower. The unusually large petals are fan-shaped and extend to the edge of the sepals, but the lip is tiny. The whole flower is only 3 to 4 mm long and covered with hairs. (Panama and Honduras.)

170. A single flower of Stelis gemma *reveals the pubescent surface and the extremely tiny petals, lip, and column.*

Stenia

A single species is known in the genus *Stenia*, a plant similar vegetatively to the *Zygopetalum* group but with distinctive flowers.

Stenia pallida lacks pseudobulbs. It has a fan of rather broad, pleated leaves 9 to 15 cm tall. The short pendent or arching flower stems come from leaf axils and bear single blossoms 4.5 to 5.5 cm across, cream color or light green, with oval dorsal sepal and petals, broad lateral sepals, and a peculiar lip. The lip is stiff and waxy, and its edges roll up to form a pointed horn with a tiny opening at its tip and a larger opening at its base, where the maroon-spotted side lobes flare out under the column. (British Guiana, Trinidad, and Venezuela; flowers variably throughout the year.)

Stenoglottis

Lovely terrestrials, the species of *Stenoglottis* make a many-leaved, basal rosette and a tall spike of small flowers arranged in a spiral. More and more blossoms are formed as the stem lengthens so that it remains in bloom for two or three months. The season's leaves die down as new ones start in midwinter or early spring. After flowering, a short dry spell is beneficial, otherwise water regularly. They have fleshy, tuberous roots, and should be potted in sandy loam.

Stenoglottis fimbriata has slender, soft leaves 5 to 10 cm long,

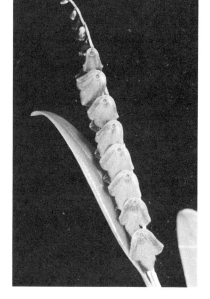

171. The flowers of Stelis *are not always three-pointed.* Stelis gemma *has a fleur-de-lis shape, and its flowers are large for the genus. 1.3 cm across. A flowering stem has crowded, overlapping blossoms.*

wavy on the edges and more or less spotted on the back. The sepals are wide triangles, the dorsal erect, the laterals spread straight to the sides [Plate 172]. The petals curve together to form a hood over the column, and the lip extends from under it. The tip of the lip is divided into several fingerlike extensions that begin at different levels across the end of the lip. The flowers are pink spotted with bright magenta, 1 to 1.2 cm long, and rather fleshy. (Malawi to South Africa; summer.)

Stenoglottis longifolia is similar vegetatively to *S. fimbriata*. It is held by some to have less spotting on the leaves, but this is purely relative. The flowers are also similar, except that the fimbriations of the lip start at the same level across the tip. (South Africa; summer.)

Stenoglottis woodii is a smaller plant than the above, although its leaves are about the same length. The flowering stem is shorter, [Plate 173], and the fewer delicate flowers are white, with a tri-lobed rather than a fimbriated lip and a short spur. (South Africa; summer.)

172. Stenoglottis fimbriata, *an African terrestrial, has a tall spike of pinkish blossoms spotted with magenta.*

Stolzia

Apparently there are several species in *Stolzia*, only one of which is much known.

Stolzia repens is an intriguing plant with a creeping rhizome on which the 2 to 3 mm pseudobulbs are mere forward-pointing swellings, something like bottles placed on their sides. Each new one comes from the "shoulder" of the preceding one. A pair of tiny oval, succulent leaves 0.5 to 1 cm long arises from the tip, as do the single flowers, which are 9 mm long on short peduncles, yellow to red-brown, striped on the inside with brown, and with a red lip. The parts are all slender and pointed, the dorsal sepal and petals erect, the laterals joined at the base to form a chin from which their ends curl into a complete circle. The plants must be grown on mounts in a rather cool, damp, shady spot. (Kenya, Tanzania, and Rhodesia; winter.)

173. Stenoglottis woodii, *a more modest species, has white flowers.*

Taenia

Members of the terrestrial genus *Taenia* are mostly quite large, but one is small and dainty.

Taenia shimadai has conical pseudobulbs 3 to 5 cm tall topped by a single, narrow leaf 16 to 20 cm long. The 15 to 20 cm flowering stem comes from the base of the pseudobulb and bears 15 or more delightful, brownish blossoms with a white lip [Plate 174]. The column peers over the lip like a bug with two dark eyes. The sepals and petals are slender, the lip spade-shaped with spotted side lobes and two tall keels. Must be kept on the dry side after leaf fall and until new growth begins. (Taiwan; summer.)

Taeniophyllum———————————————————————

This is a genus of some 200 leafless orchids that range through the Orient, New Guinea, and Australia. They require a warm, damp, shady spot and may be mounted on cork bark or small branches.

    Taeniophyllum complanatum has wide, flat, gray-green roots and 4 cm spikes of slender, tubular, pale yellow flowers, 2 to 3 mm long. (Taiwan; summer.)

    Taeniophyllum formosanum has flat roots narrower than those of the preceding species. Otherwise, its habit and flowers are similar. (Taiwan; winter.)

174. Taenia shimadai *has a buglike column peering out over the white lip; the rest of the flower is brown.*

Telipogon———————————————————————

The over 50 members of the genus *Telipogon* are beautiful but frustratingly difficult to tell apart. Many new ones are being found and as yet remain unnamed. They are so intriguing, however, that a grower can enjoy them without knowing their specific names. Two plant forms exist, one that has a short stem and few proportionately long leaves in which new growths come close together from the rhizome, and one with a long stem clothed with tiny alternate leaves. The flowers are pollinated by pseudo-copulation performed by male flies attracted by a bristly column and a hairy pad below it on the base of the lip. The beak of the column is usually long and therefore certain to make contact with the pollinator. Most species require cool temperatures, although some do well in a cool-intermediate situation. They should be mounted on small slabs or branches and have a mist spray once a day.

    Telipogon ampliflorus [Color Plate C-90] has a short stem and leaves 6 cm tall, with a flowering stem of 10 cm. The large flower has broad, fan-shaped petals whose narrow bases expose the dorsal sepal. The blossoms are yellow-green with a slightly darker border, and the lip is red at the base with a darker red cushion. The column has long bristles. (Costa Rica; fall to winter.)

    Telipogon croesus has a few 6 cm leaves and a short inflorescence bearing two or three flowers. The large flower is 3 to 5 cm across, beautifully colored. The round petals and lip are bordered with yellow, white through the central portion, and deep pink at the base, with a darker cushion. The column is slightly pubescent. (Colombia, Ecuador, and Venezuela; summer.)

    Telipogon nervosus has slender stems and alternate 2 cm leaves. It first flowers when the stem is about 10 cm tall [Plate 175]. After a stem has flowered, new growth starts from the spot where the flowering stem formed, so that the main stem increases in length *ad infinitum*. Mean-

175. Telipogon nervosus *bears its insect imitating flower on a tall stem. The plant is of the climbing type.*

176. A beautiful little monopodial that scrambles over a small mount, Thrixspermum formosanum *hangs on by just a few roots. The plant gives many flowering stems.*

177. The blossoms of Thrixspermum formosanum, *shown here in closeup, come one after another throughout the year.*

while, side branches will have developed from the lower portions. Roots form along the stem. Growing this type of *Telipogon* is much like growing a *Dichaea*, except that the plants are erect and the inflorescences are tall. Three or four blossoms develop in succession, 3.5 cm across. The slender sepals are hidden, all but their tips, behind the huge rounded petals and round lip. The flowers are greenish-ivory veined with red and the column and lip cushion are red. (Costa Rica; winter.)

Thrixspermum

In the exquisite monopodial genus *Thrixspermum* there are two different flowering habits. In one the inflorescence bears at its tip flattened alternate bracts all in the same plane, resembling in miniature the flat spikes of some bromeliads. Flowers come from beneath the bracts. In the other form, the bracts are less conspicuous and not two-ranked. A diagnostic detail of the flowers is a callus on the forward inside surface of the lip. The plants should be grown on small mounts.

Thrixspermum accuminatissimum is 5 to 8 cm tall with three or four pairs of leaves 8 to 10 cm long. The flower spike, of the large-bract type, can be short or up to 20 cm long and produces one or several spidery, yellow flowers. The sepals and petals are long and tapering, giving the blossoms a diameter of 6 cm. The pale yellow lip has a broad, red-spotted cup at the base and a long pointed white mid-lobe. (Sumatra, Malaya, and the Philippines; flowers over a long period.)

Thrixspermum formosanum [Plate 176] is small and dainty, with a stem 3 to 4 cm tall and narrow leaves 5 to 7 cm long. The plant branches freely and yet confines itself to a small area. Flowering stems come from each leaf axil and open one or two buds at a time as more continue to form for many months. The little waxy 1 cm blossoms [Plate 177] are white with a pink-spotted lip. The oval sepals and petals curve forward around the proportionately large, deep, double-chinned bucket of the lip. Grow warm or intermediate. Needs a damp, shady spot. (Taiwan; flowers all year.)

Thrixspermum kusukusense has leaves some 8 cm long and short spikes of 2 cm flowers. The blossoms are creamy white, with broad, wide-spreading sepals and petals, and a deep, bucket-shaped lip spotted with brilliant red-orange. Warm or intermediate, damp and shady. (Taiwan; flowers at intervals throughout the year.)

Thrixspermum sarumatarii has oval 4 to 5 cm leaves closer together than in the other species, and it flowers very freely. Several round, creamy white, 1.5 cm flowers come on spikes about the same length as the leaves. (Taiwan; flowers at various times of the year.)

Thysanoglossa _____

The two species of *Thysanoglossa* are related to *Ornithocephalus* but have flowers that look like (but are not related to) *Oncidium*. They are rather rare. Since they dwell natively in damp forests and are almost continually saturated with water, they need a damp and shady spot in cultivation.

 Thysanoglossa jordanensis has a tuft of four or five leaves 4 cm tall and an erect zigzig flower stem about 6 cm long that bears a handful of blossoms. The whitish flowers are 2.5 cm long, with free narrow sepals and petals, and a long, fiddle-shaped lip. The shoulderlike side lobes are edged with long pointed "fingers," and the mid-lobe is edged with short teeth. (Brazil; winter.)

 Thysanoglossa organensis is quite similar but of a darker yellow. (Brazil; winter.)

Trias _____

Ten diminutive species belong to the genus *Trias*, so named because the flowers are three-pointed stars formed by broad, triangular sepals. The plants have squat little pseudobulbs that look like small bags pulled shut with a drawstring. They make a little chain along a rhizome, each bearing a rather broad leaf. The flowers come singly on short stems from the base or side of the pseudobulbs. Where the lateral sepals come together they form a broad chin. The fleshy lip is parallel to the column for a short distance, then turns sharply out or down. The anther cap is tall and peaked like a "pixie" cap.

 Trias disciflora is the largest of the group. The plants are 12 cm tall and the flowers over 5 cm long. The large sepals are light greenish-yellow bordered with minute red dots, and the oval convex lip is covered with tiny purple-brown warts. The petals are extremely small. (Laos; fall.)

 Trias intermedia has pseudobulbs 0.6 to 1 cm in diameter, finely wrinkled and pitted when old. The leaves are thick, broadly oval, 1.4 cm long. The little flowering stem is only 5 mm tall and bears a blossom 1 cm across that is green with purplish veins. The sepals are triangular and come to a point, and the much smaller petals are oval. The fleshy lip is tongue-shaped, yellow and brown with purple spots. (Thailand; winter.)

 Trias nana has lumpy, potatolike pseudobulbs and a tiny leaf, whose combined height is about 2 cm. The yellow flowers, 1.5 cm across, come on very short stems. The sepals are narrow and pointed, the lip quite small and deep yellow. (Thailand; midwinter.)

 Trias nasuta also has lumpy pseudobulbs and a slender leaf. The plant is 6 to 9 cm tall. The fairly large flower is nearly 3 cm long, greenish-yellow, the petals tipped with purple, and the lip purple on its basal half. (Thailand and Burma; winter.)

*Triceratorhynchus*_____

One minute monopodial species makes up the genus *Triceratorhynchus*. It is a relative of *Sphyrarhynchus*, which also has only one species.

Triceratorhynchus viridiflorum is only 4 cm tall with a few pairs of strap-shaped leaves 1 to 3 cm long. Sprays 6 to 8 cm long bear four to seven, tiny, round, star-shaped, green flowers. They are 2 to 4 mm across, with pointed parts and a curved spur 3 mm long. (Kenya; winter.)

*Trichocentrum*_____

178. Trichocentrum hoegei
*is a sparkling flower with
green and brown sepals and
petals and a white lip
veined with violet.*

Trichocentrum is related to *Oncidium*, but the flowers differ, especially in that *Trichocentrum* has a spur formed by the base of the lip. The plants have an inconspicuous pseudobulb topped by a single leaf. There are about 18 species.

Trichocentrum albo-coccineum is 10 cm tall with leathery leaves. The 4.5 to 5 cm flowers come on a short inflorescence, opening one at a time over a long period. Sepals and petals are gold stippled with red-brown, widening toward the top and then ending in a point. The beautiful skirtlike lip is white except for a basal patch of purple on each side of the center line. The spur is short. (Ecuador, Peru, and Brazil; summer and fall.)

Trichocentrum capistratum has leaves 5 cm long and flowers 2 cm across. They are wide open, fleshy, with slender, dark pink sepals, and brownish-green petals. The simple lip is creamy white, with turned-up edges, and a short blunt spur. The column tip is covered with slender papillae and shows just above its wide, curving wings. Warm growing. (Costa Rica, Panama, Colombia, and Venezuela; flowers any time.)

Trichocentrum hoegei has stiff little "mule ear" leaves 4 to 6 cm long. The flowers [Plate 178] are 2 to 3 cm long, with creamy green sepals and petals centered by a broad band of brown, and a long, white oval lip whose base is decorated with rays of violet. The spur is fat and less than 1 cm long. The column has a pair of tiny "hands" curving under the anther. (Mexico; fall.)

179. Trichocentrum
tigrinum *has flowers as
long as its leaves. The
plant here is growing on
the outside of a coconut
husk.*

Trichocentrum pfavii, one of the prettiest of the genus, is 2 to 4 cm tall, with proportionately large, round, flowers. They are about 3 cm across, with white, slightly wavy sepals and petals marked by a band of rose, and much ruffled, skirtlike lip that has a band of rose toward the base. The spur is short and blunt. (Colombia; winter and spring.)

Trichocentrum pulchrum is much like *T. capistratum* in size and shape of flower, except that it has a long spur that lies straight back against the ovary. Flowers are 4 cm long, cream-green, spotted with red-purple. The column wings are toothed, the anther covered with papillae. (Colombia, Ecuador, Peru, and Venezuela; fall.)

Trichocentrum tigrinum [Plate 179] has lightly spotted leaves

5 to 6 cm long and flowers almost the same length. The sepals and petals are wide-spreading, yellow heavily spotted with brown. The long lip, which widens at the apex, is white with a rose-colored base. The spur is short and blunt. (Ecuador; spring and summer.)

Trichoceros

Among the most fascinating of American orchids, each species of *Trichoceros* mimics a different species of large fuzzy fly. Males are lured by what appear to be the females of their species to perform pseudocopulation with the flowers. Because of their furry appearance, in their native countries they are affectionately called *flor de gato*, "cat flower," or *michimichi*, "kitty kitty." We call them "fly orchids." The genus is related to *Telipogon*. The plants have small pseudobulbs that typically bear a very small or almost aborted leaf at the apex and several thick stiff ones from the base. They travel along a wandering, branching rhizome, rather widely separated, and for that reason are best grown in flats. Some people grow them on poles. When plants rise up too high or hang out too far, they can be broken off and replanted. The inflorescence continues to form flowers for six to nine months. They need constant moisture, fair shade, and cool temperatures, at least the cool end of intermediate conditions.

Trichoceros armillatus has side leaves 5 to 7 cm long and a center one of 3 cm. The flowering stem is 15 to 20 cm tall and bears a succession of blossoms 3 cm across, spotted with red-violet on a greenish-white background [Plate 180]. The oval sepals and longer, narrower petals are lightly spotted, the broadly oval lip densely so. The curved side lobes of the lip are antenna-like, striped, and covered with short hairs. The column is stubby, covered with reddish bristles, and as in all the species, exposes a large, glistening, pitlike stigma that probably simulates the cloacal cavity of the female fly. (Colombia, Ecuador, Peru, and Bolivia; spring to the following winter.)

Trichoceros bergoldii is a newly discovered species less flylike in appearance. It has slender leaves 2.5 cm long, including the center one, and a short inflorescence that bears a succession of flowers. They are 1.5 cm across, the sepals and larger petals pale yellow-green faintly veined with pink, the petals finely toothed along their lower margins. The lip is a broad oval with only short side lobes, which, along with the very base of the lip, are rosy-red and covered with hooked hairs. The dorsal surface of the column has long hairs that are four-pronged at the tip. (Venezuela.)

Trichoceros muralis has plants similar to but slightly smaller than those of *T. armillatus*. The flowers [Plate 181] are smaller, with short, blunt side lobes instead of antenna-like ones. The sepals and petals are greenish spotted with dull red. The lower end of the lip is similarly marked, but its base is a triangular cushion covered with red papillae. The red side lobes are oval with a few scattered hairs. The red column is papil-

180. Trichoceros is a genus of fly imitators, pollinated by pseudocopulation. The flowers imitate the females of different species of fly. Trichoceros armillatus is spotted with violet on a greenish ground. Note its long, barred "antennae", the side lobes of the lip.

181. Trichoceros muralis is greenish marked with red. Note the oval side lobes, and the hairy, triangular lip cushion.

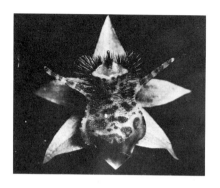

182. Trichoceros parviflorus
is yellow and brown; the
bristles from the column
continue down onto the base
of the lip.

lose in front, covered with long bristles on the back. (Ecuador and Peru; spring through fall.)

Trichoceros parviflorus has much larger plants, the leaves being broad and 6 to 10 cm long, except for the center one which is a mere pinpoint. The flowering stem is 30 to 40 cm tall, and the flowers are 2.5 to 3 cm across, tawny yellow, the pointed sepals and petals faintly blotched with brown [Plate 182]. The broad lip, its antenna-like side lobes, and the column are all marked with large brown spots. Long bristles surround the column and continue down onto the raised basal part of the lip. The scalloped rim of the stigma is yellow shading to pale green. (Colombia, Ecuador, Peru, and Bolivia; spring through the following winter.)

Trichoceros tupaipi has leaves 3 cm long and flowers 1.5 to 2 cm across, greenish-yellow marked with lines of reddish spots. The lip has a solid red, humped basal cushion and perfectly round side lobes. The column has long hairs on its dorsal surface and short ones around its base. The inflorescence is short and bears several flowers in succession. (Peru.)

Trichopilia

The genus *Trichopilia* has some 30 species, somewhat related to *Miltoniopsis*. They have flattened pseudobulbs, sometimes narrow, sometimes broad, and a single tough leaf. Two or more trumpet-shaped flowers are borne on rather short stems from the base of the plant. The best known species with the handsomest flowers, some of which are deliciously fragrant, are either too large—such as *T. suavis*, *T. marginata*, and *T. fragrans*— or borderline. Some of the smaller species are difficult to identify with certainty. A characteristic of the genus is that the lip is united to the column by a partition down its center. The column is hooded with a fringed bonnet.

Trichopilia maculata is about 19 cm tall, with only slightly compressed pseudobulbs about 5 cm high, covered with purple-spotted sheaths. The fragrant flowers, which come singly or in pairs, are 7 cm across. The wavy sepals and petals are narrow and slightly twisted, pale yellow-green. The lip is white with a yellow throat veined with red, its outer margin wide and slightly ruffled. (Guatemala, El Salvador, and Panama; spring.)

Trichopilia oicophylax has pale yellow-green, slightly curved pseudobulbs up to 6 cm tall and leaves to 12 cm. The dainty paired flowers are 8 cm across, with slender, flat, pale green sepals and petals, and a white lip whose sides overlap around the column. The ruffled front lobe flares wide. (Colombia and Venezuela; fall.)

Trichopilia subulata may stay about 10 cm high but can be taller. The pseudobulbs are 1 to 2.5 cm tall, while the fleshy, narrow or semi-terete leaves are 9 to 22 cm long. The flowers are 4 to 5 cm across, three to eight on a pendulous stem. They have pointed, white sepals and white or yellow petals, and a very pretty lip that is white, spotted with rose-purple. The front lobe is edged with long, uneven teeth. (Colombia and Jamaica; spring.)

Trichopilia tortilis is one of the prettiest species, with pseudo-bulbs 4 to 7 cm tall and leaves 14 cm. The fragrant, waxy flowers are 10 cm across, with ribbonlike, much twisted green sepals and petals tinged with brown down the center. The lip is white or cream color, scalloped on the edges, and the yellow throat is spotted with crimson. (Mexico and Honduras; spring and summer.)

Trichopilia turialbae is 15 cm or more tall with slender pseudo-bulbs 4 to 7 cm high. The fragrant, 5 cm flowers [Plate 183] have plain narrow, almost translucent sepals and petals, pure white or slightly tinged with cream or lavender. The lateral sepals are united to or beyond the middle. The lip is white with a few yellow lines in the throat and distinctive for its very long tube. (Costa Rica, Panama, and Colombia; fall.)

183. Trichopilia *is a genus of trumpet-shaped flowers. Shown here is* T. turialbae, *with a long white lip and near-white sepals and petals.*

Trigonidium

The flowers of *Trigonidium* have curious eyespots, shiny pads on the tips of the petals that lure male bees to perform pseudocopulation with the blossoms. The genus is related to *Maxillaria*. The plants have slender, conical pseudobulbs and narrow leaves. Flowers come singly on tall slender stems.

Trigonidium acuminatum is 15 to 18 cm tall, with fluted pseudobulbs, and a narrow, limber leaf that curves over at the tip. The flowering stem is a bit taller than the leaves and bears a blossom 1.7 cm across, yellow-brown, striped with a darker tone [Plate 184]. The long pointed sepals are joined for half their length to form an urn-shaped cup from whose top they turn gracefully down. Within the tube shine the reddish eye spots of the small petals, which are themselves oval, tapering at the tip, and colored like the sepals. The tiny lip and column are well hidden within the tube. (Colombia to Bolivia, British Guiana, and Surinam to Venezuela and Brazil; throughout the year.)

Trigonidium obtusum is about 15 cm tall, with flower stems shorter than that. The blossom is pinkish with purple veins, and the eye spots are shiny blue. The flower is a bit over 1 cm across, and its sepals are broader and less tapering than in the foregoing species. (Brazil; flowers in summer and at other times.)

184. Trigonidium acuminatum *is another insect deceiver. The bright eye spots on the tips of its petals are the lure that brings its pollinator.*

Tuberolabium

This is a small genus of monopodials with lovely little waxy flowers.

Tuberolabium kotoense (syn. *quisumbingii*) is a trim plant 8 to 12 cm tall with seven or eight oval, rather fleshy, horizontal leaves 7 to 13 cm long. A young plant's pendent inflorescence is about 10 cm long with a dozen flowers, but on a mature or well-established plant it can reach 20 to 25 cm and bear 30 to 50 flowers [Plate 185]. The blossoms are arranged spirally on the thick, fleshy inflorescence, which is interesting in itself for the concave trough below each flower. The round waxy flowers [Color Plate C-91] are 1.2 cm across, creamy white tinged with green, and have a sparkling texture. The sepals are broadly oval and pointed, the petals more slender. The lip is a broad compressed cone, almost closed on top, with three purple-tinged points that project upward. The out-curving side lobes of the lip are edged with red-brown. (Taiwan; winter.)

Uncifera

This is a genus of small monopodials, some of which have been transferred from the related genus *Saccolabium*. The one given here is, however, a new species.

Uncifera thailandica is a diminutive plant 7 to 8 cm tall with narrow leaves 10 cm long. It has a short flower spike from near the base, which is crowded with some 20 blossoms. They are fat and round, 1.5 cm in diameter, with broad sepals and petals curved forward, and a funnel-shaped lip with a short hooked spur. The sepals are pale purple with white edges, the petals light green with a purple spot in the center, and the lip is white with a purple spot. (Thailand; spring and summer.)

Vanda

There are a few small species in the beautiful and popular genus *Vanda*, some of which come close to borderline but are tiny in comparison with their large relatives. As with many monopodials, they gradually increase in stem length, and the grower can remove the top section and pot it anew. They need bright light except as noted.

Vanda coerulescens ranges from 15 cm to rarely over 25 cm in height and has closely set leaves 15 cm long. Flower spikes are about the same length as the leaves, bearing 12 to 20 lovely purplish blue flowers with a violet lip. They are 3 cm across, with oval sepals and petals that broaden toward the tip. The petals twist at the base so that the dorsal surface faces front. The lip juts out at a right angle to the broad column, its outer edges turned down. It needs warm temperatures and medium light—less light than the usual vanda. (Burma and Thailand; early summer.)

Vanda lilacina (syn. *laotica*) is an exquisite species reaching 12 cm in height with leaves about 12 cm long. Twenty or more beautiful flowers are borne on an erect stem, almost all of them opening at once. They are 2 cm across, and the slender (sometimes broad) sepals and petals

185. Tuberolabium kotoense *is a charming species that gives stems of thick, waxy little flowers.*

flowers are borne on an erect stem, almost all of them opening at once. They are 2 cm across, and the slender (sometimes broad) sepals and petals are white with lavender tips. The lip is broad, vertical at the base, with its bright rose-colored tip turned down, and it has a narrow·spur. (Thailand, Laos, and possibly Cambodia; winter.)

Vanda parviflora is a dainty plant usually under 15 cm in height, with leaves 10 to 20 cm long, close together and curved downward. The erect flower spike carries 10 to 20 yellow flowers arranged around the stem on rather long pedicels. They are 2 cm across, with broad sepals, narrow, twisted petals, and an upright, funnel-shaped lip with a short spur. (Sri Lanka, India, Burma, and Thailand; summer.)

Vandopsis

Very much like *Vanda*, the genus *Vandopsis* has about ten species, most of which are large sturdy plants.

Vandopsis parishii is sturdy but of short stature, resembling a phalaenopsis in habit, with a few broadly oval leaves. The large round flowers are borne five to seven on an erect stem. Two forms are known. The less frequently grown type has yellow, red-spotted flowers with broadly oval, widely spreading sepals and petals and a pink lip. (Thailand, Indochina, and Burma; rarely blooms.) The preferred one, variety *marriottiana*, has flowers with nearly overlapping round parts and is more richly colored: sepals and petals are gold at the ends, pink at the base, so densely spotted with magenta that they appear a solid color. Warm or warm-intermediate. (Thailand; spring.)

Ypsilopus

This a genus of just two or three small monopodial species, and there is some question as to just which is which. We hope the one given here is correct.

Ypsilopus longifolius [Plate 186] is a delicate plant with a short stem and a few narrow, channeled leaves up to 20 cm long and 5 mm wide. The 10 to 12 cm inflorescence comes from the base of the plant and bears seven or eight lovely flowers. They are 1 cm across, star-shaped, with oval sepals whose tips are rounded, and smaller, pointed petals. The lip is spear-shaped, with sharp side points, and a long pointed tip. The rose-colored anther gives a charming accent to the pure white blossom. The delicate spur is 4 cm long. The plant can be mounted or grown in a pot in a damp, shady spot. (Kenya and Malawi; winter or spring.)

186. Ypsilopus longifolius, despite its name, is a small plant with lovely, star-shaped white blossoms that have an arrow-shaped lip and a long spur.

175

187. Zygostates lunata *has dense sprays of tiny golden flowers, arranged all around the stem.*

Zygostates

About a dozen species of *Zygostates* are present in Brazil, one of which is rather well-known and completely delightful. The genus is related to *Ornithocephalus*.

   Zygostates lunata [Plate 187] has a fan of five to seven rather soft leaves 4 to 4.5 cm long. From the leaf axils arise numerous pendulous stems, bearing 30 or more tiny green or deep gold flowers, each 8 mm across [Color Plate C-92]. They have smooth oval sepals and broad, shiny fan-shaped petals toothed on the edges and covered with minute bumps. The cup-shaped lip is toothed on its edges, and over it sits the fantastic column with its red, long-beaked head and outstretched arms that end in yellow thickenings. (Brazil; fall or winter.)

Selected References

(Note: Some of the references listed are available only through libraries. Many are sold by book dealers, orchid companies, and the American Orchid Society, Inc.)

Books

American Orchid Society *Handbook on Pests and Diseases*. 1975. Botanical Museum of Harvard University, Cambridge, Mass.

Ames, Oakes, and Donovan S. Correll. *Orchids of Guatemala*. 1952–53. 2 vols. Fieldiana: Botany, vol. 26, nos. 1 and 2. Field Museum of Natural History, Chicago. Supplement, 1965, by Correll.

Burnett, Harry C. *Orchid Diseases,* 1974. Florida Department of Agriculture and Consumer Services. Division of Plant Industry. Gainesville, Fla.

Cady, Leo, and E. R. Rotherham. *Australian Native Orchids in Colour*. 1970. A. H. and A. W. Reed, Sydney, Australia.

Cheng, Chow. *Taiwan Native Orchids*, 1967. Chow Cheng Orchids, 194 Litoh Street, Taichung, Taiwan.

Davis, Reg. S., and Mona Lisa Steiner. *Philippine Orchids*. 1952. The William Frederick Press, New York.

da la Bathie, H. Perrier. *Flore de Madagascar: Orchidées.* 1941. Tananarive, Imprimerie Officielle. Museum National d'Histoire Naturelle, Paris. Reprinted, 1977. Margaret Ilgenfritz, Monroe, Michigan.

Dockrill, A. W. *Australian Indigenous Orchids*. 1969. Halstead Press, Sydney, Australia.

Dressler, Robert, and Glenn E. Pollard. *The Genus Encyclia in Mexico*. 1974. Asociación Mexicana de Orquideología, Apartado Postal 53-123, Mexico, 17, D.F.

Dressler, Robert L. *Field Guide to the Orchids of Costa Rica and Panama*. 1974. Comstock Publishing Associates, 1994. Ithaca and London.

Dunsterville, G. C. K., and Leslie A. Garay. *Venezuelan Orchids Illustrated*, 1959–1976. 6 vols. Andre Deutsch Ltd., London.

Fawcett, W., and A. B. Rendle. *Flora of Jamaica*: Vol. 1, *Orchids*. British Museum, London, 1910. Reproduced with permission by George W. Hart, P.O. Box 283, Kingston, Jamaica, 1963.

Foldats, Ernesto. *Flora de Venezuela: Orchidaceae,* vol. XV, 5 parts. 1969. Instituto Botánico, Caracas, Venezuela.

Garay, Leslie A., and Herman R. Sweet. *Flora of the Lesser Antilles: Orchidaceae*, 1974. Arnold Arboretum, Harvard University, Cambridge, Mass.

—— *Orchids of Southern Ryukyu Islands*, 1974. Botanical Museum, Harvard University, Cambridge, Mass.

Ghose, B. N. *Beautiful Indian Orchids*. 1968. G. Ghose and Co., Town-End, Darjeeling, India.

Graf, Alfred Byrd. *Exotica, Pictorial Cyclopedia of Exotic Plants*. 1963. Roehrs Co., Rutherford, N.J.

Hamer, Fritz. *Las Orquideas de El Salvador*. 1974. 2 vols. Text in Spanish, English, and German. Ministerio de Educación, Dirección de publicaciones, San Salvador, El Salvador.

Hamilton, Robert M. *Orchid Flower Index: A World List of Reproductions in Color, in Books and Periodicals*. 1736–1966. Published by the author, 9211 Beckwith Road, Richmond, B.C. Canada. Vol. 2, 1966–1979.

—— *Index to Plant Illustrations in the American Orchid Society Bulletin*. 1932–1971. vols. 1–40. Published by the author. Supplementary List 1972–1977, Vols. 41–46, 1978.

—— *When Does It Flower?* Flowering dates of 3500 orchid species in the United States, 1977. Published by the author.

Harrison, E. R. *Epiphytic Orchids of Southern Africa*. 1972. Natal Branch of the Wildlife Protection and Conservation Society of South Africa.

Harvard University, *Botanical Museum Leaflets*. By subscription, or separately from American Orchid Society, Cambridge, Mass.

Hawkes, Alex. D. *Encyclopaedia of Cultivated Orchids*. 1961. Faber and Faber, Ltd., London.

Hoehne, F. C. *Flora Brasilica: Orchidaceae*. 1940–45, 1953. vol. XII, nos. I, II, and III. Instituto de Botánica, Secretaria de Agricultura, São Paulo, Brasil.

—— *Iconografía de Orchidaceas do Brasil*. 1949. Published as for the preceding.

Holttum, R. E. *A Revised Flora of Malaya*. Vol. 1, *Orchids of Malaya*, 1953. Government Printing Office, Singapore, Malaya.

King, R., and R. Pantling. *The Orchids of the Sikkim Himalaya*. 1898. Reprinted 1967.

Lindley, Professor John. *Folia Orchidacea*. Vol. I, parts 1–9. 1853–1855. London. Reprinted by A. Asher and Co., Amsterdam, 1964.

Miller, Andreé. *Orchids of Papua New Guinea*, 1978, University of Washington Press, Seattle, and London.

Morris, Brian. *Epiphytic Orchids of Malawi*, 1970. The Society of Malawi, Blantyre, Malawi.

Nicholls, W. H. *Orchids of Australia*. 1969. Thomas Nelson Ltd., Sydney, Australia.

Northen, Rebecca Tyson. *Home Orchid Growing*, 4th rev. ed., 1990. Prentice-Hall, Englewood Cliffs, New Jersey.

—— *Orchids as House Plants*, 2nd rev. ed. 1976. Dover Publications, New York.

Ortiz, V., Pedro. *Orquideas de Colombia*. 1976. Published by the author, Carrera 10, No. 65–48, Bogotá 2, Colombia.

Pabst, G. F. J., and F. Dungs. *Orchidaceae Brasilienses*. Vol. 1, 1975; Vol. 2, 1977. Text in English, German, and Portuguese. Brüke-Verlag Kurt Schmerson, Hildesheim, Germany.

Piers, Frank. *Orchids of East Africa*, 2nd ed. 1968. Available from Wheldon and Wesley Ltd., Codicote/Herts, England.

Pradhan, Udai C. *Indian Orchids: Guide to Identification and Culture*. Vol. 1, 1976; Vol. 2, 1977. Published by the author, Rishi Road, P.O. Kalimpong 734381, Dist. Darjeeling, India.

Santapau, H., and Z. Kapadia. *The Orchids of Bombay*. 1966. Government of India Press, Calcutta.

Schelpe, E. A. *An Introduction to the South African Orchids*. 1966. MacDonald and Co., Ltd., London.

Schlechter, Rudolph. *Die Orchideen*. In process of revision and editing by F. G. Brieger, R. Maatsch, and K. Senghas. Several sections published, others to follow. Verlag Paul Parry, Berlin and Hamburg.

—— *Orchideen von Deutsch Neu-Guinea*. 1911–14. Two parts, Text and Figuren Atlas. Reprinted 1974 by Otto Koeltz Antiquariat, Koenigstein, Germany.

Schultes, Richard Evans. *Native Orchids of Trinidad and Tobago*. 1960. Pergamon Press, New York.

—— and Arthur Stanley Pease. *Generic Names of Orchids, Their Meaning and Origin*. 1963. Academic Press, New York and London.

Schweinfurth, Charles. *Orchids of Peru*. 1958–61. Fieldiana: Botany, vol. 30, nos. 1, 2, 3, 4. Field Museum of Natural History, Chicago.

Seidenfaden, Gunnar. *Notes on Cirrhopetalum* Lindl. 1973. Dansk Botanisk Arkiv, Udgivet of Dansk Botanisk Forenung, Copenhagen, Denmark.

—— *Orchid Genera of Thailand*, I-III, 1975. Dansk Botanisk Arkiv, Udgivet of Dansk Botanisk Forenung, Copenhagen, Denmark.

—— and Tem Smitinand. *The Orchids of Thailand: A Preliminary List.* 1959-1965. Parts I; II, 1 and 2; III; and IV, 1 and 2. The Siam Society, Bangkok, Thailand.

Stewart, Joyce, and Bob Campbell. *Orchids of Tropical Africa.* 1970. A. S. Barnes and Co., South Brunswick and New York.

Veitch and Sons. *Manual of Orchidaceous Plants.* 1887. 2 vols. London. Reprinted 1962.

Williams, B. S., and H. Williams. *The Orchid Grower's Manual*, 7th rev. ed. 1894. Reprinted 1960. Wheldon and Wesley, Ltd., Codicote/ Herts, England, and Hafner Publishing Co., New York.

Williams, L. O. *The Orchidaceae of Mexico.* 1952. Ceiba Vol. 2, nos. 1-4, 1951. Reprinted 1965. Escuela Agricola Panamericana, Tegucigalpa, Honduras.

—— and Paul H. Allen. *Flora of Panama*, Part III, Fascicles 2, 3, 4, *Orchidaceae*, 1946-49. Annals of the Missouri Botanical Garden, St. Louis.

Williamson, Graham. *The Orchids of South Central Africa*, 1977. J. W. Dent & Sons, Ltd., London.

Woolfson, George E. *Ten Year Index to Plant Illustrations in 10 Influential Orchid Periodicals, 1968 thru 1977.* 1978. Twin Oaks Books, Lowell, Michigan.

Glossaries

American Orchid Society. *An Orchidist's Glossary.* 1974.
Oregon Orchid Society. *An Orchidist's Lexicon.* 1969.

Periodicals

American Orchid Society Bulletin, Botanical Museum of Harvard University, Cambridge, Mass. 02138

Australian Orchid Review, Harbour Press, P.O. Box M60, Sydney Mail Exchange, N.S.W., Australia 2012.

The Florida Orchidist, 1333 S. Miami Ave., Miami, Florida 33130.

Orchid Digest, 25 Ash Avenue, Corte Madera, Calif. 94925

Orchid Digest, P.O. Box 916, Carmichael, CA 95608.

The Orchid Review, 5 Orchid Ave., Kingsteignton, Newton Abbot, Devon, England TQ12 3HG.
53-123, Mexico 17, D.F.

Orquideología, Sociedad Colombiana de Orquideología, Apartado Aéreo 4725, Medellín, Colombia.

South African Orchid Journal, P.O. Box 9516, Johannesburg, South Africa.

Appendix: _____

Orchid Pest Control
(Courtesy of Don Lingrell, Horticulturist)

The most serious problem with orchid pest control is virus, because there is no cure for a virused plant. Plants proven to be virused should be discarded. The most serious other pests are *(a)* aphids; *(b)* scale insects; *(c)* thrips; *(d)* mites (spider relatives); and *(e)* slugs and snails (mollusks). Most insecticides will not be effective against mites. Following is a list of chemicals that I have used to control these pests (with the kinds of pests each controls, its method of operation, and any suggestions for use). In a closed environment such as a greenhouse a respirator should be worn when applying chemicals. Follow label instructions carefully.

Orthene 75WP: aphids, scale insects and thrips; works both systemically and on contact
Mavrik EC: aphids, thrips, mites and caterpillars; works on contact
Permethrin (Spectracide): aphids, scale insects, thrips and mites; works on contact
Safe-T-Side and other spray oils: aphids, scale insects, thrips and mites; use with care
Pentac: mites
Metaldehyde: slugs and snails; bait or spray regularly
Malathion: aphids, scale insects and thrips

There are numerous fungus and bacterial problems that afflict orchids. Sanitation, proper watering, fertilizers, and control over humidity, temperature and air movement, together with timely repotting, are the best way to control the most serious problems. Once or twice a year the growing area should be sanitized with Clorox if no plants are present or Physan if they are. Following is a list of chemicals I have used, with some of the diseases they control.

Physan 20: algae, bacteria and fungi; has no residual effect.
Kocide 101: bacterial and fungal leaf spots; use no more than three times a year (it contains copper, which is toxic to plants)
Bayleton: various fungal leaf spots and rusts
Cleary's 3336: rhizoctonia root rots, botrytis, some leaf spots
Subdue: pythium and phytophthera root rots; use very sparingly
Banrot: pythium and phytophtera, rhizoctonia, etc.

Refer to the AOS handbook on disease control or your local grower for more information.

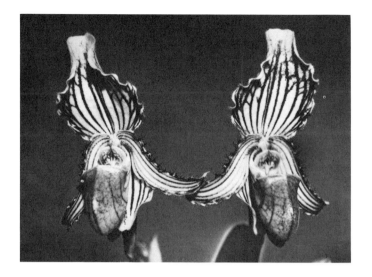

Index